HUNT FOR WOLVERINE

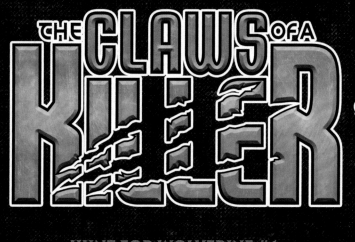

THE CLAWS OF A KILLER

HUNT FOR WOLVERINE #1

WRITER **Charles Soule**

"SECRETS AND LIES"

ARTIST **David Marquez**

COLOR ARTIST **Rachelle Rosenberg**

"HUNTER'S PRYDE"

PENCILER **Paulo Siqueira**

INKER **Walden Wong**

COLOR ARTIST **Ruth Redmond**

COVER ART **Steve McNiven, Jay Leisten & Laura Martin**

CLAWS OF A KILLER #1-4

WRITER **Mariko Tamaki**

PENCILERS **Butch Guice** (#1-4) & **Mack Chater** (#2-4)

INKERS **Cam Smith** (#1-4) & **Mack Chater** (#2-4)

COLOR ARTISTS **Dan Brown** (#1-3) & **Jordan Boyd** (#4)

COVER ART **Greg Land, Jay Leisten & Marte Gracia** (#1); **Greg Land & Jason Keith** (#2); **Giuseppe Camuncoli, Roberto Poggi & Dean White** (#3); AND **Giuseppe Camuncoli, Roberto Poggi & Carlos Lopez** (#4)

LETTERER **VC's Joe Sabino**

ASSISTANT EDITORS **Christina Harrington** & **Annalise Bissa**

EDITORS **Mark Paniccia** & **Jordan D. White**

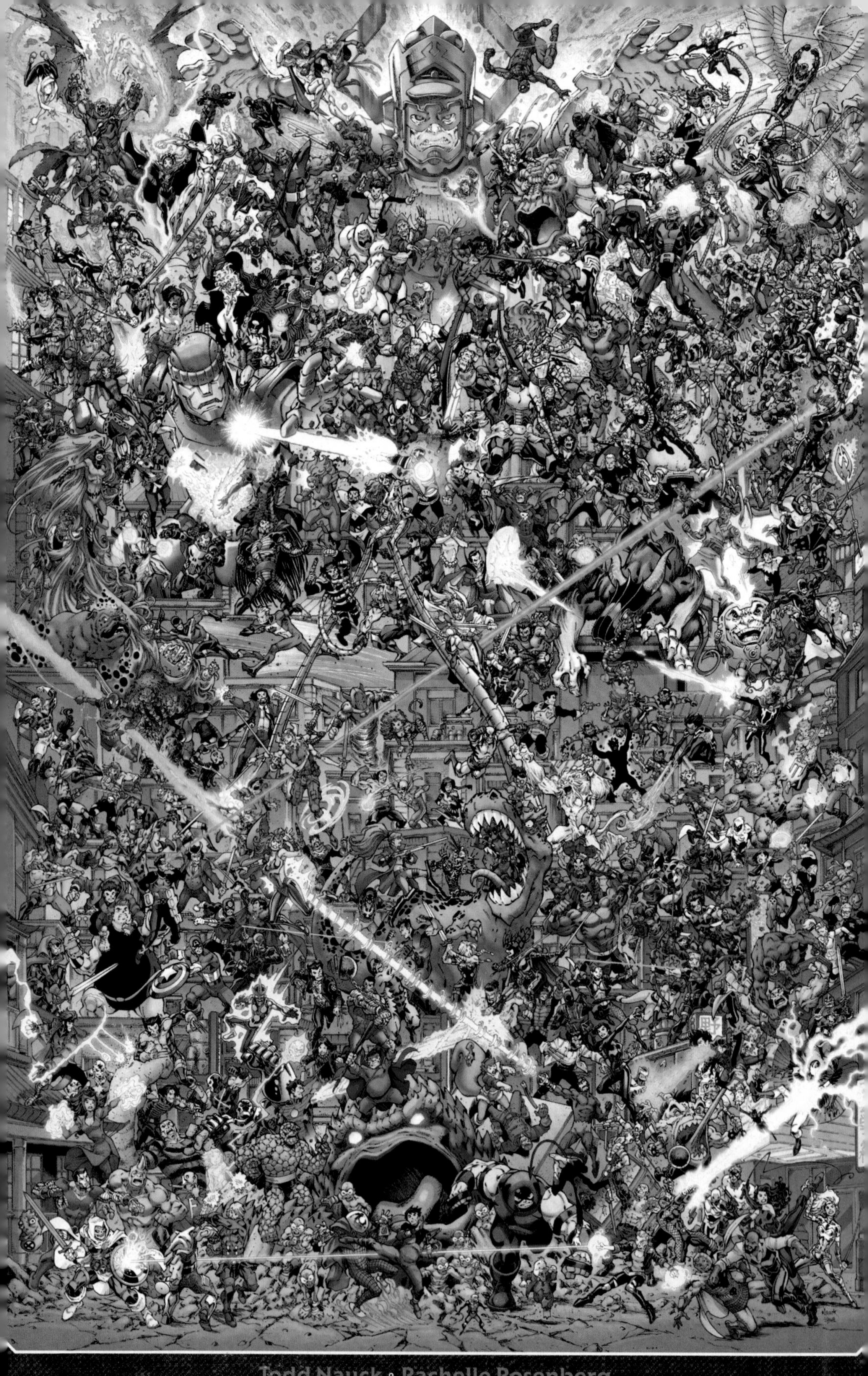

Todd Nauck & Rachelle Rosenberg

WEAPON LOST #1, ADAMANTIUM AGENDA #1, CLAWS OF A KILLER #1 & MYSTERY IN MADRIPOOR #1 CONNECTING VARIANTS

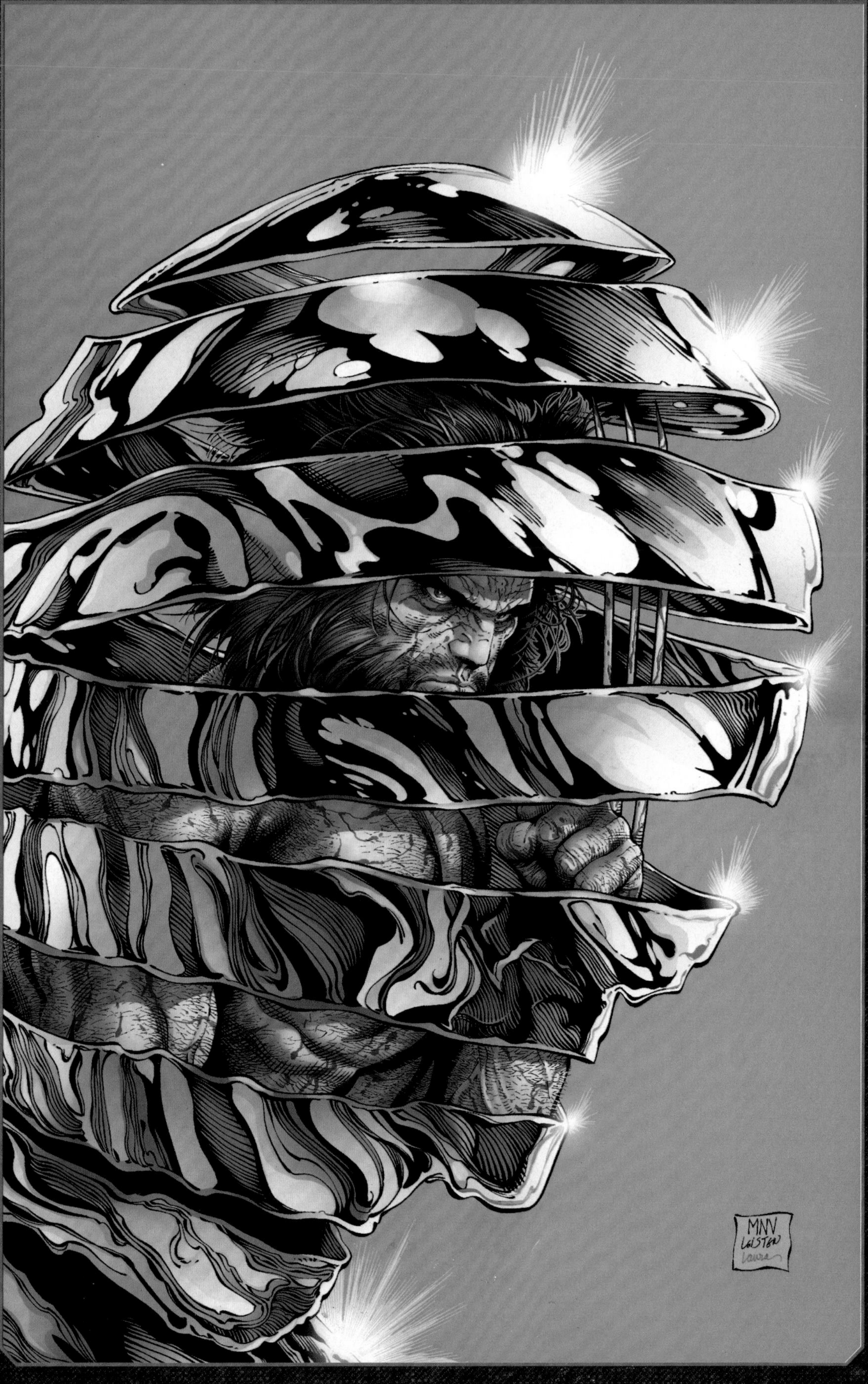

HUNT FOR WOLVERINE 1

WOLVERINE DIED,
ENTOMBED IN
MOLTEN ADAMANTIUM.

THE X-MEN TOOK HIS
METAL-ENCASED BODY
AND HID IT AWAY,
KEEPING ITS LOCATION SECRET.

BUT NOTHING STAYS BURIED.

IT WAS ONLY A MATTER OF TIME.

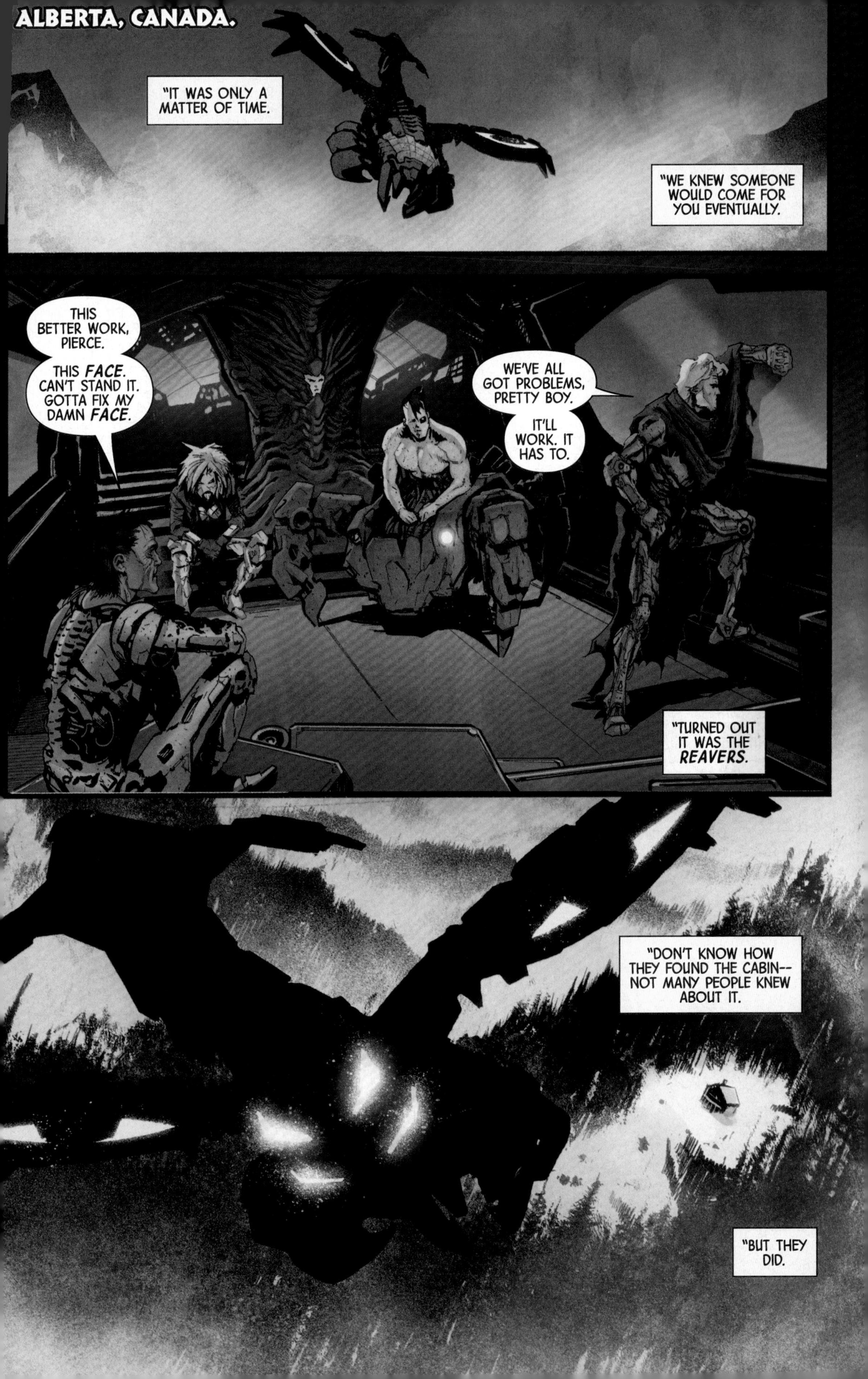
ALBERTA, CANADA.
"IT WAS ONLY A MATTER OF TIME.
"WE KNEW SOMEONE WOULD COME FOR YOU EVENTUALLY.
THIS BETTER WORK, PIERCE.
THIS FACE. CAN'T STAND IT. GOTTA FIX MY DAMN FACE.
WE'VE ALL GOT PROBLEMS, PRETTY BOY.
IT'LL WORK. IT HAS TO.
"TURNED OUT IT WAS THE REAVERS.
"DON'T KNOW HOW THEY FOUND THE CABIN-- NOT MANY PEOPLE KNEW ABOUT IT.
"BUT THEY DID.

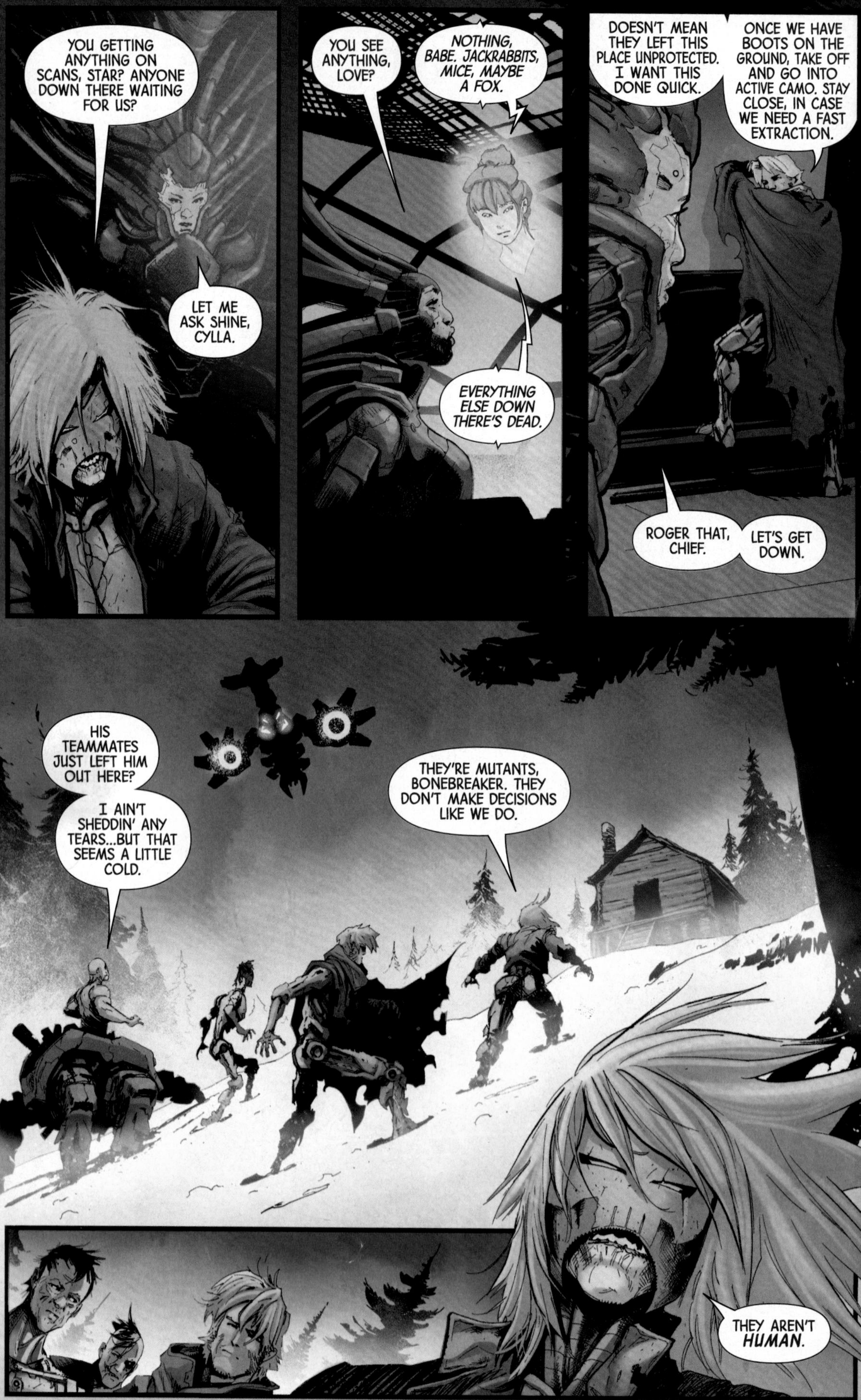
YOU GETTING ANYTHING ON SCANS, STAR? ANYONE DOWN THERE WAITING FOR US?
LET ME ASK SHINE, CYLLA.
YOU SEE ANYTHING, LOVE?
NOTHING, BABE. JACKRABBITS, MICE, MAYBE A FOX.
EVERYTHING ELSE DOWN THERE'S DEAD.
DOESN'T MEAN THEY LEFT THIS PLACE UNPROTECTED. I WANT THIS DONE QUICK.
ONCE WE HAVE BOOTS ON THE GROUND, TAKE OFF AND GO INTO ACTIVE CAMO. STAY CLOSE, IN CASE WE NEED A FAST EXTRACTION.
ROGER THAT, CHIEF.
LET'S GET DOWN.
HIS TEAMMATES JUST LEFT HIM OUT HERE?
I AIN'T SHEDDIN' ANY TEARS...BUT THAT SEEMS A LITTLE COLD.
THEY'RE MUTANTS, BONEBREAKER. THEY DON'T MAKE DECISIONS LIKE WE DO.
THEY AREN'T *HUMAN*.

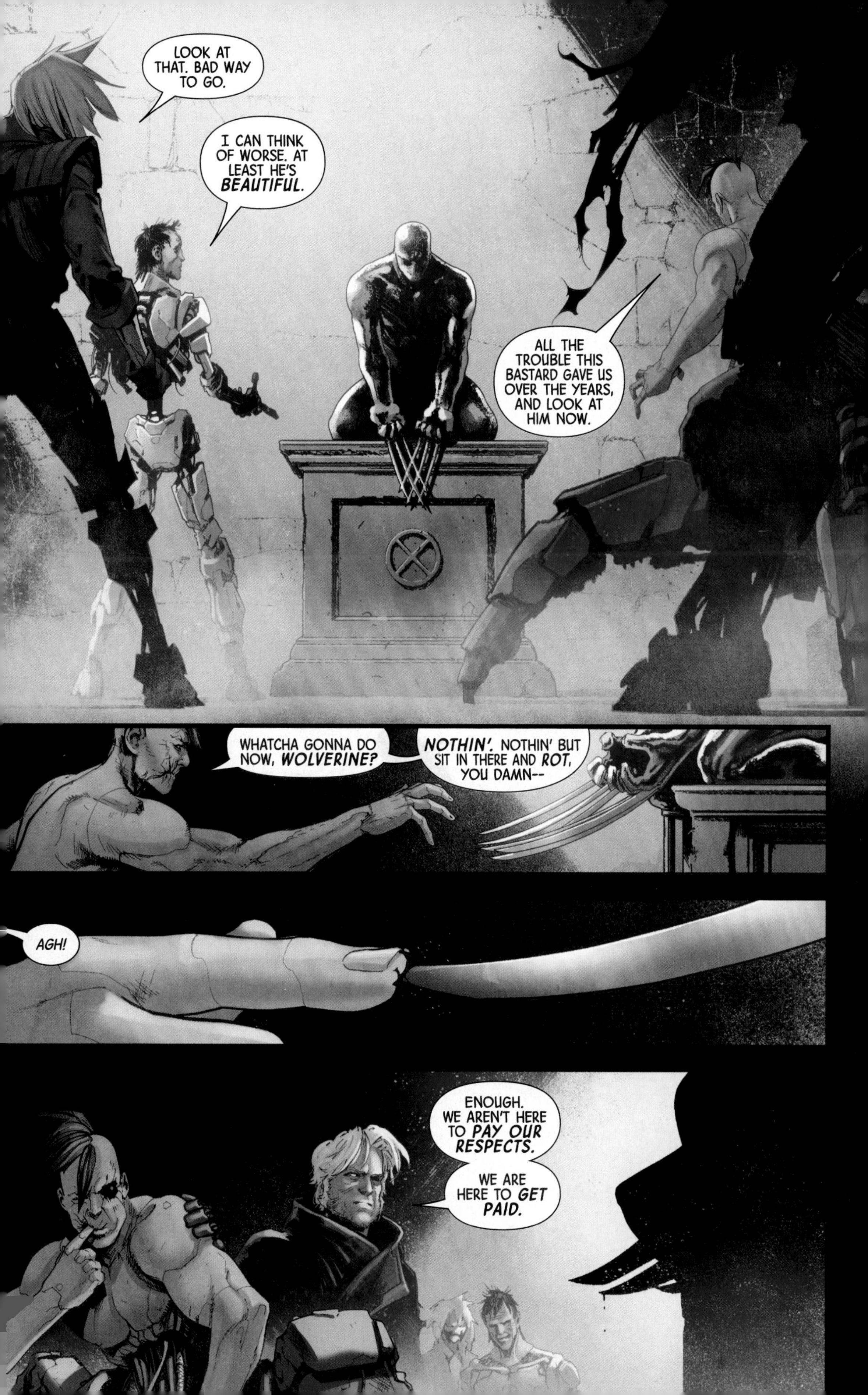
LOOK AT THAT. BAD WAY TO GO.
I CAN THINK OF WORSE. AT LEAST HE'S BEAUTIFUL.
ALL THE TROUBLE THIS BASTARD GAVE US OVER THE YEARS, AND LOOK AT HIM NOW.
WHATCHA GONNA DO NOW, WOLVERINE?
NOTHIN'. NOTHIN' BUT SIT IN THERE AND ROT, YOU DAMN--
AGH!
ENOUGH. WE AREN'T HERE TO PAY OUR RESPECTS.
WE ARE HERE TO GET PAID.

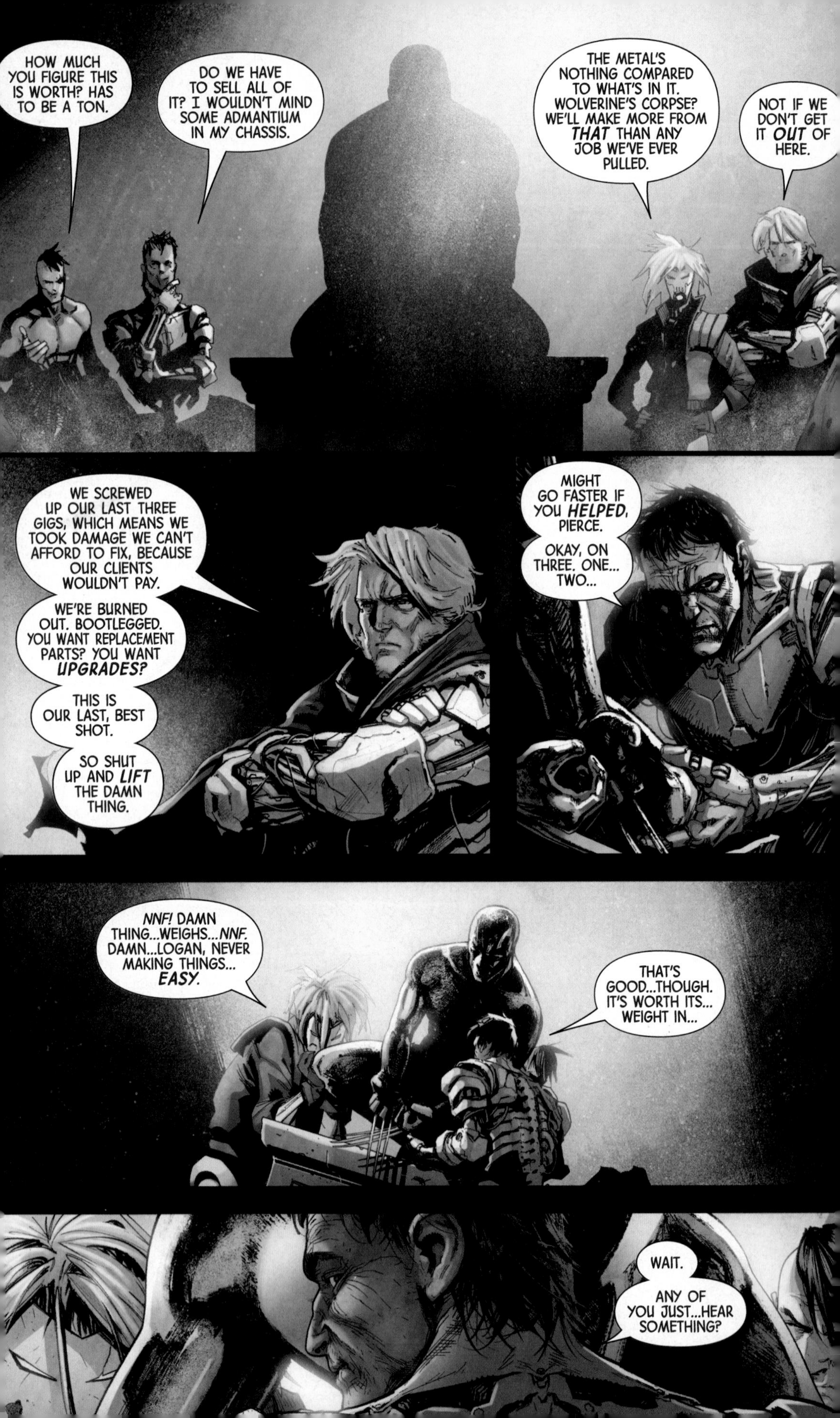
HOW MUCH YOU FIGURE THIS IS WORTH? HAS TO BE A TON.
DO WE HAVE TO SELL ALL OF IT? I WOULDN'T MIND SOME ADMANTIUM IN MY CHASSIS.
THE METAL'S NOTHING COMPARED TO WHAT'S IN IT. WOLVERINE'S CORPSE? WE'LL MAKE MORE FROM THAT THAN ANY JOB WE'VE EVER PULLED.
NOT IF WE DON'T GET IT OUT OF HERE.
WE SCREWED UP OUR LAST THREE GIGS, WHICH MEANS WE TOOK DAMAGE WE CAN'T AFFORD TO FIX, BECAUSE OUR CLIENTS WOULDN'T PAY.
WE'RE BURNED OUT. BOOTLEGGED. YOU WANT REPLACEMENT PARTS? YOU WANT UPGRADES?
THIS IS OUR LAST, BEST SHOT.
SO SHUT UP AND LIFT THE DAMN THING.
MIGHT GO FASTER IF YOU HELPED, PIERCE.
OKAY, ON THREE. ONE... TWO...
NNF! DAMN THING...WEIGHS...NNF. DAMN...LOGAN, NEVER MAKING THINGS... EASY.
THAT'S GOOD...THOUGH. IT'S WORTH ITS... WEIGHT IN...
WAIT.
ANY OF YOU JUST...HEAR SOMETHING?

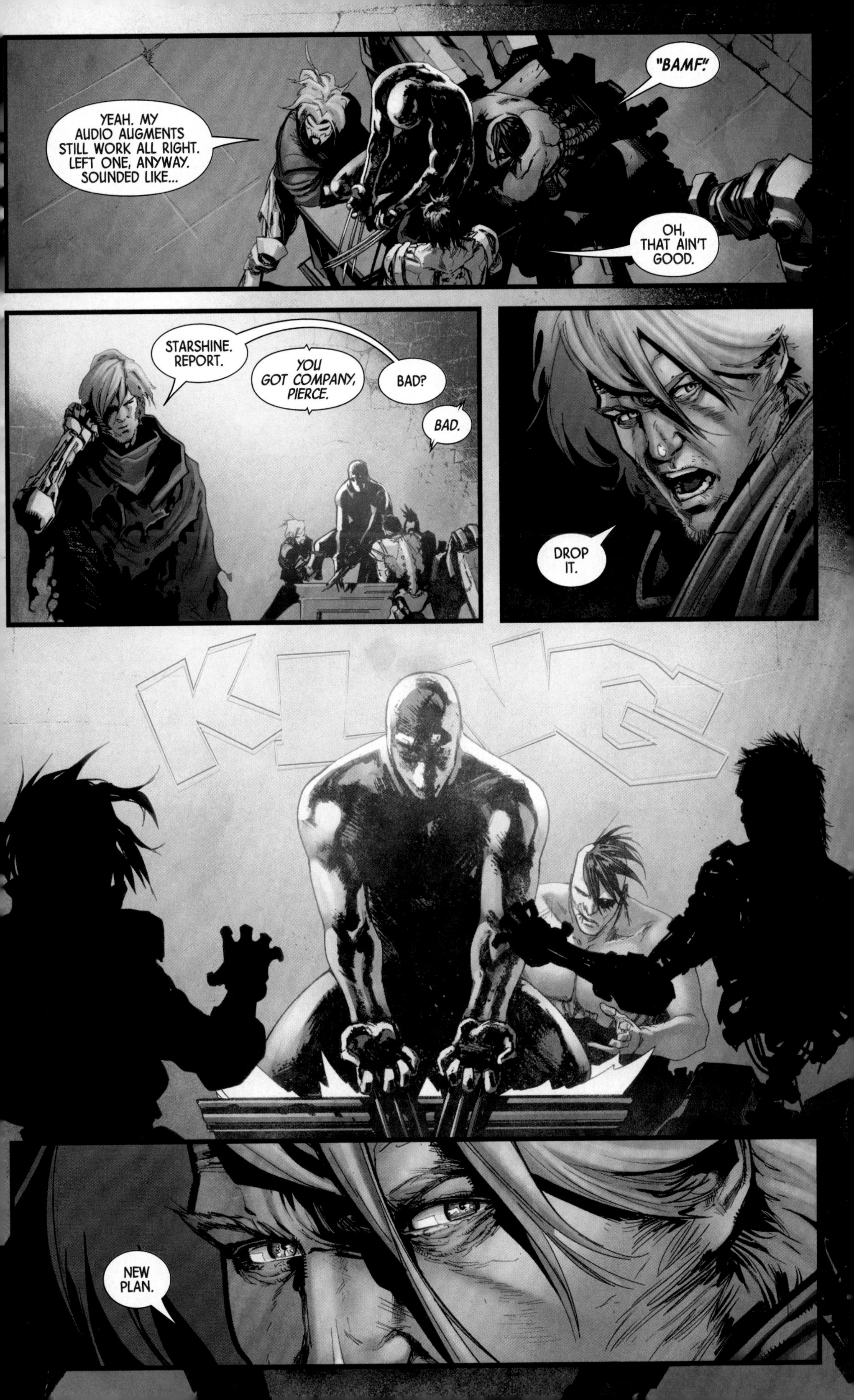
YEAH. MY AUDIO AUGMENTS STILL WORK ALL RIGHT. LEFT ONE, ANYWAY. SOUNDED LIKE...
"BAMF!"
OH, THAT AIN'T GOOD.
STARSHINE. REPORT.
YOU GOT COMPANY, PIERCE.
BAD?
BAD.
DROP IT.
KLANG
NEW PLAN.

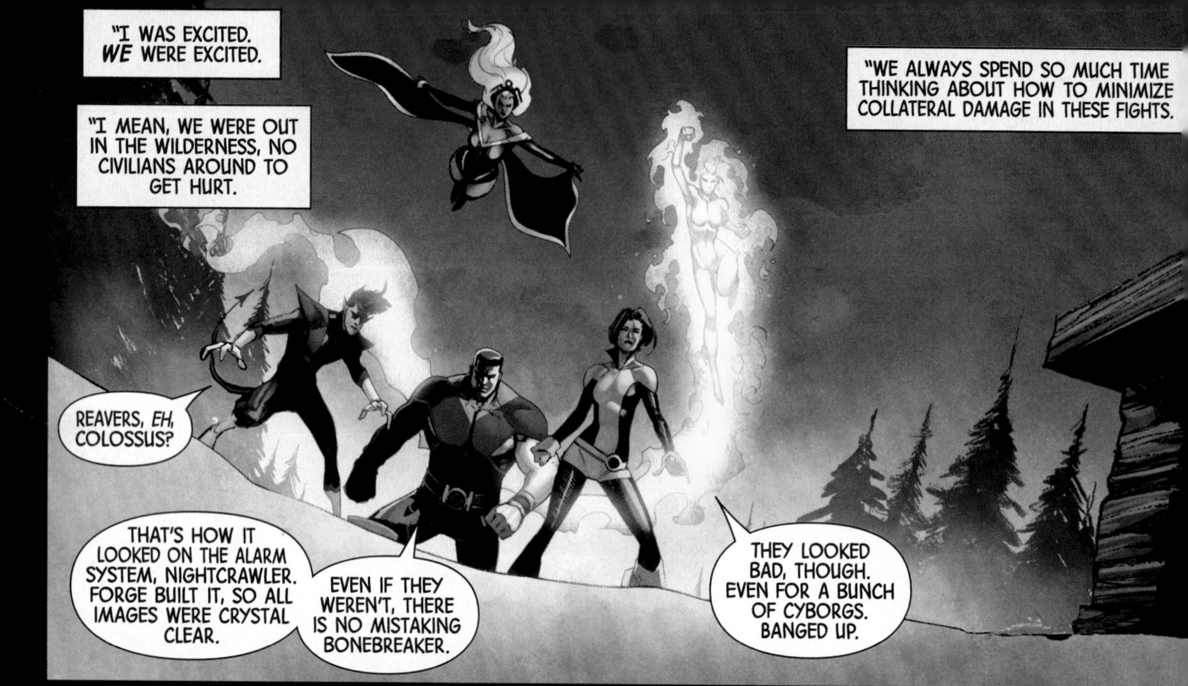
"I WAS EXCITED. *WE* WERE EXCITED.
"I MEAN, WE WERE OUT IN THE WILDERNESS, NO CIVILIANS AROUND TO GET HURT.
"WE ALWAYS SPEND SO MUCH TIME THINKING ABOUT HOW TO MINIMIZE COLLATERAL DAMAGE IN THESE FIGHTS.
REAVERS, *EH,* COLOSSUS?
THAT'S HOW IT LOOKED ON THE ALARM SYSTEM, NIGHTCRAWLER. FORGE BUILT IT, SO ALL IMAGES WERE CRYSTAL CLEAR.
EVEN IF THEY WEREN'T, THERE IS NO MISTAKING BONEBREAKER.
THEY LOOKED BAD, THOUGH. EVEN FOR A BUNCH OF CYBORGS. BANGED UP.
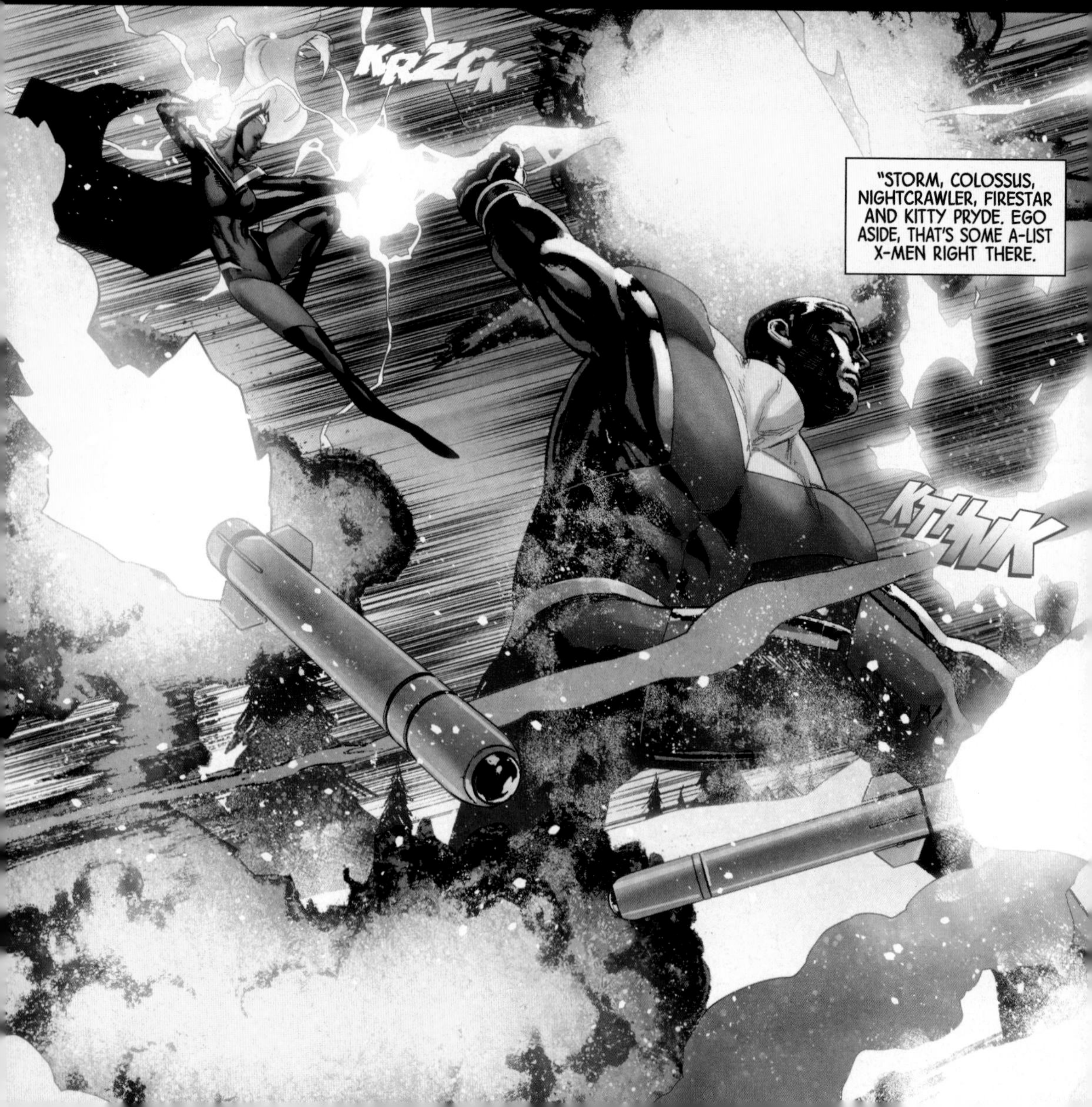
KRZCK
"STORM, COLOSSUS, NIGHTCRAWLER, FIRESTAR AND KITTY PRYDE. EGO ASIDE, THAT'S SOME A-LIST X-MEN RIGHT THERE.
KTHNK

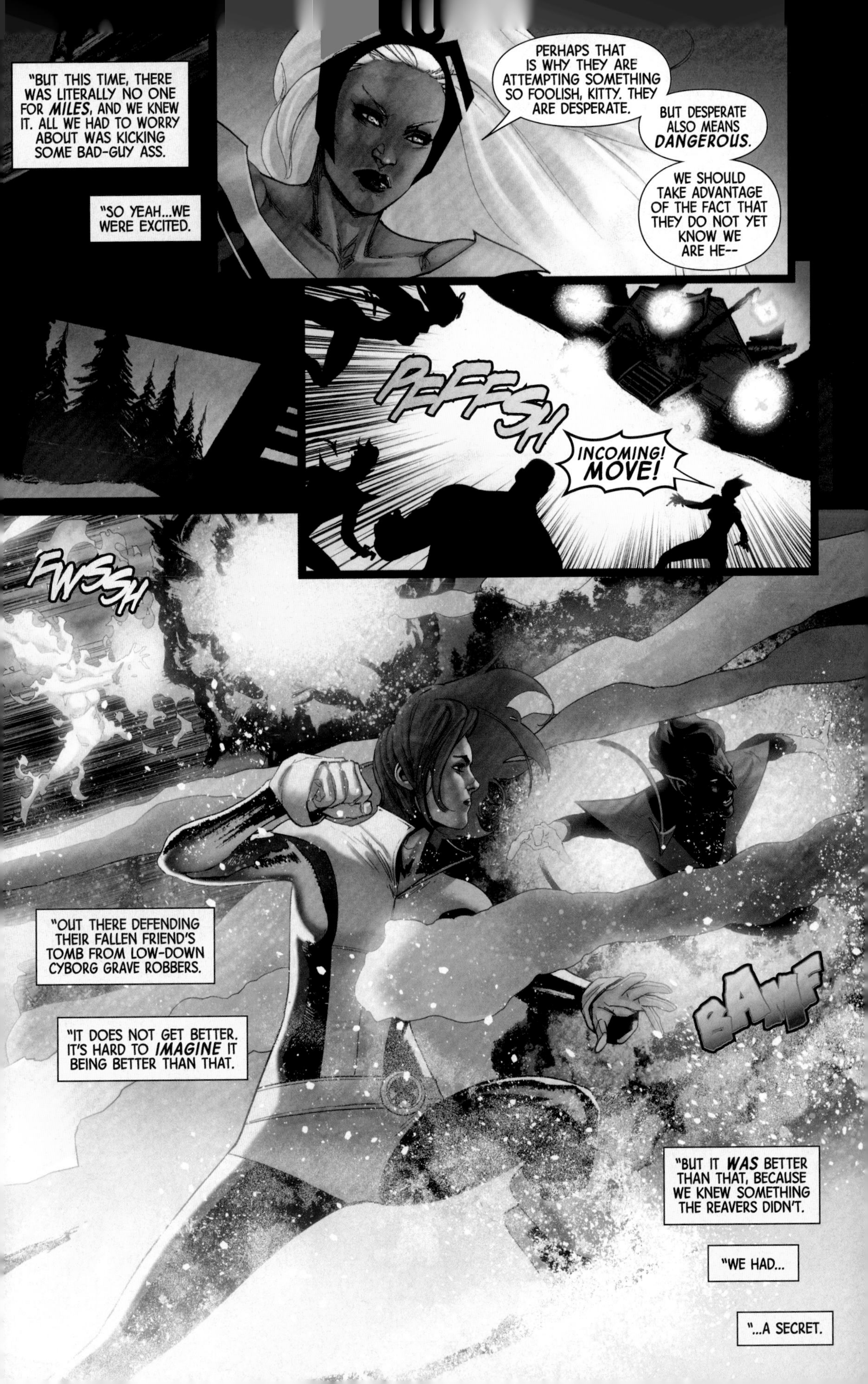
"BUT THIS TIME, THERE WAS LITERALLY NO ONE FOR MILES, AND WE KNEW IT. ALL WE HAD TO WORRY ABOUT WAS KICKING SOME BAD-GUY ASS.
"SO YEAH...WE WERE EXCITED.
PERHAPS THAT IS WHY THEY ARE ATTEMPTING SOMETHING SO FOOLISH, KITTY. THEY ARE DESPERATE.
BUT DESPERATE ALSO MEANS DANGEROUS.
WE SHOULD TAKE ADVANTAGE OF THE FACT THAT THEY DO NOT YET KNOW WE ARE HE--
PFFFSH
INCOMING! MOVE!
FWSSH
"OUT THERE DEFENDING THEIR FALLEN FRIEND'S TOMB FROM LOW-DOWN CYBORG GRAVE ROBBERS.
"IT DOES NOT GET BETTER. IT'S HARD TO IMAGINE IT BEING BETTER THAN THAT.
BAMF
"BUT IT WAS BETTER THAN THAT, BECAUSE WE KNEW SOMETHING THE REAVERS DIDN'T.
"WE HAD...
"...A SECRET.

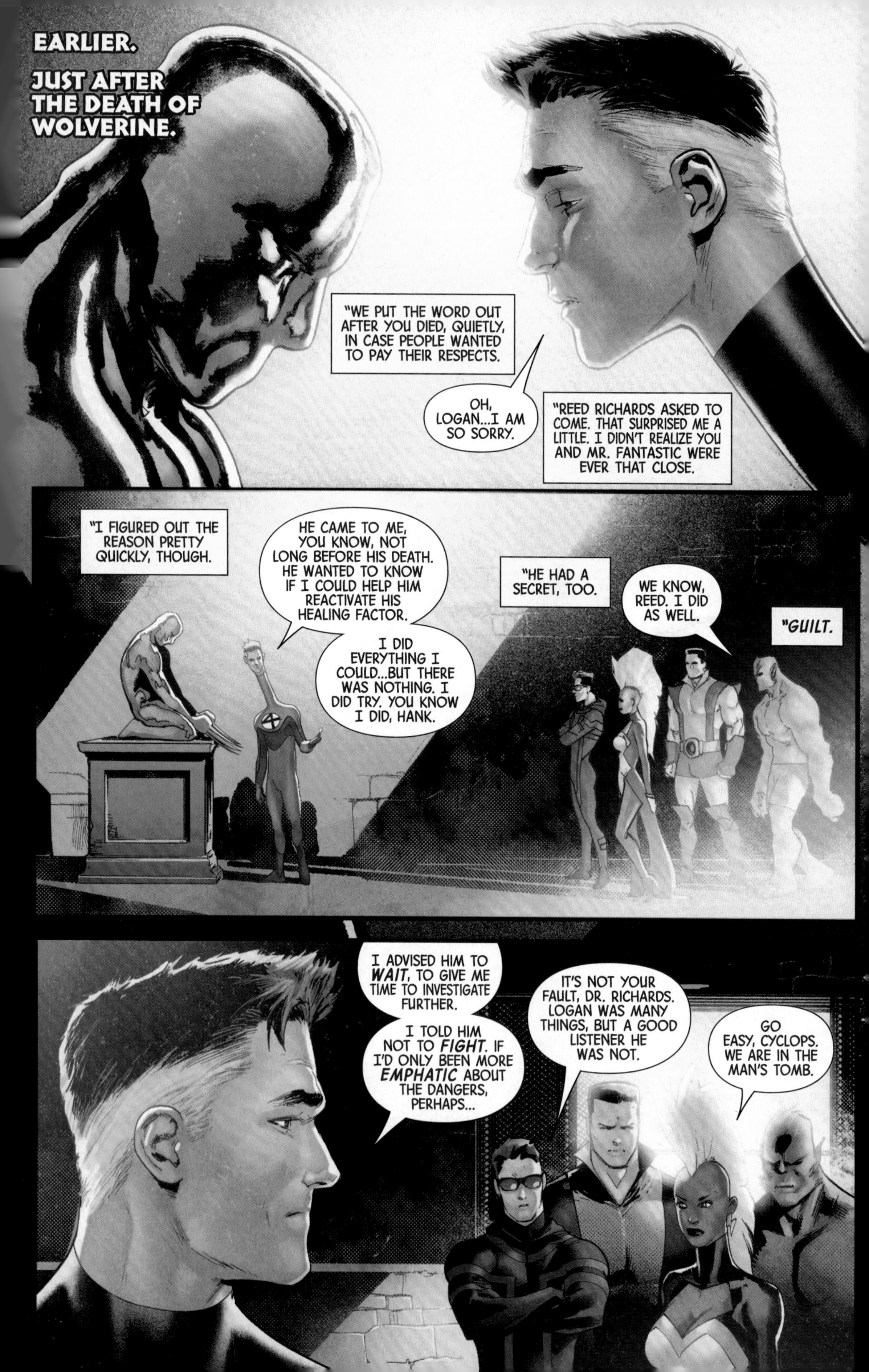
EARLIER.
JUST AFTER THE DEATH OF WOLVERINE.
"WE PUT THE WORD OUT AFTER YOU DIED, QUIETLY, IN CASE PEOPLE WANTED TO PAY THEIR RESPECTS.
OH, LOGAN...I AM SO SORRY.
"REED RICHARDS ASKED TO COME. THAT SURPRISED ME A LITTLE. I DIDN'T REALIZE YOU AND MR. FANTASTIC WERE EVER THAT CLOSE.
"I FIGURED OUT THE REASON PRETTY QUICKLY, THOUGH.
HE CAME TO ME, YOU KNOW, NOT LONG BEFORE HIS DEATH. HE WANTED TO KNOW IF I COULD HELP HIM REACTIVATE HIS HEALING FACTOR.
I DID EVERYTHING I COULD...BUT THERE WAS NOTHING. I DID TRY. YOU KNOW I DID, HANK.
"HE HAD A SECRET, TOO.
WE KNOW, REED. I DID AS WELL.
"GUILT.
I ADVISED HIM TO WAIT, TO GIVE ME TIME TO INVESTIGATE FURTHER.
I TOLD HIM NOT TO FIGHT. IF I'D ONLY BEEN MORE EMPHATIC ABOUT THE DANGERS, PERHAPS...
IT'S NOT YOUR FAULT, DR. RICHARDS. LOGAN WAS MANY THINGS, BUT A GOOD LISTENER HE WAS NOT.
GO EASY, CYCLOPS. WE ARE IN THE MAN'S TOMB.

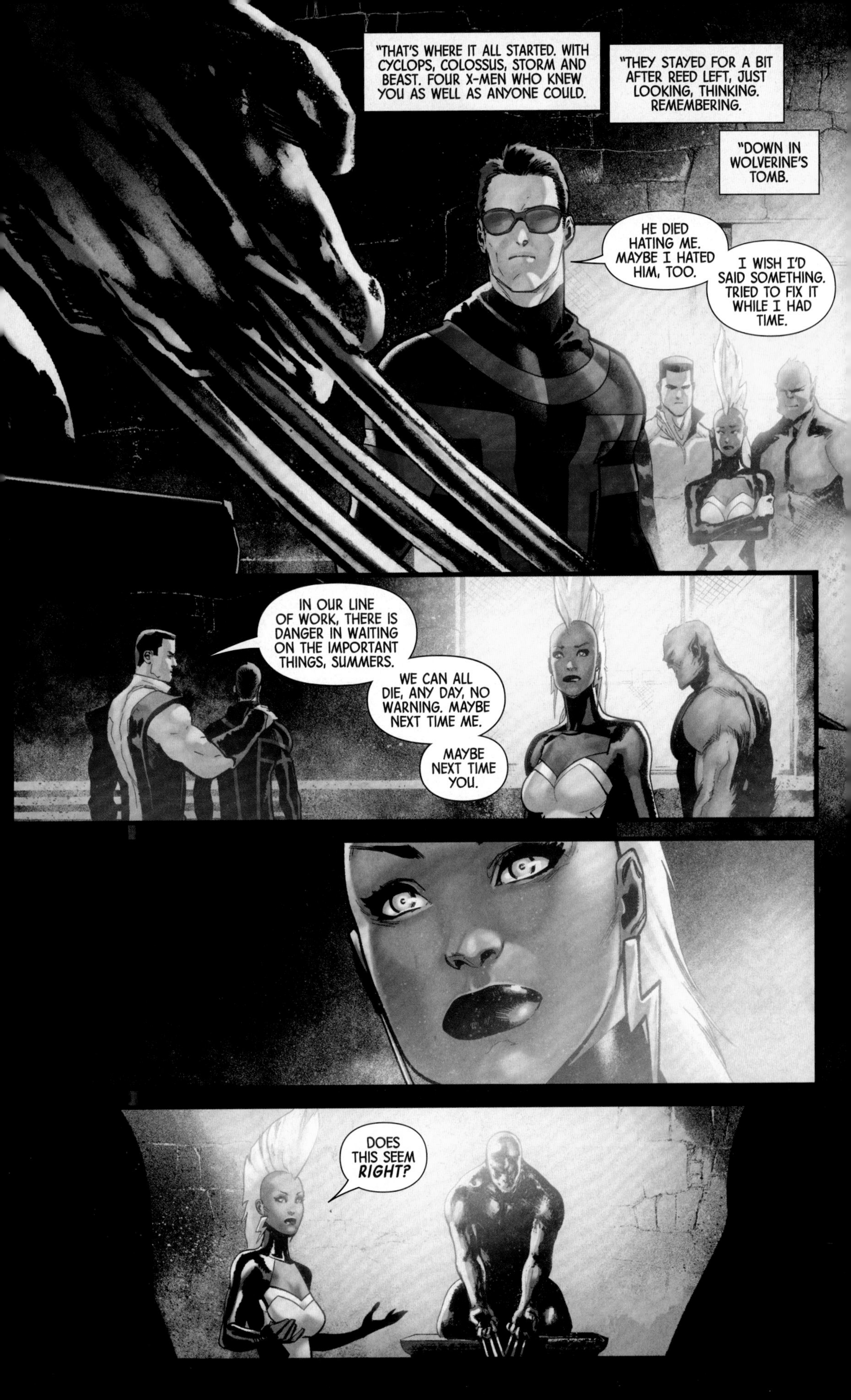

"THAT'S WHERE IT ALL STARTED. WITH CYCLOPS, COLOSSUS, STORM AND BEAST. FOUR X-MEN WHO KNEW YOU AS WELL AS ANYONE COULD.
"THEY STAYED FOR A BIT AFTER REED LEFT, JUST LOOKING, THINKING. REMEMBERING.
"DOWN IN WOLVERINE'S TOMB.
HE DIED HATING ME. MAYBE I HATED HIM, TOO.
I WISH I'D SAID SOMETHING. TRIED TO FIX IT WHILE I HAD TIME.
IN OUR LINE OF WORK, THERE IS DANGER IN WAITING ON THE IMPORTANT THINGS, SUMMERS.
WE CAN ALL DIE, ANY DAY, NO WARNING. MAYBE NEXT TIME ME.
MAYBE NEXT TIME YOU.
DOES THIS SEEM *RIGHT?*

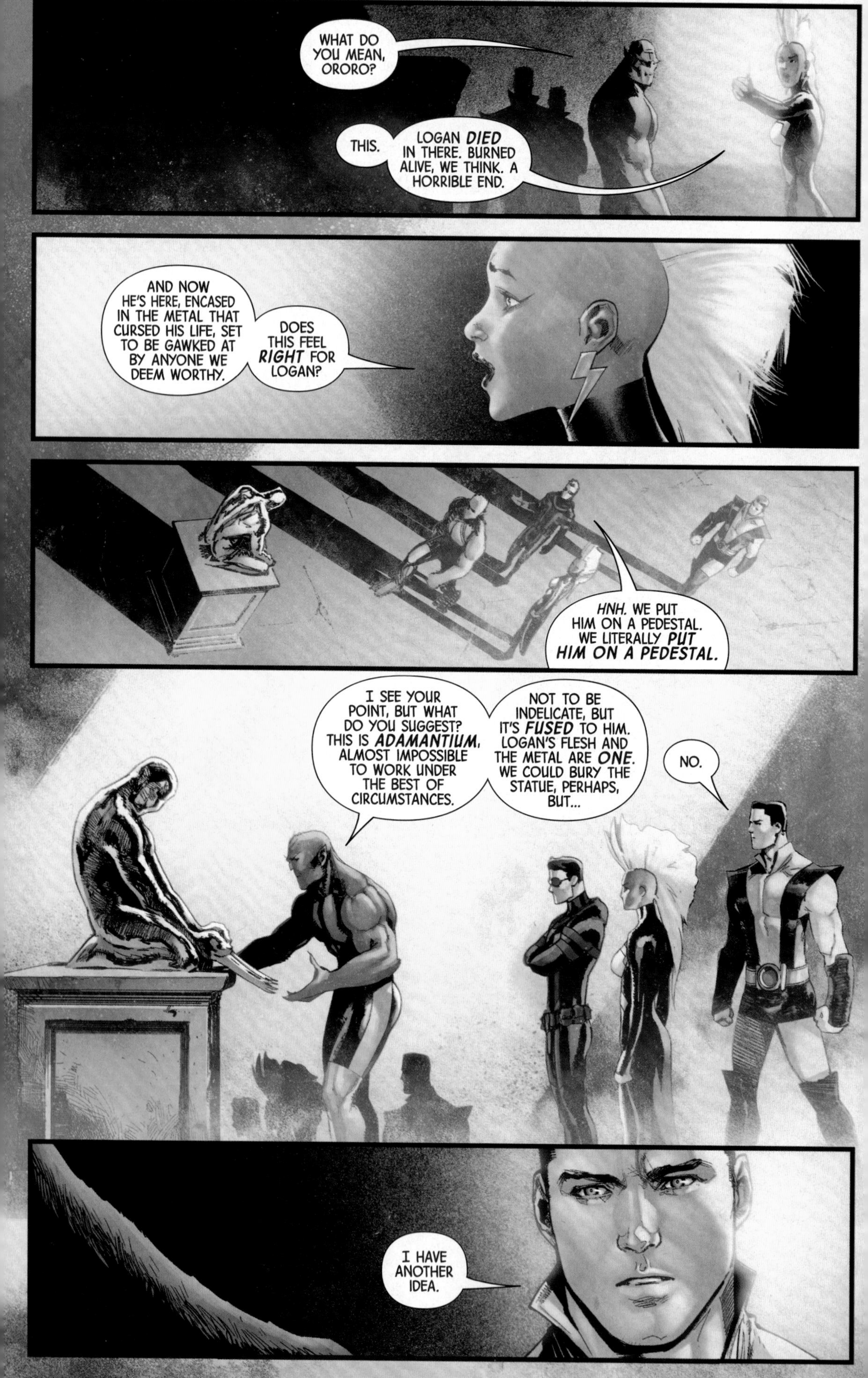
WHAT DO YOU MEAN, ORORO?
THIS.
LOGAN *DIED* IN THERE. BURNED ALIVE, WE THINK. A HORRIBLE END.
AND NOW HE'S HERE, ENCASED IN THE METAL THAT CURSED HIS LIFE, SET TO BE GAWKED AT BY ANYONE WE DEEM WORTHY.
DOES THIS FEEL *RIGHT* FOR LOGAN?
HNH. WE PUT HIM ON A PEDESTAL. WE LITERALLY *PUT HIM ON A PEDESTAL.*
I SEE YOUR POINT, BUT WHAT DO YOU SUGGEST? THIS IS *ADAMANTIUM*, ALMOST IMPOSSIBLE TO WORK UNDER THE BEST OF CIRCUMSTANCES.
NOT TO BE INDELICATE, BUT IT'S *FUSED* TO HIM. LOGAN'S FLESH AND THE METAL ARE *ONE*. WE COULD BURY THE STATUE, PERHAPS, BUT...
NO.
I HAVE ANOTHER IDEA.

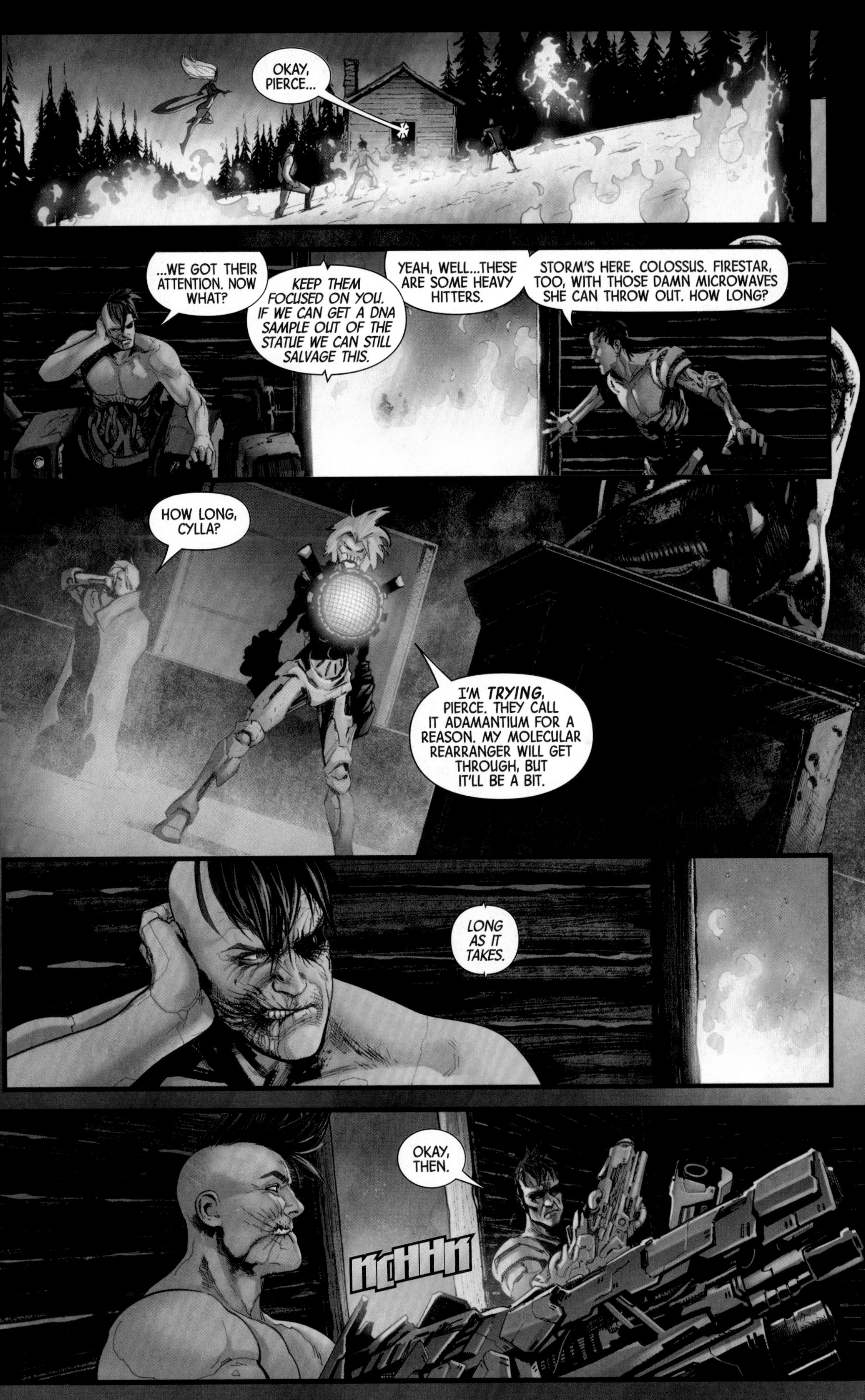

OKAY, PIERCE...
...WE GOT THEIR ATTENTION. NOW WHAT?
KEEP THEM FOCUSED ON YOU. IF WE CAN GET A DNA SAMPLE OUT OF THE STATUE WE CAN STILL SALVAGE THIS.
YEAH, WELL...THESE ARE SOME HEAVY HITTERS.
STORM'S HERE. COLOSSUS. FIRESTAR, TOO, WITH THOSE DAMN MICROWAVES SHE CAN THROW OUT. HOW LONG?
HOW LONG, CYLLA?
I'M TRYING, PIERCE. THEY CALL IT ADAMANTIUM FOR A REASON. MY MOLECULAR REARRANGER WILL GET THROUGH, BUT IT'LL BE A BIT.
LONG AS IT TAKES.
OKAY, THEN.
KCHHH

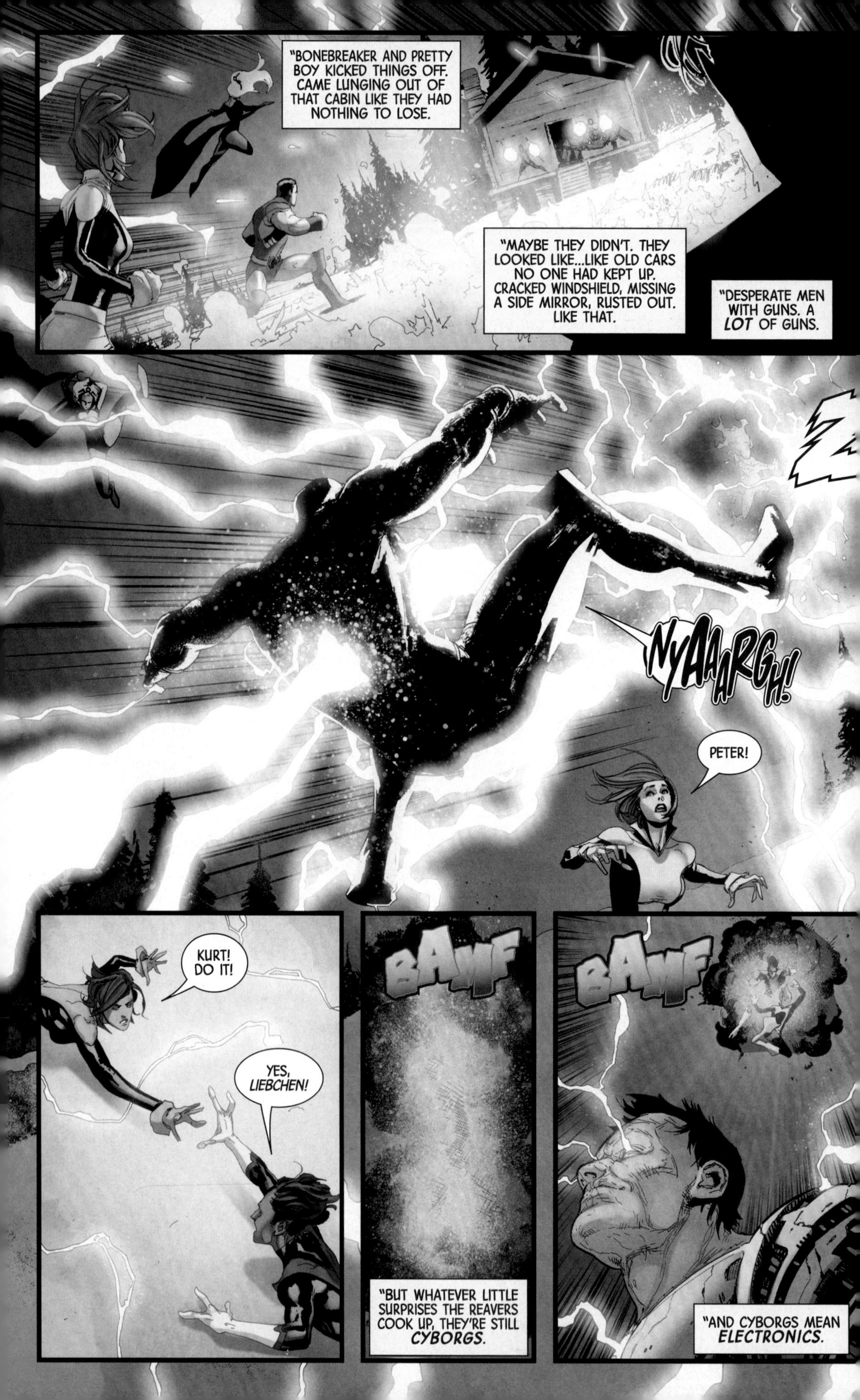
"BONEBREAKER AND PRETTY BOY KICKED THINGS OFF. CAME LUNGING OUT OF THAT CABIN LIKE THEY HAD NOTHING TO LOSE.
"MAYBE THEY DIDN'T. THEY LOOKED LIKE...LIKE OLD CARS NO ONE HAD KEPT UP. CRACKED WINDSHIELD, MISSING A SIDE MIRROR, RUSTED OUT. LIKE THAT.
"DESPERATE MEN WITH GUNS. A LOT OF GUNS.
NYAAARGH!
PETER!
KURT! DO IT!
YES, LIEBCHEN!
BAMF
"BUT WHATEVER LITTLE SURPRISES THE REAVERS COOK UP, THEY'RE STILL CYBORGS.
BAMF
"AND CYBORGS MEAN ELECTRONICS.

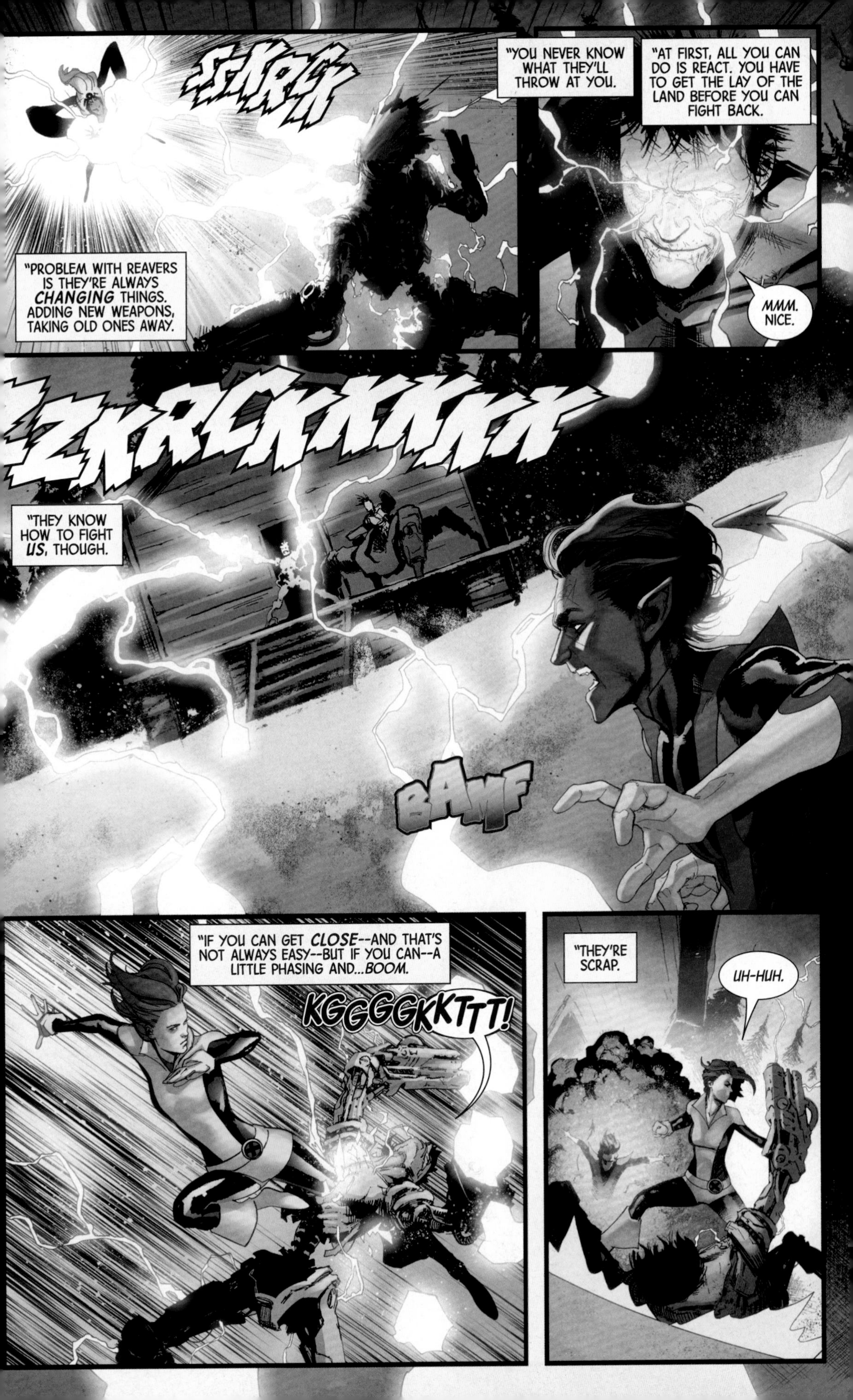
SKRAK
"PROBLEM WITH REAVERS IS THEY'RE ALWAYS CHANGING THINGS. ADDING NEW WEAPONS, TAKING OLD ONES AWAY.
"YOU NEVER KNOW WHAT THEY'LL THROW AT YOU.
"AT FIRST, ALL YOU CAN DO IS REACT. YOU HAVE TO GET THE LAY OF THE LAND BEFORE YOU CAN FIGHT BACK.
MMM. NICE.
ZKRCKKKKK
"THEY KNOW HOW TO FIGHT US, THOUGH.
BAMF
"IF YOU CAN GET CLOSE--AND THAT'S NOT ALWAYS EASY--BUT IF YOU CAN--A LITTLE PHASING AND...BOOM.
KGGGGKKTTT!
"THEY'RE SCRAP.
UH-HUH.

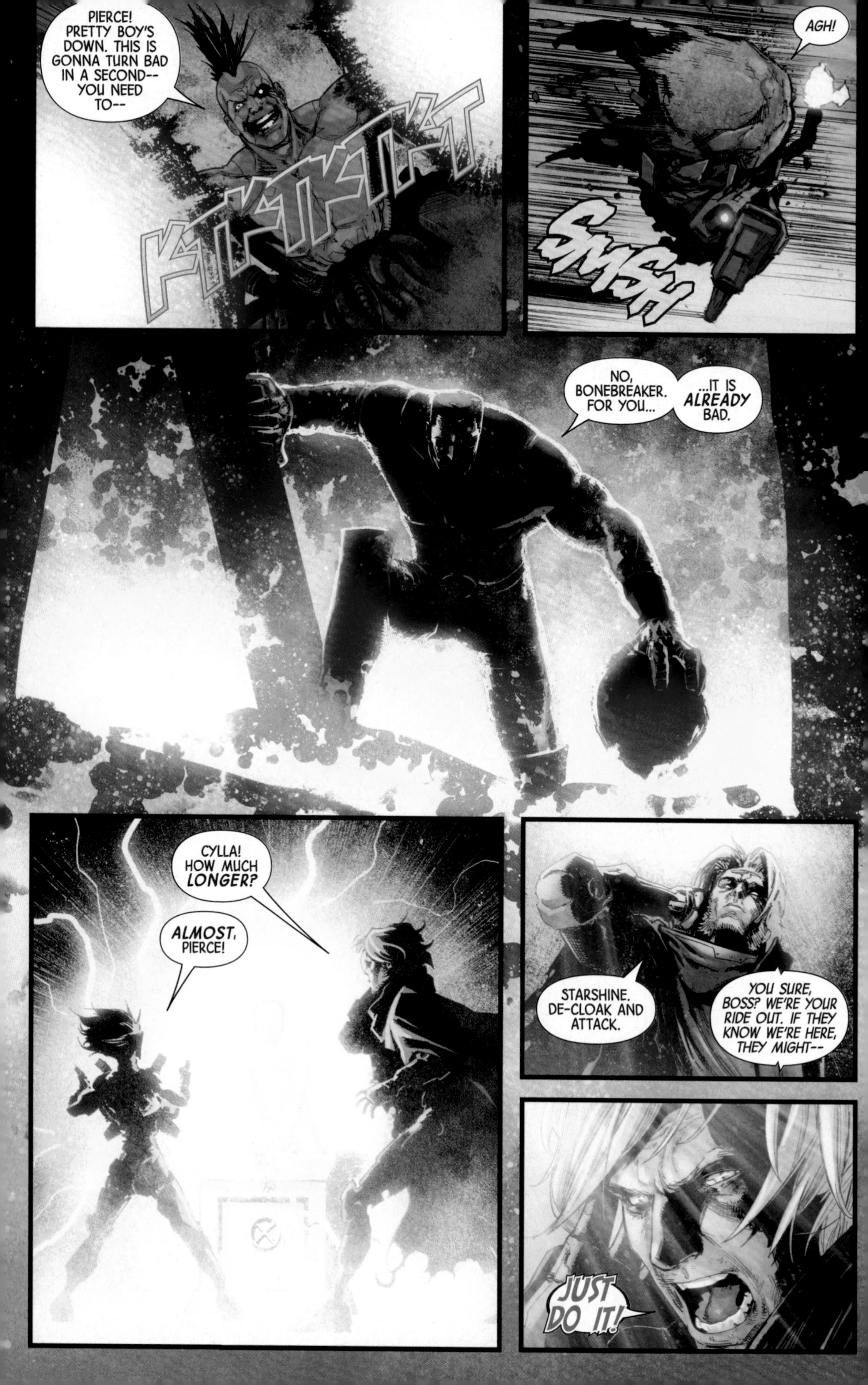
PIERCE! PRETTY BOY'S DOWN. THIS IS GONNA TURN BAD IN A SECOND-- YOU NEED TO--
KTKTKTKT
AGH!
SMSH
NO, BONEBREAKER. FOR YOU...
...IT IS ALREADY BAD.
CYLLA! HOW MUCH LONGER?
ALMOST, PIERCE!
STARSHINE. DE-CLOAK AND ATTACK.
YOU SURE, BOSS? WE'RE YOUR RIDE OUT. IF THEY KNOW WE'RE HERE, THEY MIGHT--
JUST DO IT!

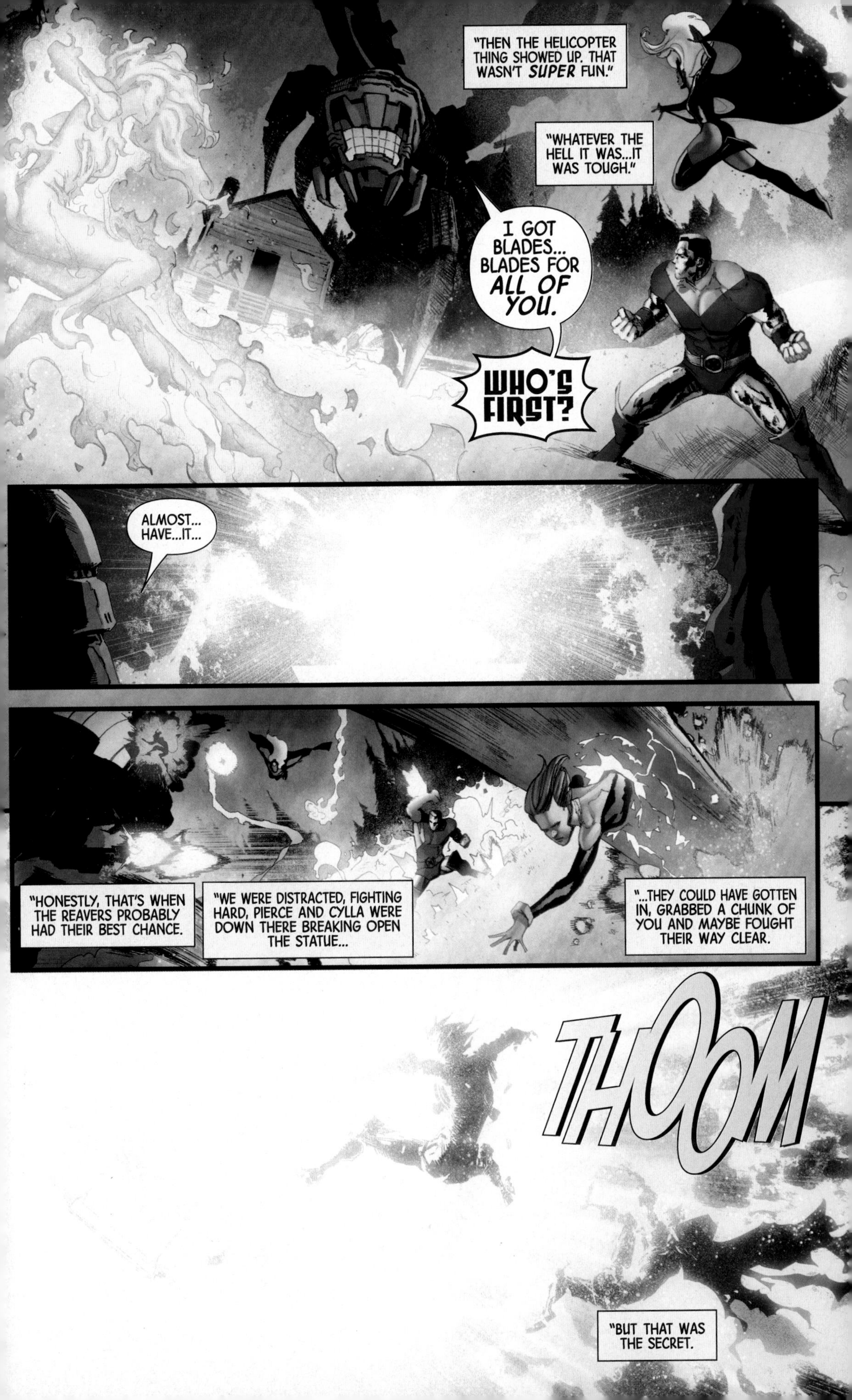
"THEN THE HELICOPTER THING SHOWED UP. THAT WASN'T *SUPER* FUN."
"WHATEVER THE HELL IT WAS...IT WAS TOUGH."
I GOT BLADES... BLADES FOR *ALL OF YOU.*
WHO'S FIRST?
ALMOST... HAVE...IT...
"HONESTLY, THAT'S WHEN THE REAVERS PROBABLY HAD THEIR BEST CHANCE.
"WE WERE DISTRACTED, FIGHTING HARD, PIERCE AND CYLLA WERE DOWN THERE BREAKING OPEN THE STATUE...
"...THEY COULD HAVE GOTTEN IN, GRABBED A CHUNK OF YOU AND MAYBE FOUGHT THEIR WAY CLEAR.
THOOM
"BUT THAT WAS THE SECRET.

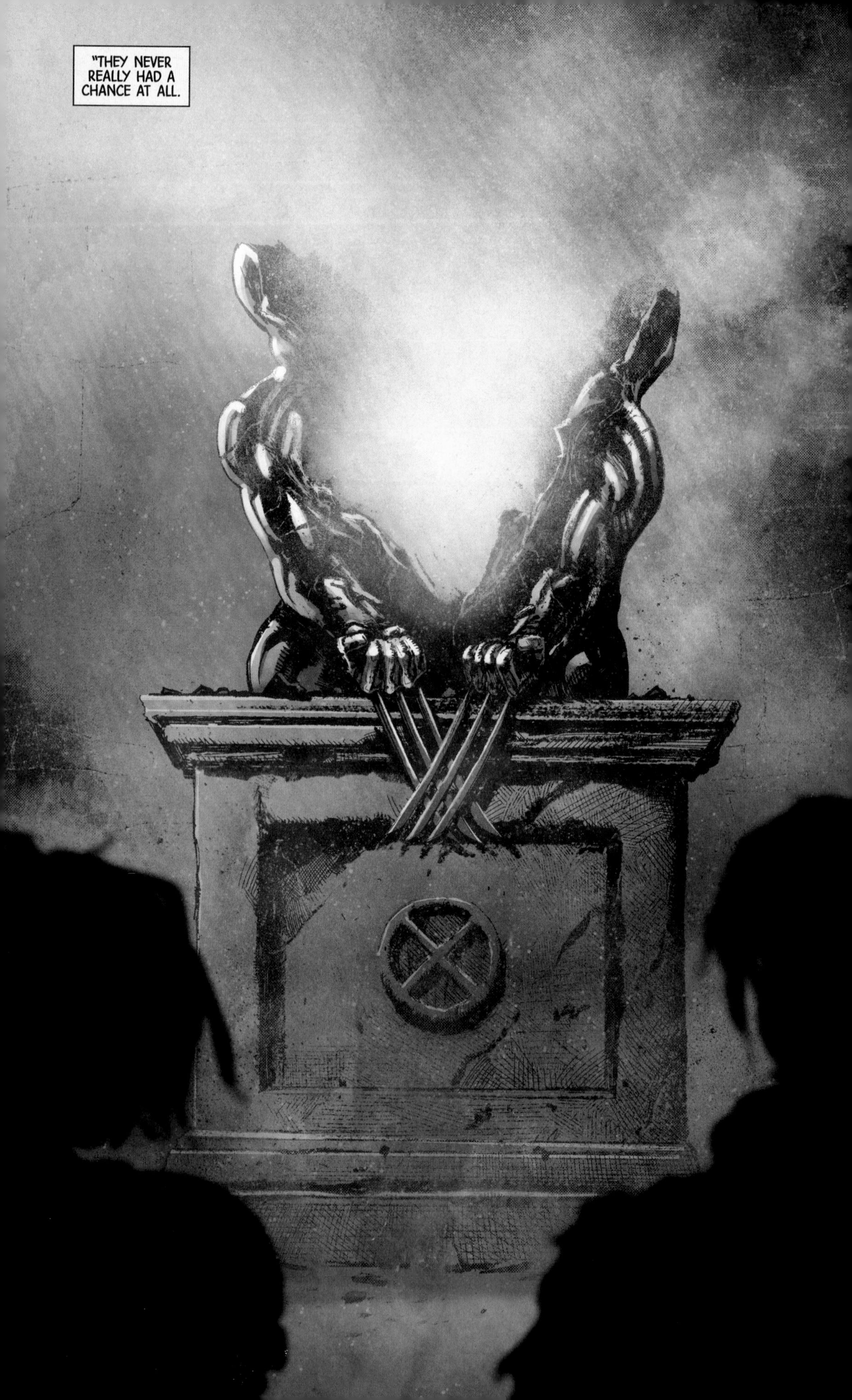
"THEY NEVER REALLY HAD A CHANCE AT ALL.

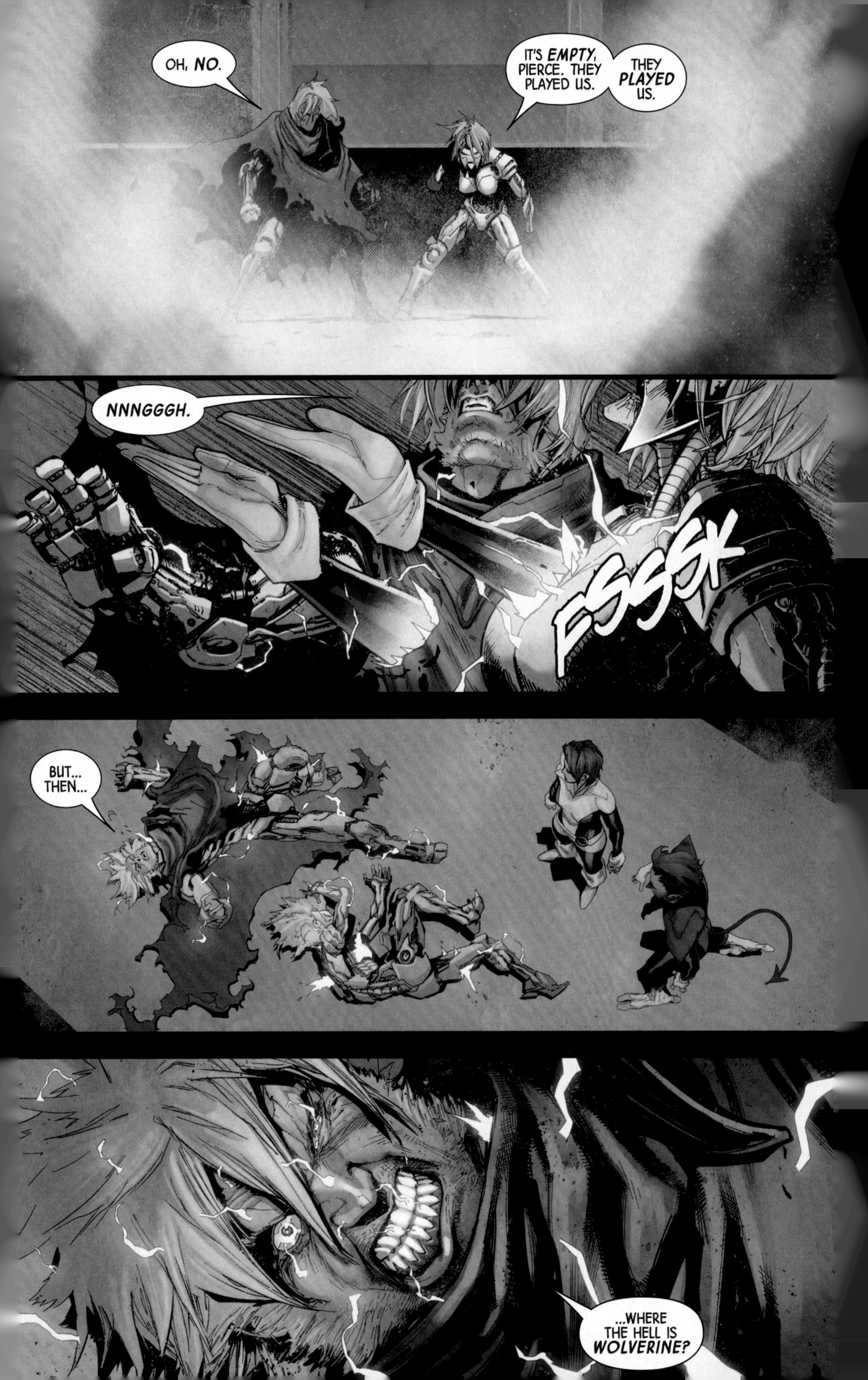

OH, NO.
IT'S EMPTY, PIERCE. THEY PLAYED US.
THEY PLAYED US.
NNNGGGH.
FSSSK
BUT... THEN...
...WHERE THE HELL IS WOLVERINE?

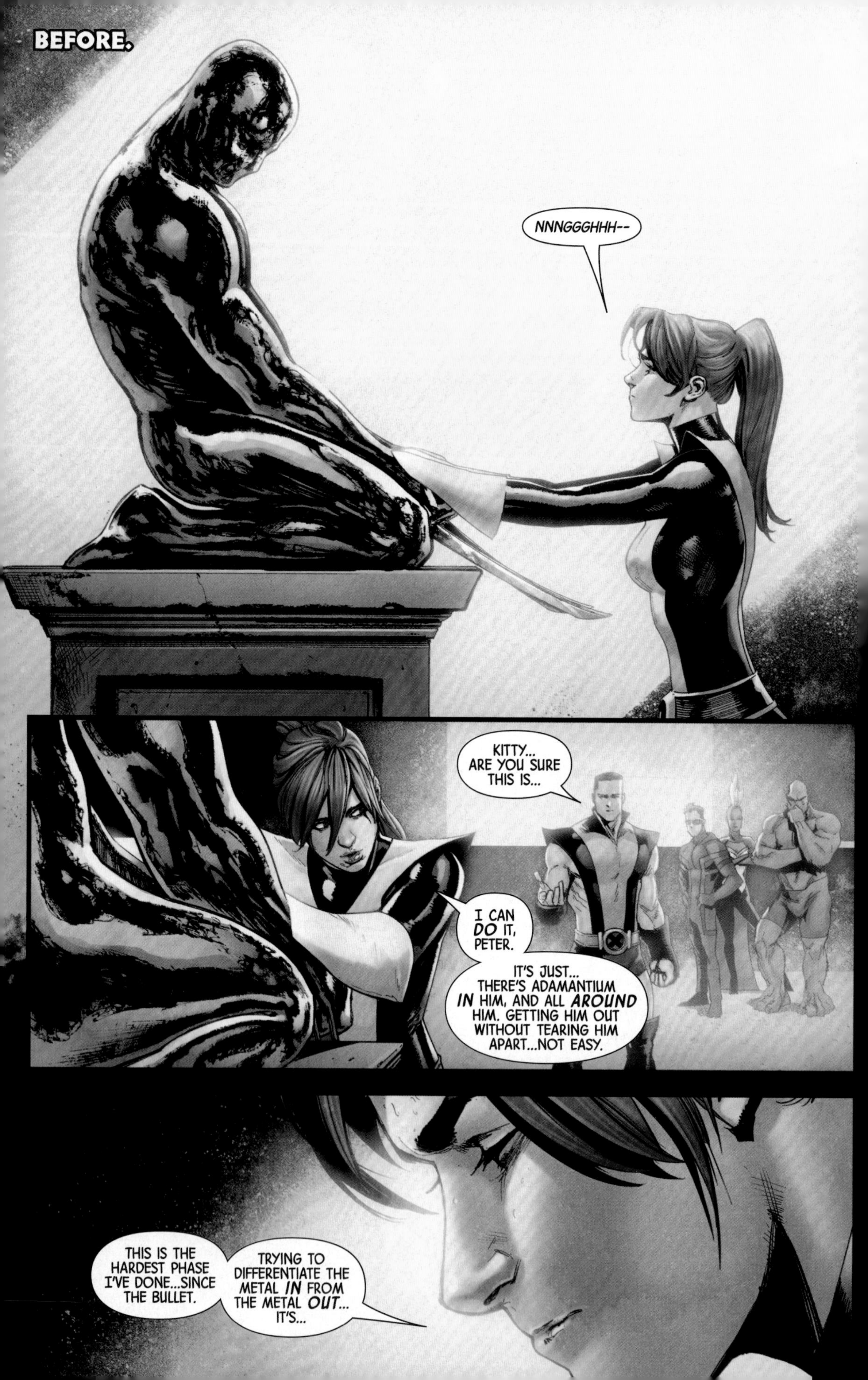

BEFORE.
NNNGGGHHH--
KITTY... ARE YOU SURE THIS IS...
I CAN DO IT, PETER.
IT'S JUST... THERE'S ADAMANTIUM IN HIM, AND ALL AROUND HIM. GETTING HIM OUT WITHOUT TEARING HIM APART...NOT EASY.
THIS IS THE HARDEST PHASE I'VE DONE...SINCE THE BULLET.
TRYING TO DIFFERENTIATE THE METAL IN FROM THE METAL OUT... IT'S...

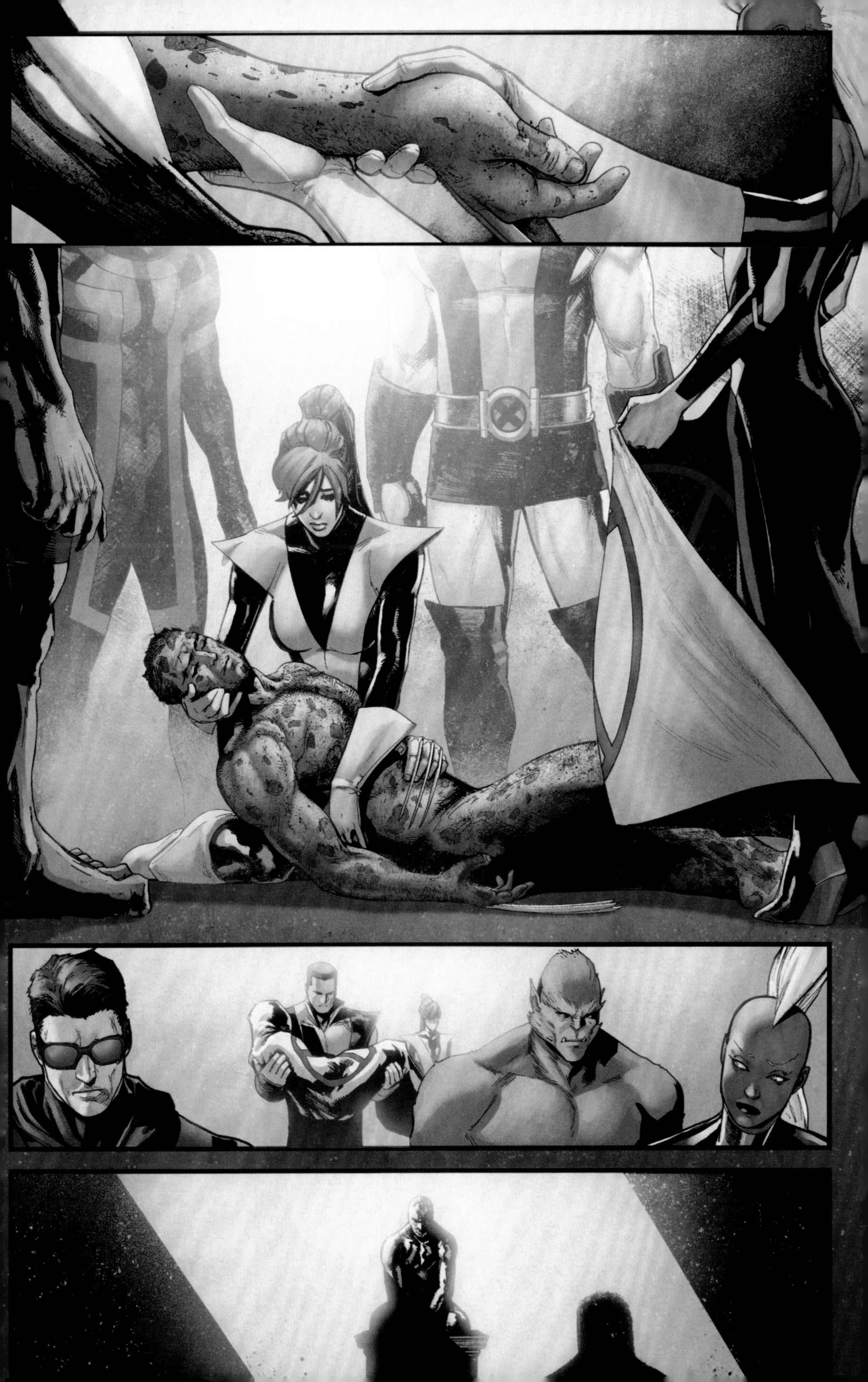

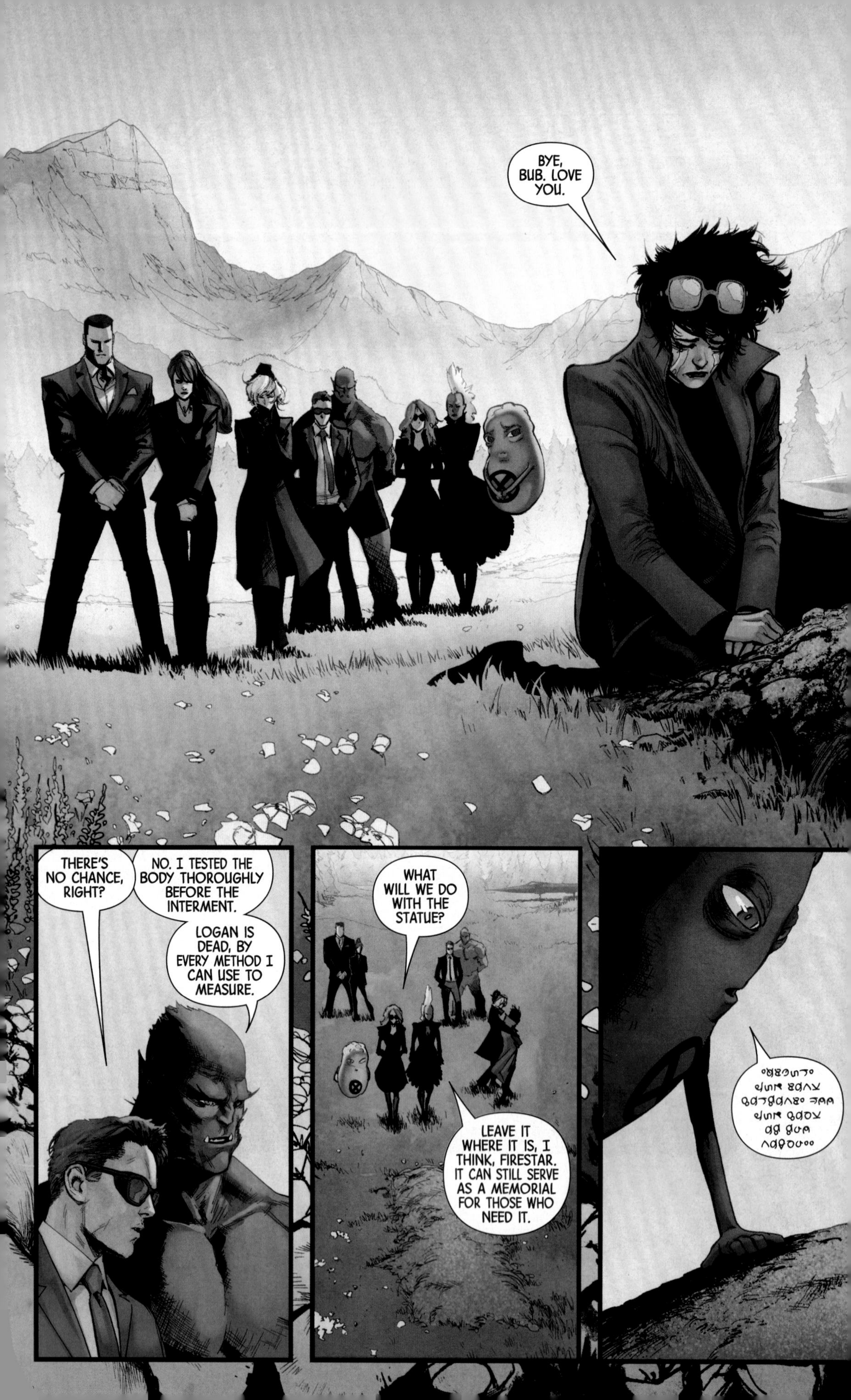
BYE, BUB. LOVE YOU.
THERE'S NO CHANCE, RIGHT?
NO. I TESTED THE BODY THOROUGHLY BEFORE THE INTERMENT.
LOGAN IS DEAD, BY EVERY METHOD I CAN USE TO MEASURE.
WHAT WILL WE DO WITH THE STATUE?
LEAVE IT WHERE IT IS, I THINK, FIRESTAR. IT CAN STILL SERVE AS A MEMORIAL FOR THOSE WHO NEED IT.

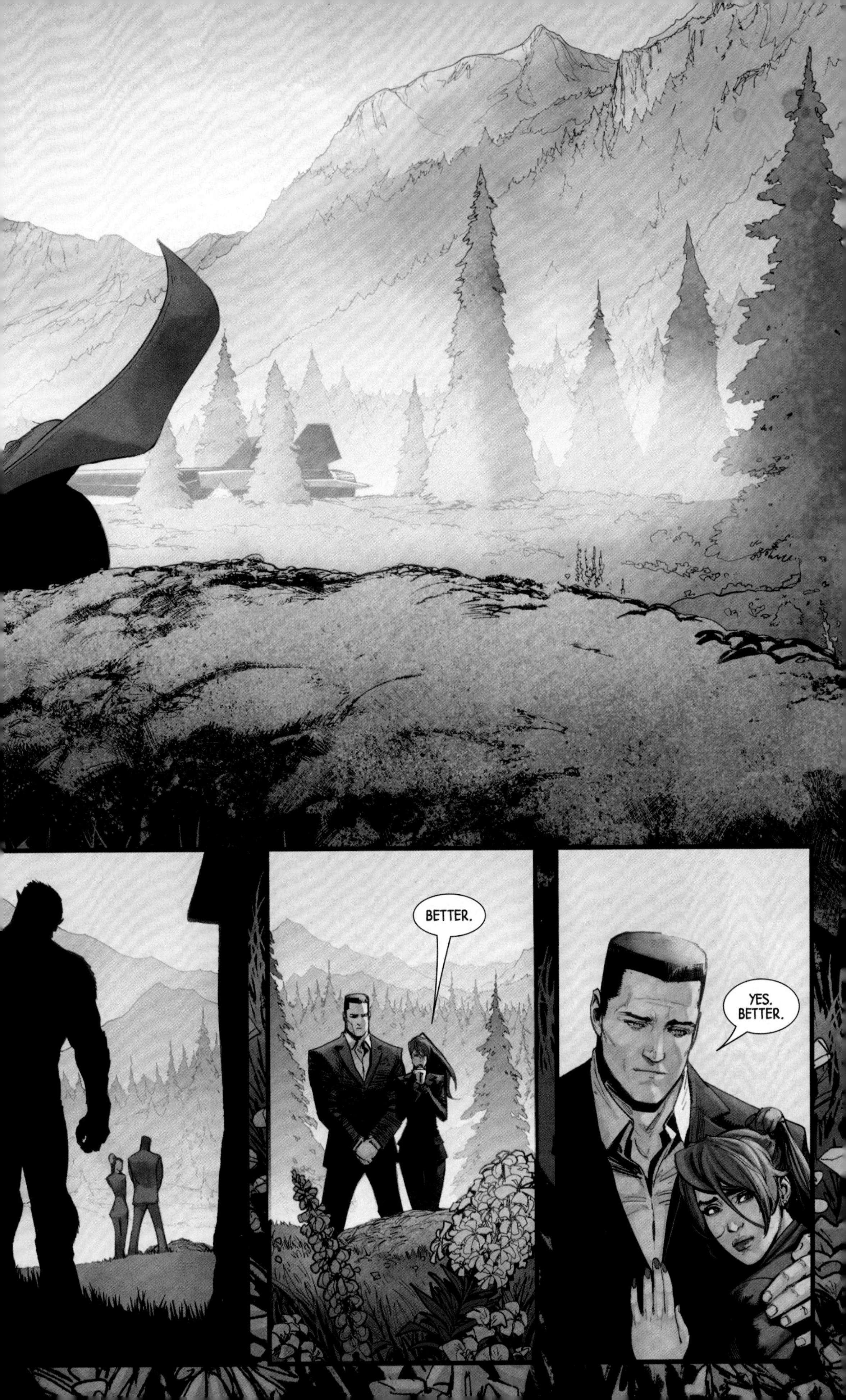
BETTER.
YES. BETTER.

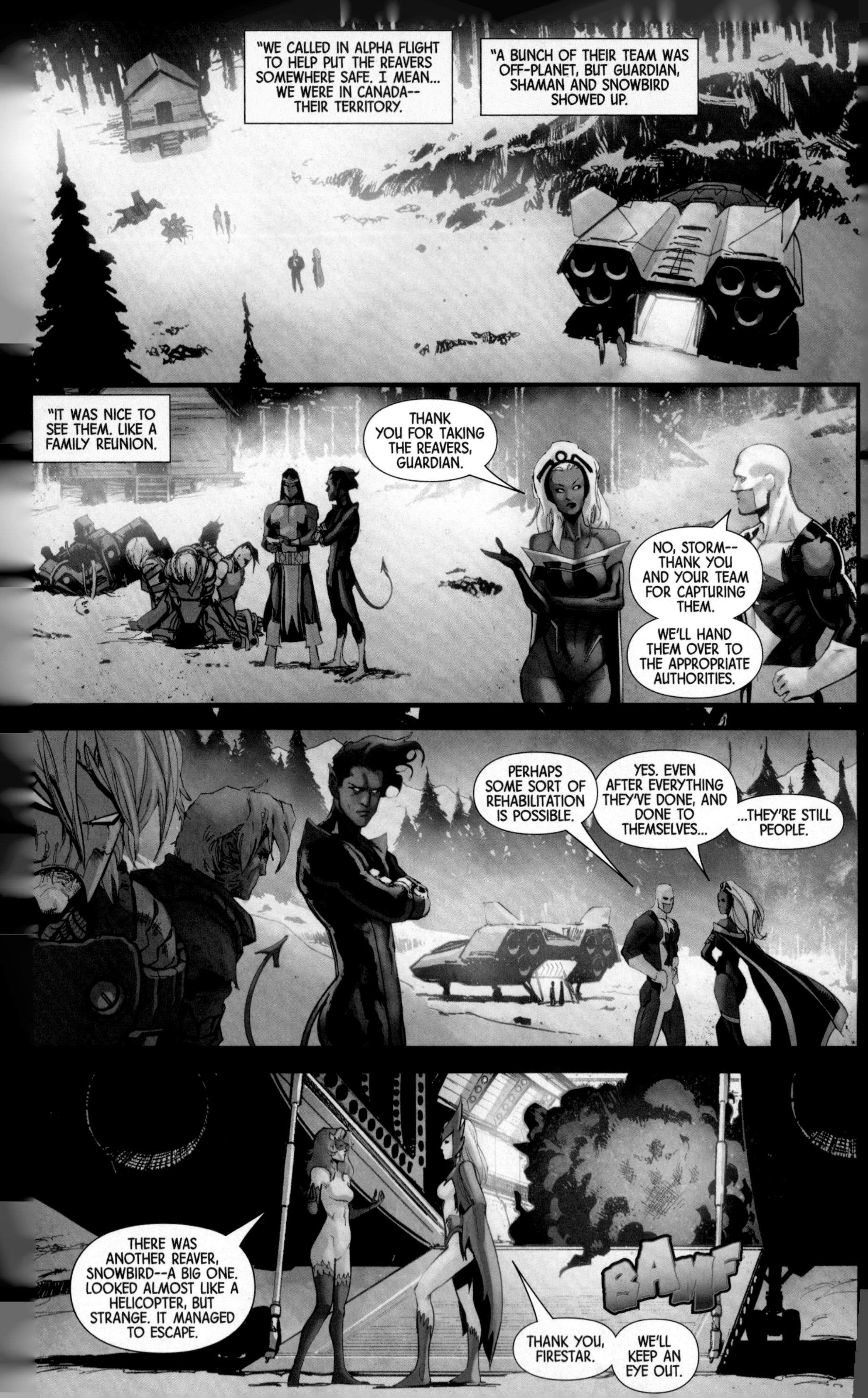
"WE CALLED IN ALPHA FLIGHT TO HELP PUT THE REAVERS SOMEWHERE SAFE. I MEAN... WE WERE IN CANADA-- THEIR TERRITORY.
"A BUNCH OF THEIR TEAM WAS OFF-PLANET, BUT GUARDIAN, SHAMAN AND SNOWBIRD SHOWED UP.
"IT WAS NICE TO SEE THEM. LIKE A FAMILY REUNION.
THANK YOU FOR TAKING THE REAVERS, GUARDIAN.
NO, STORM-- THANK YOU AND YOUR TEAM FOR CAPTURING THEM.
WE'LL HAND THEM OVER TO THE APPROPRIATE AUTHORITIES.
PERHAPS SOME SORT OF REHABILITATION IS POSSIBLE.
YES. EVEN AFTER EVERYTHING THEY'VE DONE, AND DONE TO THEMSELVES...
...THEY'RE STILL PEOPLE.
THERE WAS ANOTHER REAVER, SNOWBIRD--A BIG ONE. LOOKED ALMOST LIKE A HELICOPTER, BUT STRANGE. IT MANAGED TO ESCAPE.
BAMF
THANK YOU, FIRESTAR.
WE'LL KEEP AN EYE OUT.

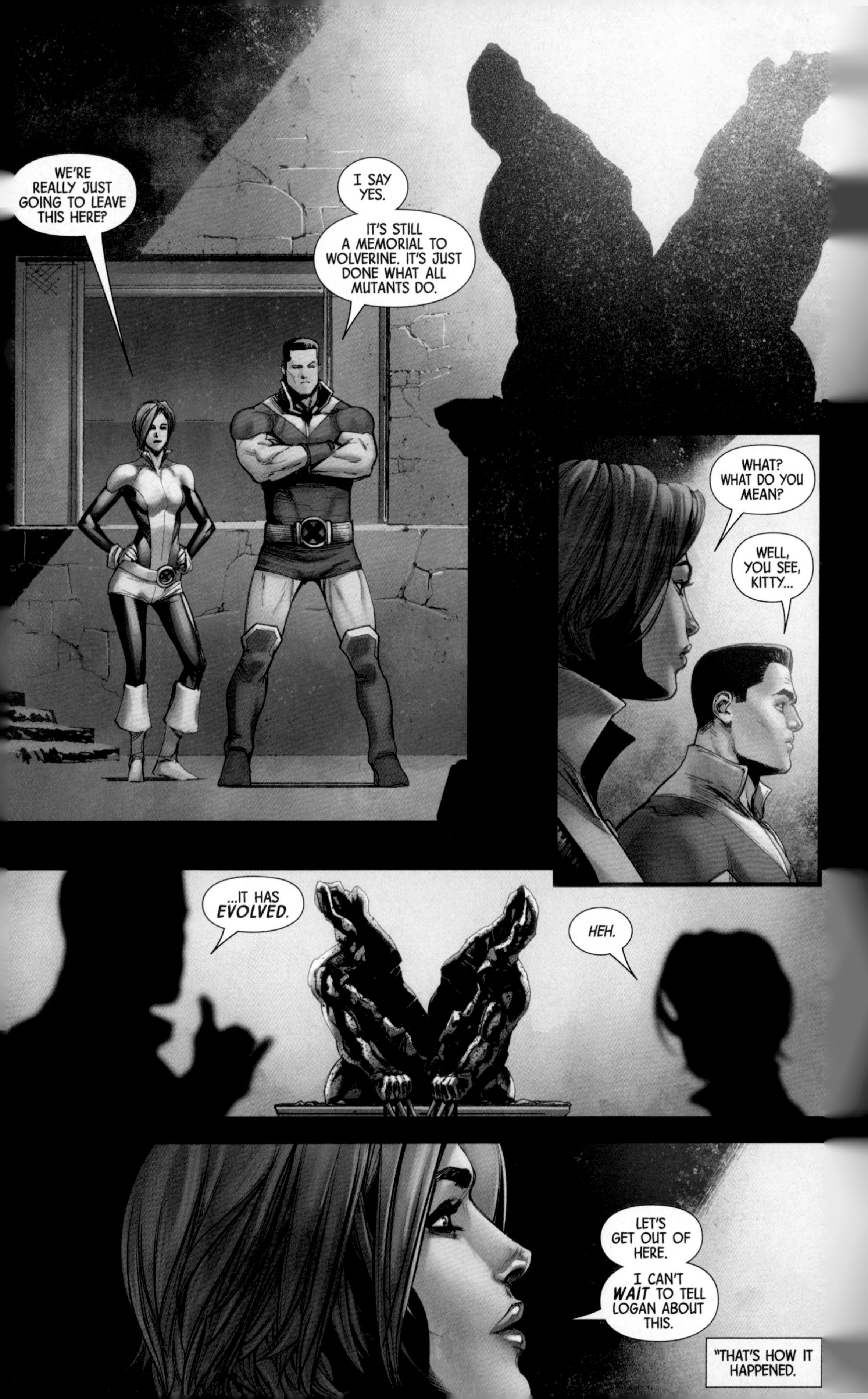

WE'RE REALLY JUST GOING TO LEAVE THIS HERE?
I SAY YES.
IT'S STILL A MEMORIAL TO WOLVERINE. IT'S JUST DONE WHAT ALL MUTANTS DO.
WHAT? WHAT DO YOU MEAN?
WELL, YOU SEE, KITTY...
...IT HAS *EVOLVED.*
HEH.
LET'S GET OUT OF HERE.
I CAN'T *WAIT* TO TELL LOGAN ABOUT THIS.
"THAT'S HOW IT HAPPENED.

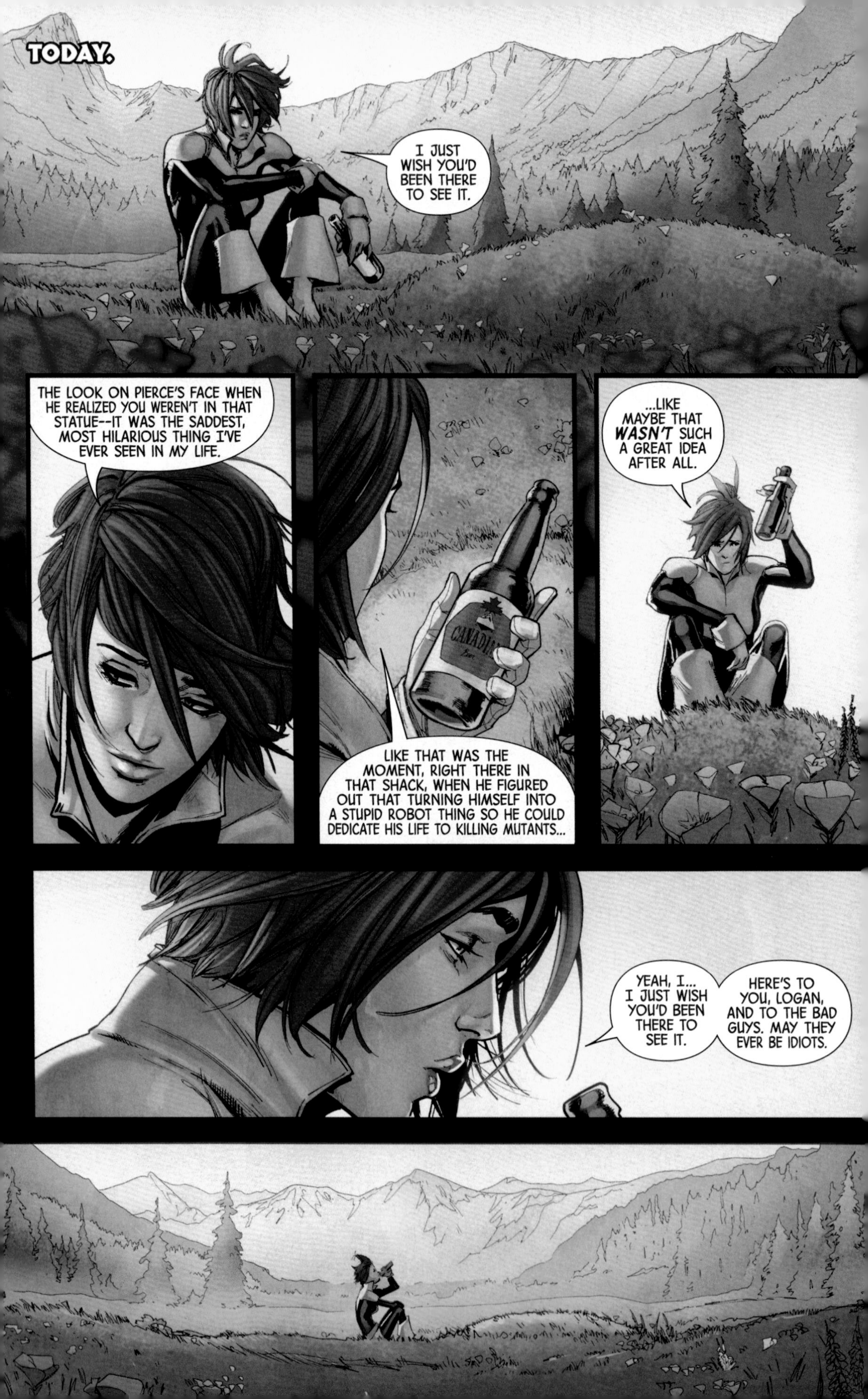
TODAY.
I JUST WISH YOU'D BEEN THERE TO SEE IT.
THE LOOK ON PIERCE'S FACE WHEN HE REALIZED YOU WEREN'T IN THAT STATUE--IT WAS THE SADDEST, MOST HILARIOUS THING I'VE EVER SEEN IN MY LIFE.
LIKE THAT WAS THE MOMENT, RIGHT THERE IN THAT SHACK, WHEN HE FIGURED OUT THAT TURNING HIMSELF INTO A STUPID ROBOT THING SO HE COULD DEDICATE HIS LIFE TO KILLING MUTANTS...
...LIKE MAYBE THAT WASN'T SUCH A GREAT IDEA AFTER ALL.
YEAH, I... I JUST WISH YOU'D BEEN THERE TO SEE IT.
HERE'S TO YOU, LOGAN, AND TO THE BAD GUYS. MAY THEY EVER BE IDIOTS.

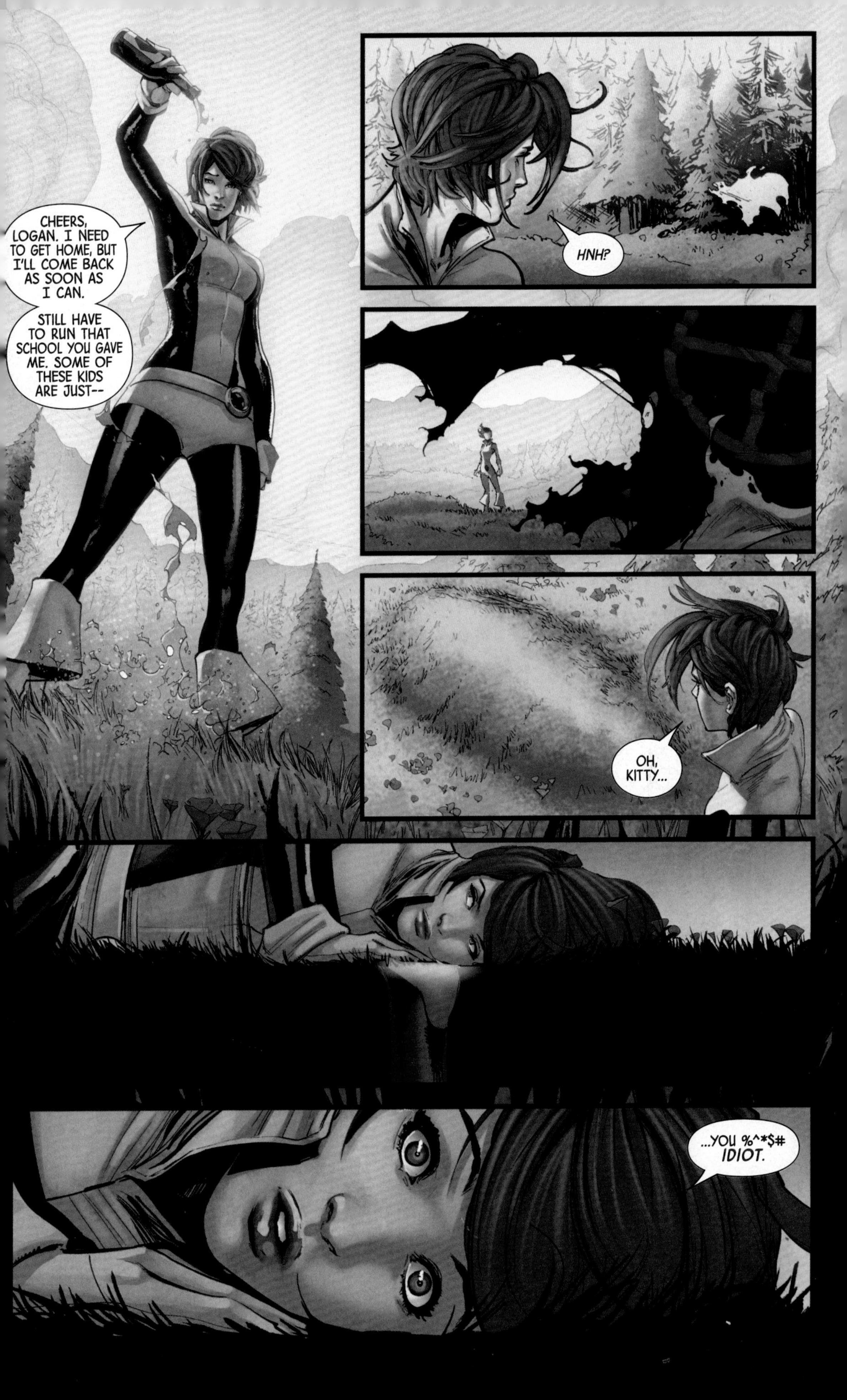
CHEERS, LOGAN. I NEED TO GET HOME, BUT I'LL COME BACK AS SOON AS I CAN.
STILL HAVE TO RUN THAT SCHOOL YOU GAVE ME. SOME OF THESE KIDS ARE JUST--
HNH?
OH, KITTY...
...YOU %^*$# IDIOT.

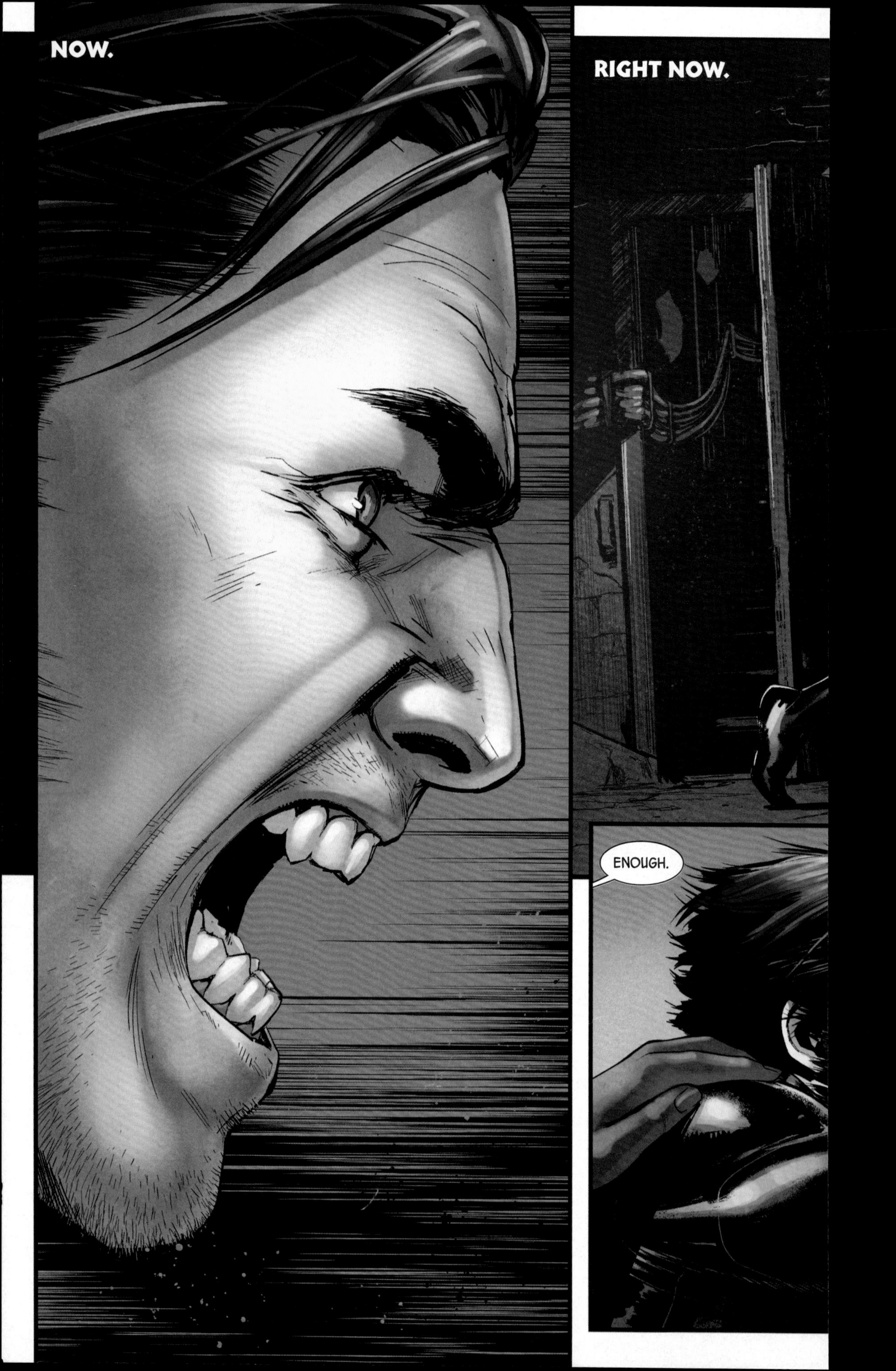
NOW.
RIGHT NOW.
ENOUGH.

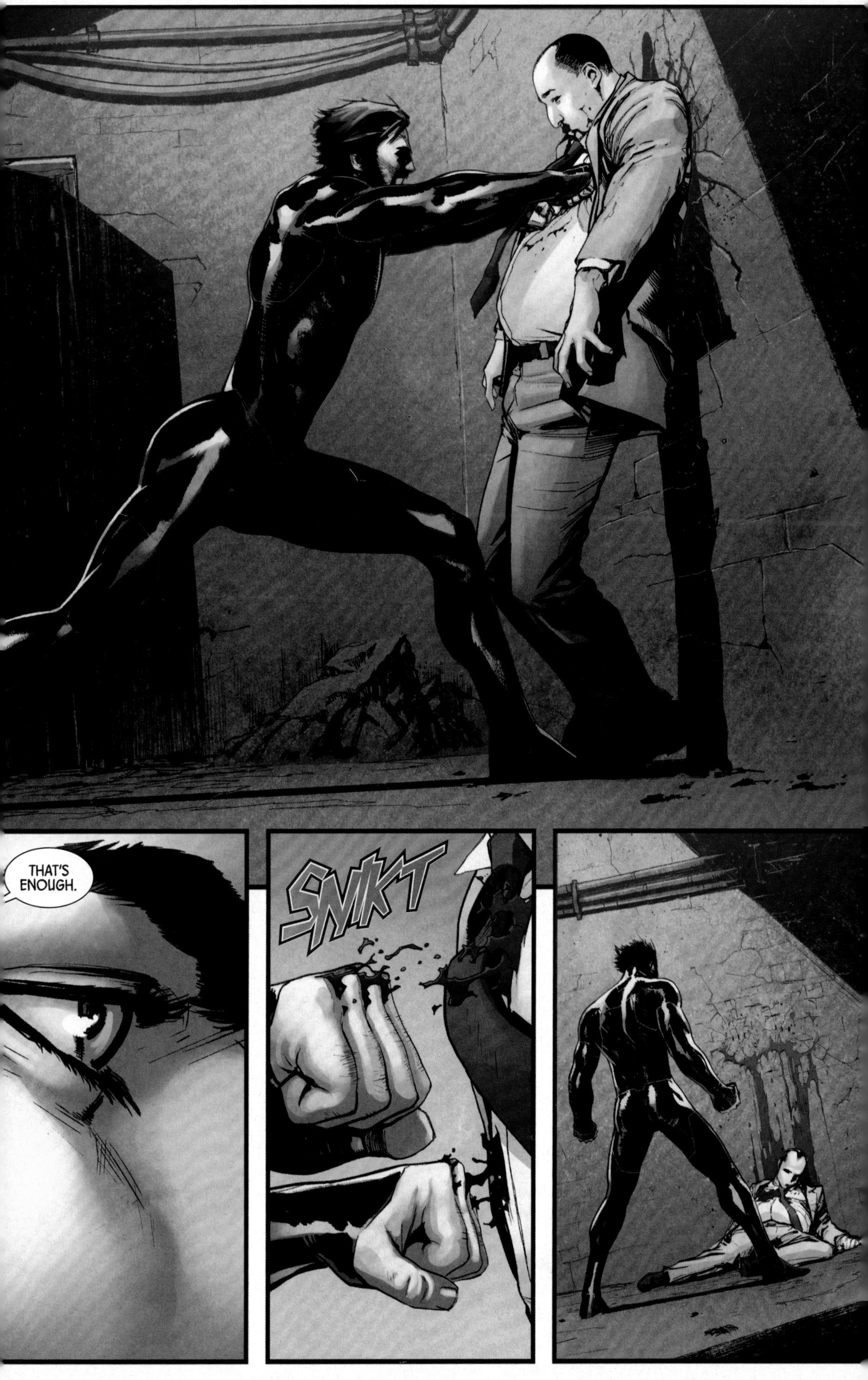
THAT'S ENOUGH.
SNIKT

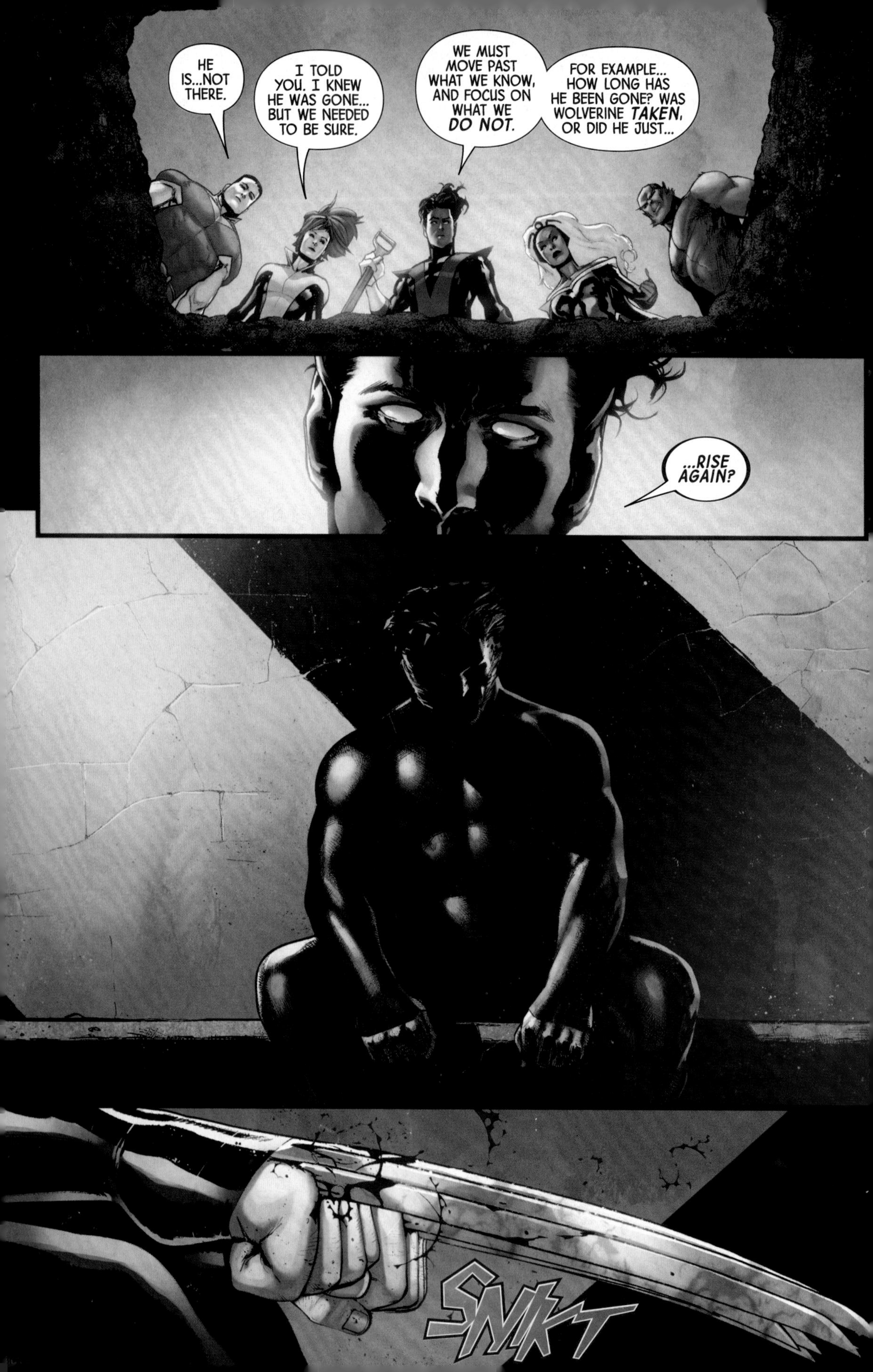
HE IS...NOT THERE.
I TOLD YOU. I KNEW HE WAS GONE... BUT WE NEEDED TO BE SURE.
WE MUST MOVE PAST WHAT WE KNOW, AND FOCUS ON WHAT WE *DO NOT*.
FOR EXAMPLE... HOW LONG HAS HE BEEN GONE? WAS WOLVERINE *TAKEN*, OR DID HE JUST...
...RISE AGAIN?
SNIKT

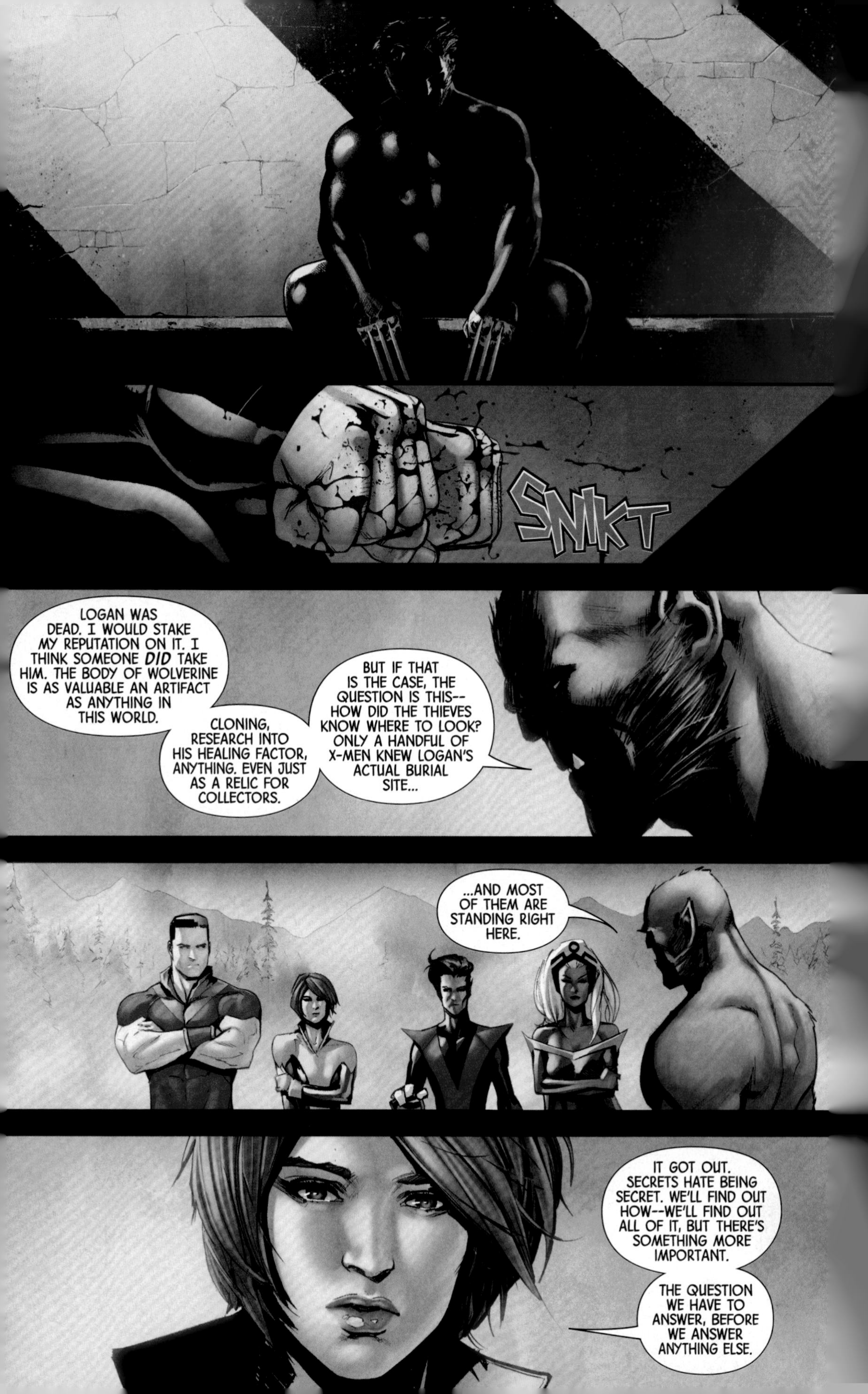
SNIKT
LOGAN WAS DEAD. I WOULD STAKE MY REPUTATION ON IT. I THINK SOMEONE *DID* TAKE HIM. THE BODY OF WOLVERINE IS AS VALUABLE AN ARTIFACT AS ANYTHING IN THIS WORLD.
CLONING, RESEARCH INTO HIS HEALING FACTOR, ANYTHING. EVEN JUST AS A RELIC FOR COLLECTORS.
BUT IF THAT IS THE CASE, THE QUESTION IS THIS--HOW DID THE THIEVES KNOW WHERE TO LOOK? ONLY A HANDFUL OF X-MEN KNEW LOGAN'S ACTUAL BURIAL SITE...
...AND MOST OF THEM ARE STANDING RIGHT HERE.
IT GOT OUT. SECRETS HATE BEING SECRET. WE'LL FIND OUT HOW--WE'LL FIND OUT ALL OF IT, BUT THERE'S SOMETHING MORE IMPORTANT.
THE QUESTION WE HAVE TO ANSWER, BEFORE WE ANSWER ANYTHING ELSE.

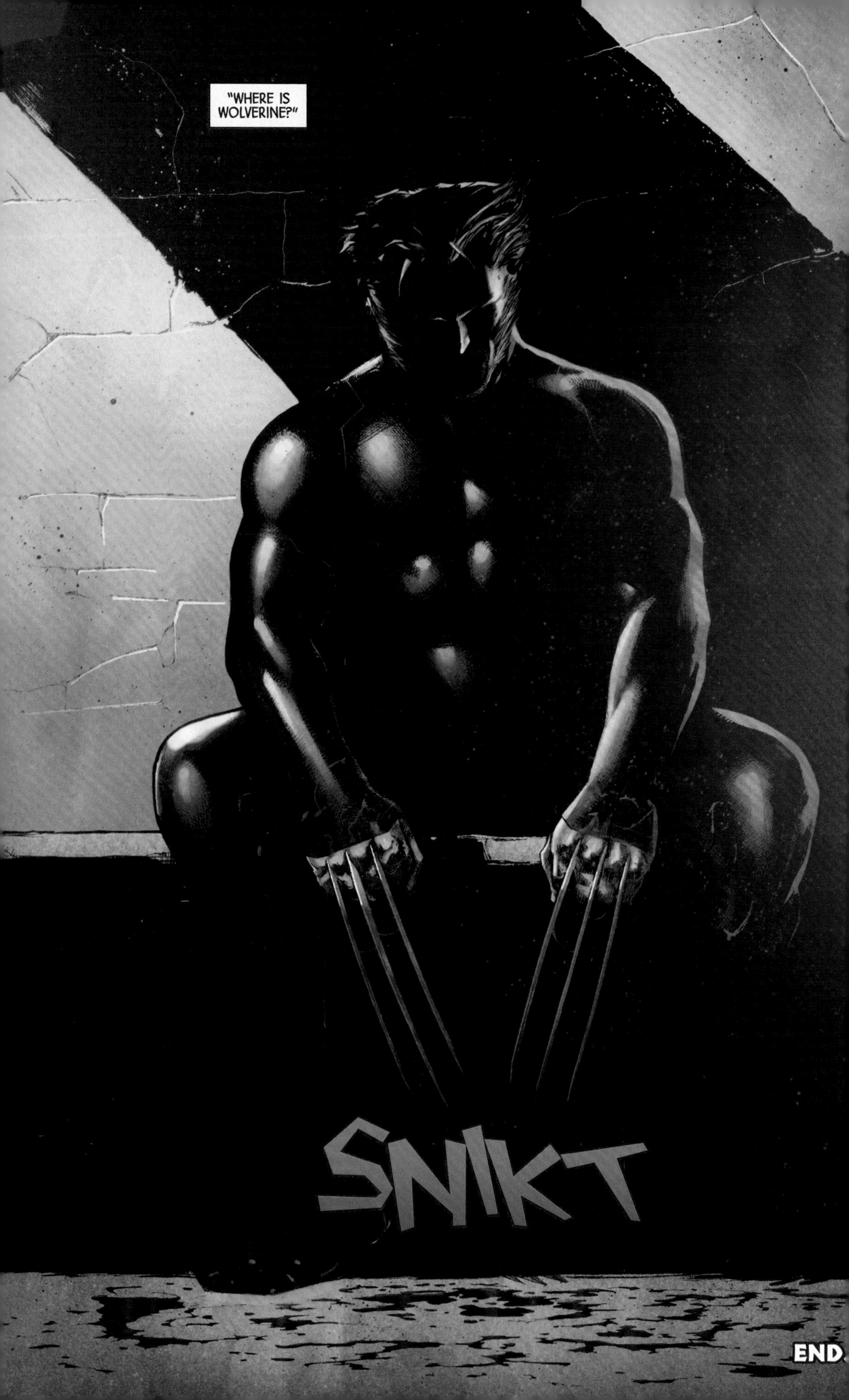
"WHERE IS WOLVERINE?"
SNIKT
END.

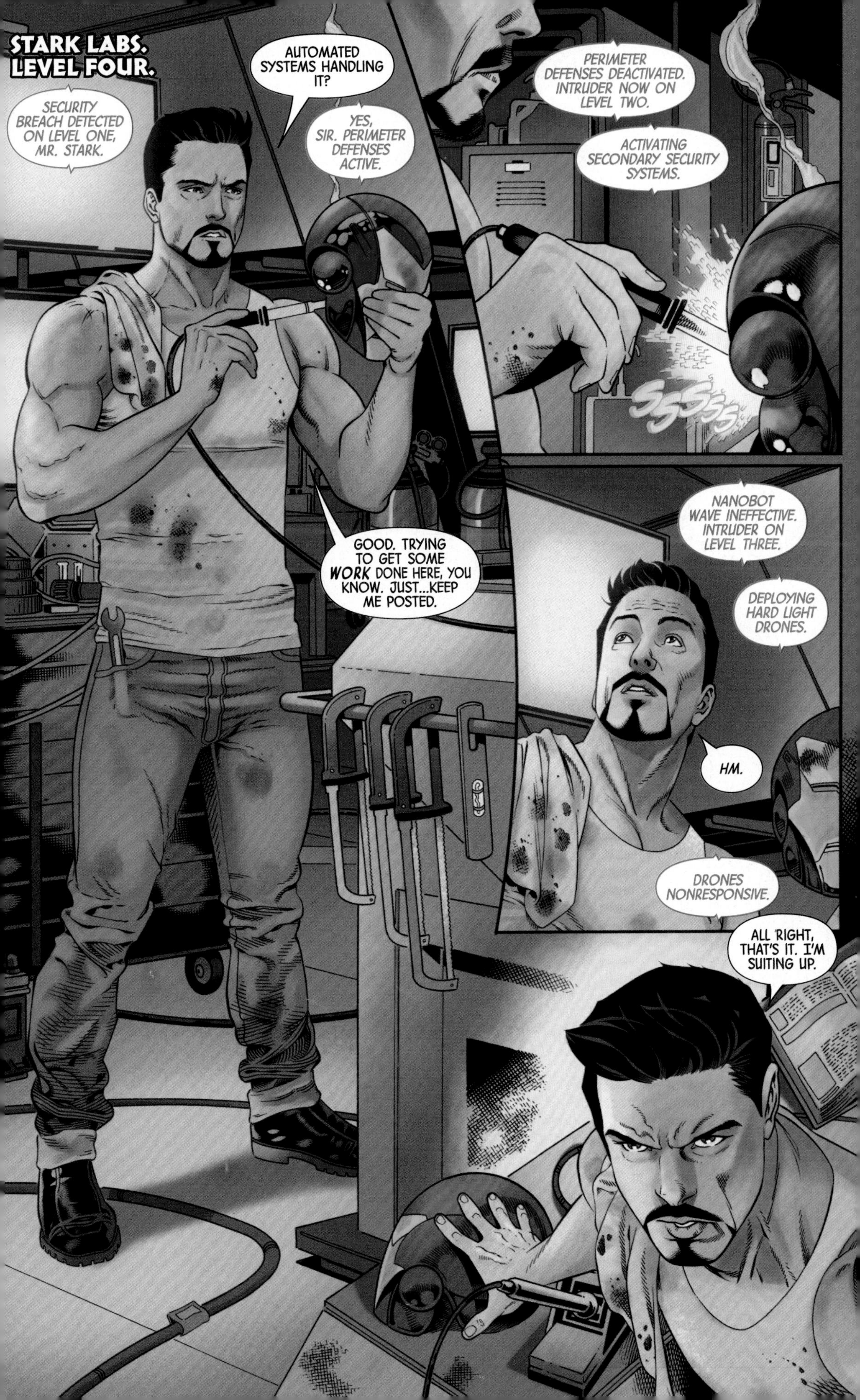
STARK LABS. LEVEL FOUR.
SECURITY BREACH DETECTED ON LEVEL ONE, MR. STARK.
AUTOMATED SYSTEMS HANDLING IT?
YES, SIR. PERIMETER DEFENSES ACTIVE.
GOOD. TRYING TO GET SOME WORK DONE HERE, YOU KNOW. JUST...KEEP ME POSTED.
PERIMETER DEFENSES DEACTIVATED. INTRUDER NOW ON LEVEL TWO.
ACTIVATING SECONDARY SECURITY SYSTEMS.
SSSSS
NANOBOT WAVE INEFFECTIVE. INTRUDER ON LEVEL THREE.
DEPLOYING HARD LIGHT DRONES.
HM.
DRONES NONRESPONSIVE.
ALL RIGHT, THAT'S IT. I'M SUITING UP.

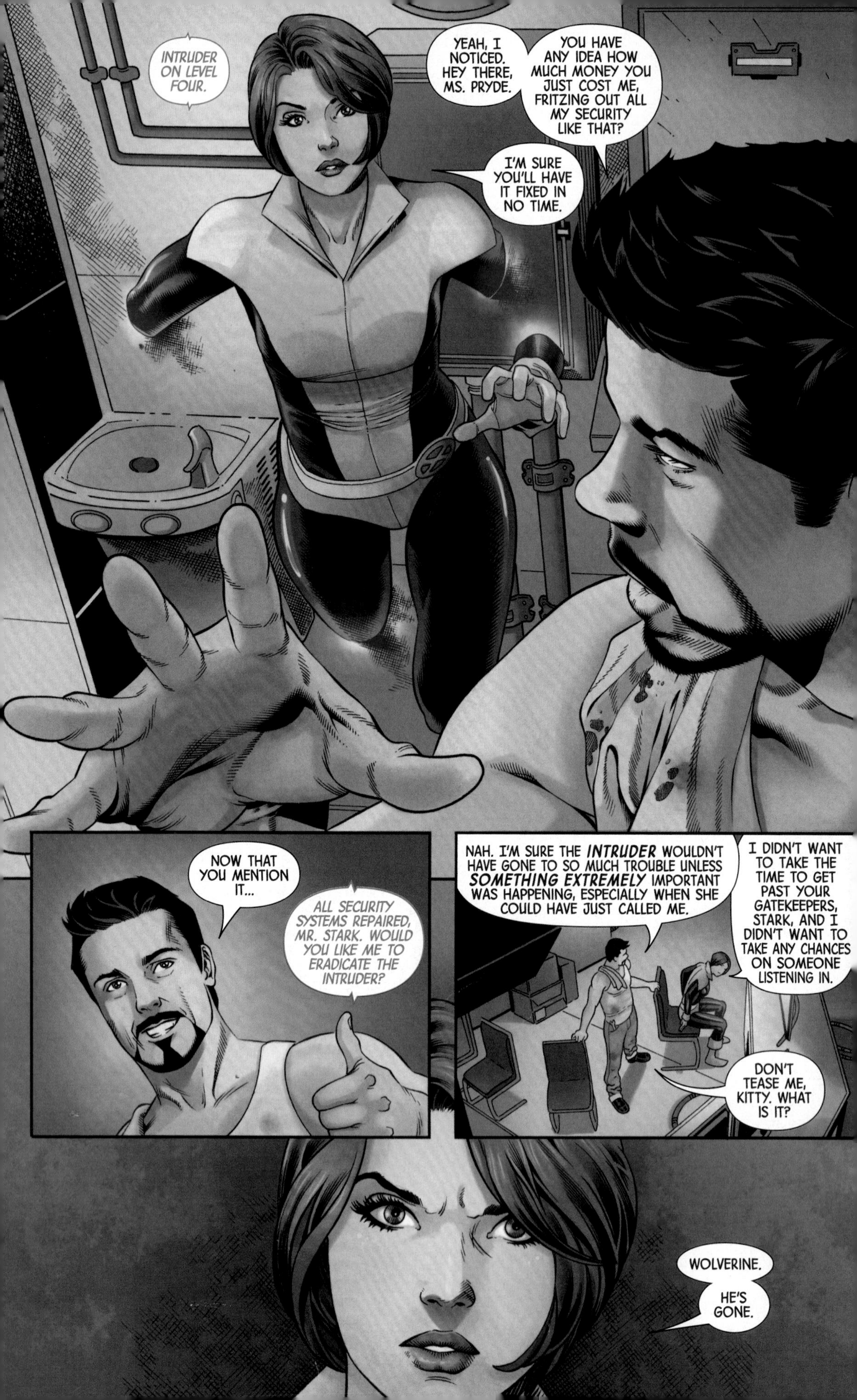
INTRUDER ON LEVEL FOUR.
YEAH, I NOTICED. HEY THERE, MS. PRYDE.
YOU HAVE ANY IDEA HOW MUCH MONEY YOU JUST COST ME, FRITZING OUT ALL MY SECURITY LIKE THAT?
I'M SURE YOU'LL HAVE IT FIXED IN NO TIME.
NOW THAT YOU MENTION IT...
ALL SECURITY SYSTEMS REPAIRED, MR. STARK. WOULD YOU LIKE ME TO ERADICATE THE INTRUDER?
NAH. I'M SURE THE INTRUDER WOULDN'T HAVE GONE TO SO MUCH TROUBLE UNLESS SOMETHING EXTREMELY IMPORTANT WAS HAPPENING, ESPECIALLY WHEN SHE COULD HAVE JUST CALLED ME.
I DIDN'T WANT TO TAKE THE TIME TO GET PAST YOUR GATEKEEPERS, STARK, AND I DIDN'T WANT TO TAKE ANY CHANCES ON SOMEONE LISTENING IN.
DON'T TEASE ME, KITTY. WHAT IS IT?
WOLVERINE.
HE'S GONE.

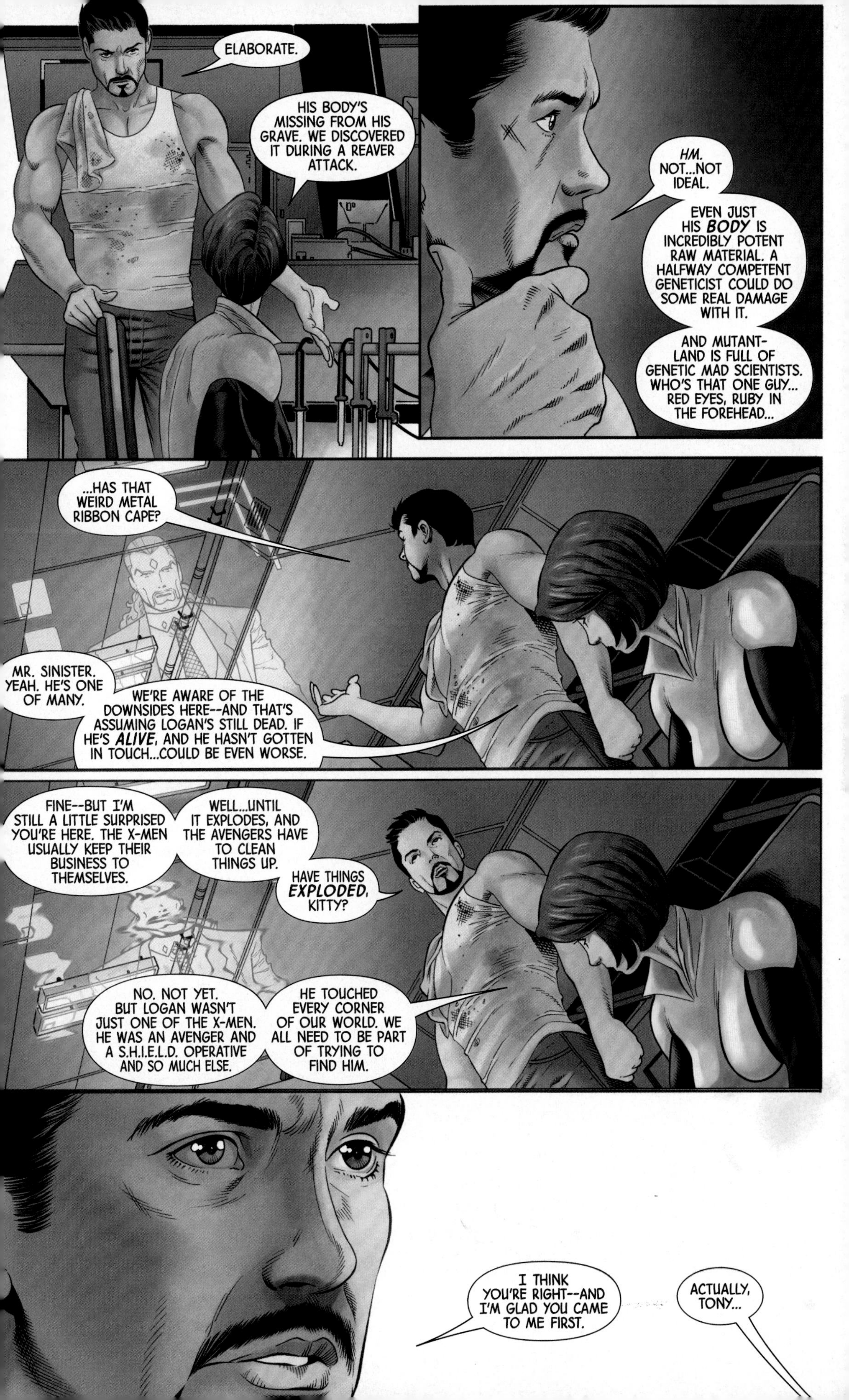
ELABORATE.
HIS BODY'S MISSING FROM HIS GRAVE. WE DISCOVERED IT DURING A REAVER ATTACK.
HM. NOT...NOT IDEAL.
EVEN JUST HIS BODY IS INCREDIBLY POTENT RAW MATERIAL. A HALFWAY COMPETENT GENETICIST COULD DO SOME REAL DAMAGE WITH IT.
AND MUTANT-LAND IS FULL OF GENETIC MAD SCIENTISTS. WHO'S THAT ONE GUY... RED EYES, RUBY IN THE FOREHEAD...
...HAS THAT WEIRD METAL RIBBON CAPE?
MR. SINISTER. YEAH. HE'S ONE OF MANY.
WE'RE AWARE OF THE DOWNSIDES HERE--AND THAT'S ASSUMING LOGAN'S STILL DEAD. IF HE'S ALIVE, AND HE HASN'T GOTTEN IN TOUCH...COULD BE EVEN WORSE.
FINE--BUT I'M STILL A LITTLE SURPRISED YOU'RE HERE. THE X-MEN USUALLY KEEP THEIR BUSINESS TO THEMSELVES.
WELL...UNTIL IT EXPLODES, AND THE AVENGERS HAVE TO CLEAN THINGS UP.
HAVE THINGS EXPLODED, KITTY?
NO. NOT YET. BUT LOGAN WASN'T JUST ONE OF THE X-MEN. HE WAS AN AVENGER AND A S.H.I.E.L.D. OPERATIVE AND SO MUCH ELSE.
HE TOUCHED EVERY CORNER OF OUR WORLD. WE ALL NEED TO BE PART OF TRYING TO FIND HIM.
I THINK YOU'RE RIGHT--AND I'M GLAD YOU CAME TO ME FIRST.
ACTUALLY, TONY...

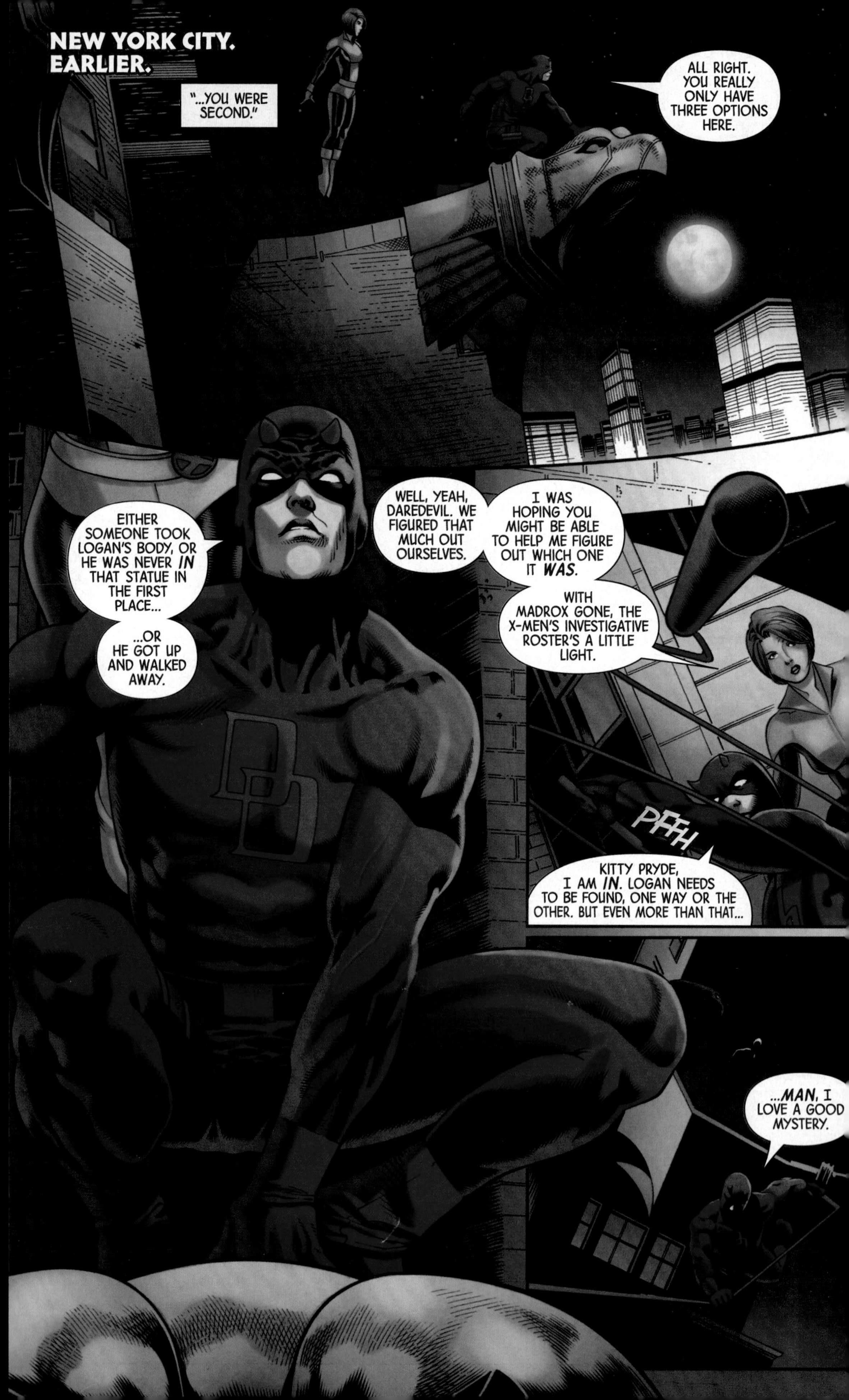

NEW YORK CITY. EARLIER.
"...YOU WERE SECOND."
ALL RIGHT. YOU REALLY ONLY HAVE THREE OPTIONS HERE.
EITHER SOMEONE TOOK LOGAN'S BODY, OR HE WAS NEVER IN THAT STATUE IN THE FIRST PLACE...
...OR HE GOT UP AND WALKED AWAY.
WELL, YEAH, DAREDEVIL. WE FIGURED THAT MUCH OUT OURSELVES.
I WAS HOPING YOU MIGHT BE ABLE TO HELP ME FIGURE OUT WHICH ONE IT WAS.
WITH MADROX GONE, THE X-MEN'S INVESTIGATIVE ROSTER'S A LITTLE LIGHT.
PFFH
KITTY PRYDE, I AM IN. LOGAN NEEDS TO BE FOUND, ONE WAY OR THE OTHER. BUT EVEN MORE THAN THAT...
...MAN, I LOVE A GOOD MYSTERY.

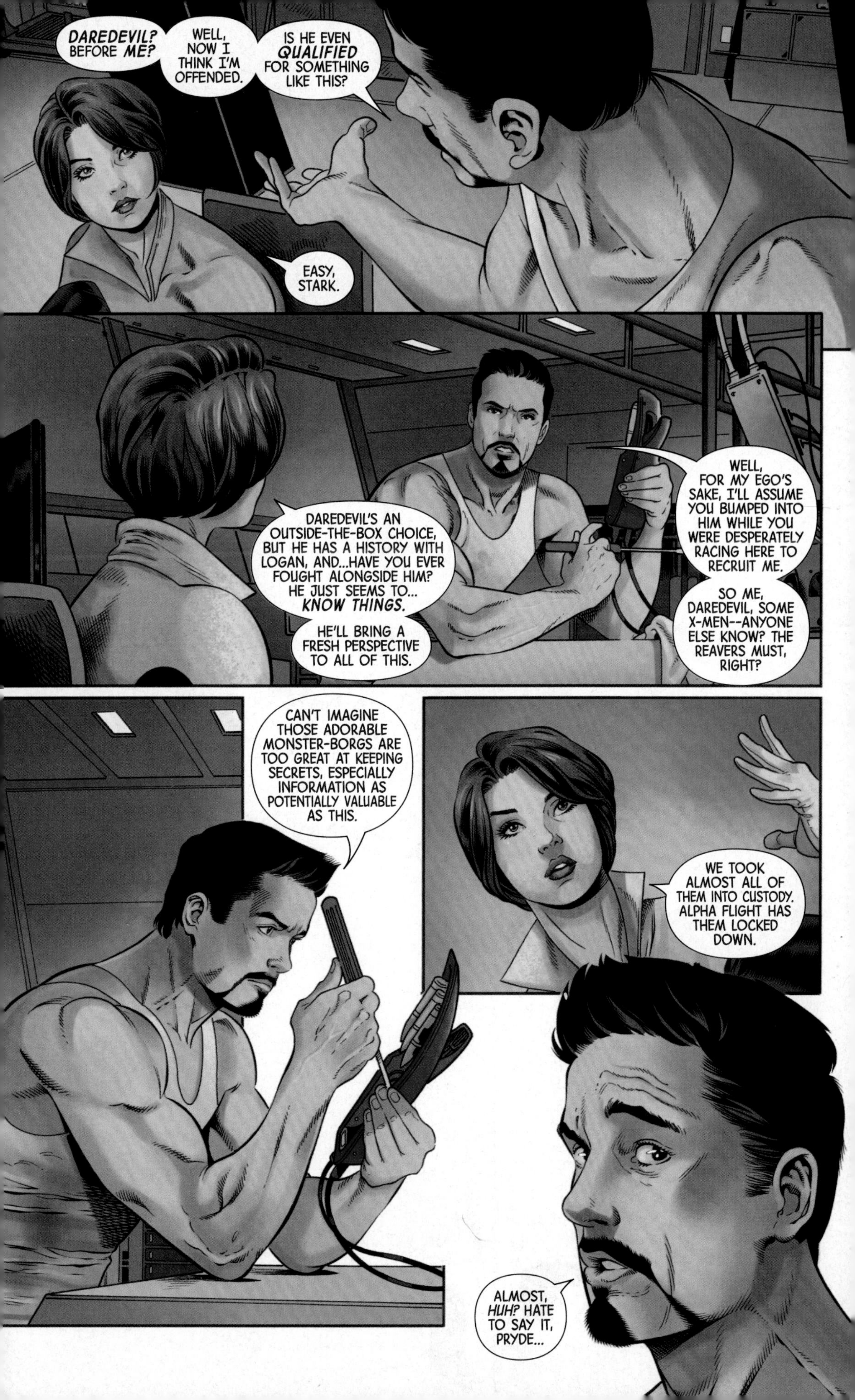
DAREDEVIL? BEFORE ME?
WELL, NOW I THINK I'M OFFENDED.
IS HE EVEN QUALIFIED FOR SOMETHING LIKE THIS?
EASY, STARK.
DAREDEVIL'S AN OUTSIDE-THE-BOX CHOICE, BUT HE HAS A HISTORY WITH LOGAN, AND...HAVE YOU EVER FOUGHT ALONGSIDE HIM? HE JUST SEEMS TO... KNOW THINGS.
HE'LL BRING A FRESH PERSPECTIVE TO ALL OF THIS.
WELL, FOR MY EGO'S SAKE, I'LL ASSUME YOU BUMPED INTO HIM WHILE YOU WERE DESPERATELY RACING HERE TO RECRUIT ME.
SO ME, DAREDEVIL, SOME X-MEN--ANYONE ELSE KNOW? THE REAVERS MUST, RIGHT?
CAN'T IMAGINE THOSE ADORABLE MONSTER-BORGS ARE TOO GREAT AT KEEPING SECRETS, ESPECIALLY INFORMATION AS POTENTIALLY VALUABLE AS THIS.
WE TOOK ALMOST ALL OF THEM INTO CUSTODY. ALPHA FLIGHT HAS THEM LOCKED DOWN.
ALMOST, HUH? HATE TO SAY IT, PRYDE...

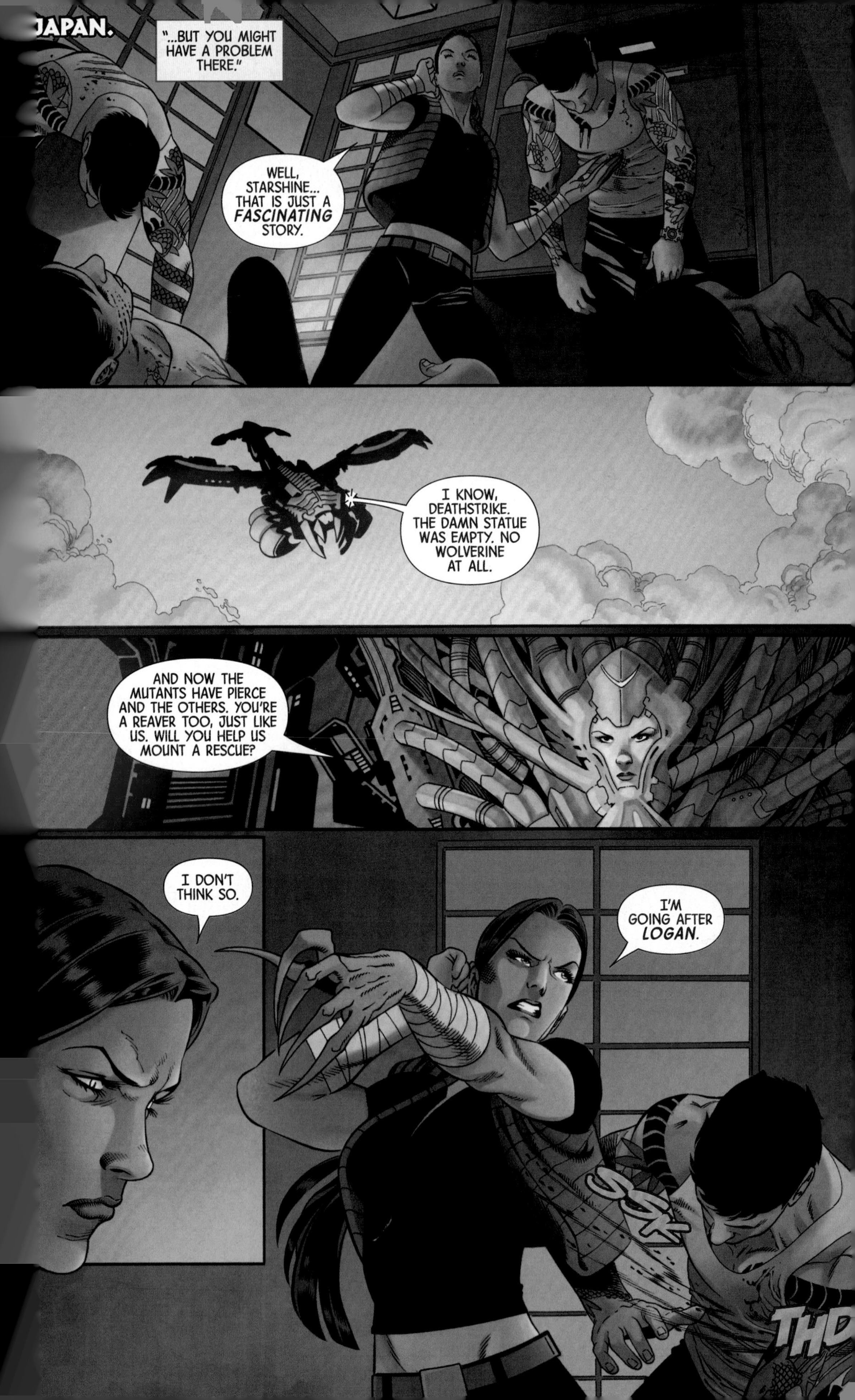
JAPAN.
"...BUT YOU MIGHT HAVE A PROBLEM THERE."
WELL, STARSHINE... THAT IS JUST A FASCINATING STORY.
I KNOW, DEATHSTRIKE. THE DAMN STATUE WAS EMPTY. NO WOLVERINE AT ALL.
AND NOW THE MUTANTS HAVE PIERCE AND THE OTHERS. YOU'RE A REAVER TOO, JUST LIKE US. WILL YOU HELP US MOUNT A RESCUE?
I DON'T THINK SO.
I'M GOING AFTER LOGAN.
SSK
THD

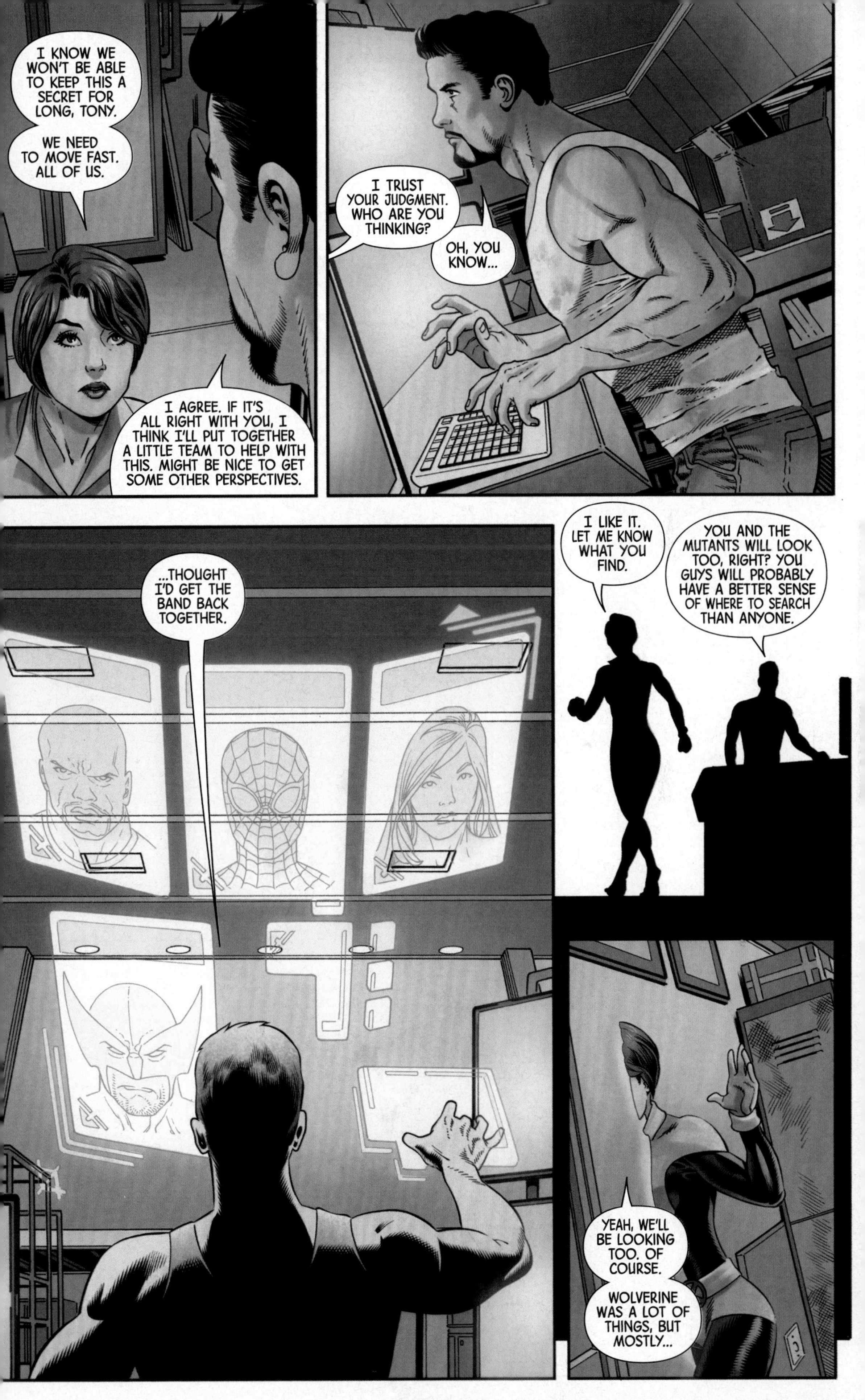
I KNOW WE WON'T BE ABLE TO KEEP THIS A SECRET FOR LONG, TONY.
WE NEED TO MOVE FAST. ALL OF US.
I AGREE. IF IT'S ALL RIGHT WITH YOU, I THINK I'LL PUT TOGETHER A LITTLE TEAM TO HELP WITH THIS. MIGHT BE NICE TO GET SOME OTHER PERSPECTIVES.
I TRUST YOUR JUDGMENT. WHO ARE YOU THINKING?
OH, YOU KNOW...
...THOUGHT I'D GET THE BAND BACK TOGETHER.
I LIKE IT. LET ME KNOW WHAT YOU FIND.
YOU AND THE MUTANTS WILL LOOK TOO, RIGHT? YOU GUYS WILL PROBABLY HAVE A BETTER SENSE OF WHERE TO SEARCH THAN ANYONE.
YEAH, WE'LL BE LOOKING TOO. OF COURSE.
WOLVERINE WAS A LOT OF THINGS, BUT MOSTLY...

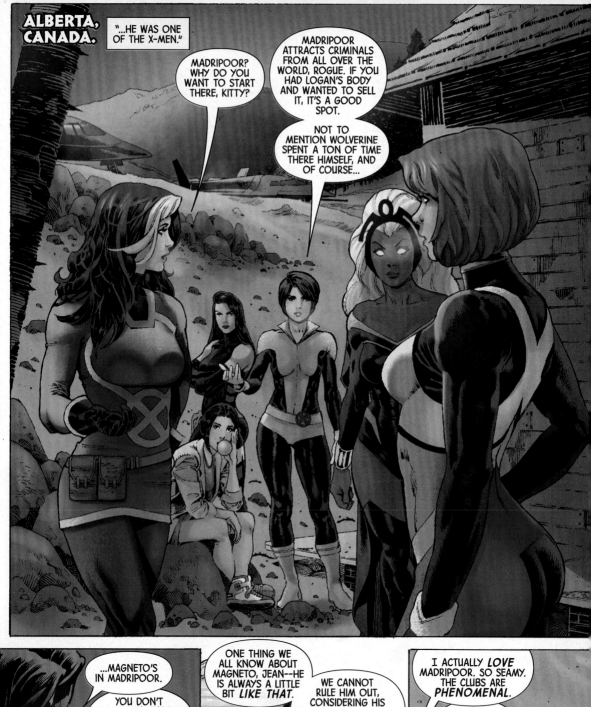

"...HE WAS ONE OF THE X-MEN."

MADRIPOOR? WHY DO YOU WANT TO START THERE, KITTY?

MADRIPOOR ATTRACTS CRIMINALS FROM ALL OVER THE WORLD, ROGUE. IF YOU HAD LOGAN'S BODY AND WANTED TO SELL IT, IT'S A GOOD SPOT.

NOT TO MENTION WOLVERINE SPENT A TON OF TIME THERE HIMSELF, AND OF COURSE...

...MAGNETO'S IN MADRIPOOR.

YOU DON'T THINK *MAGNETO* TOOK HIM, DO YOU? I KNOW HE'S HAD HIS MOMENTS, BUT HE'S NOT REALLY LIKE THAT ANYMORE.

ONE THING WE ALL KNOW ABOUT MAGNETO, JEAN--HE IS ALWAYS A LITTLE BIT *LIKE THAT.*

WE CANNOT RULE HIM OUT, CONSIDERING HIS LONG-STANDING HATRED FOR LOGAN. MADRIPOOR IS A GOOD PLACE TO BEGIN.

I ACTUALLY *LOVE* MADRIPOOR. SO SEAMY. THE CLUBS ARE *PHENOMENAL.*

NOT SURE WE'LL HAVE TIME FOR CLUBBING, JUBILEE.

I DUNNO, PSYLOCKE. MAYBE WE'LL FIND LOGAN. IF *I* DIED HORRIBLY AND CAME BACK TO LIFE, I'D GO DANCING THE VERY FIRST THING.

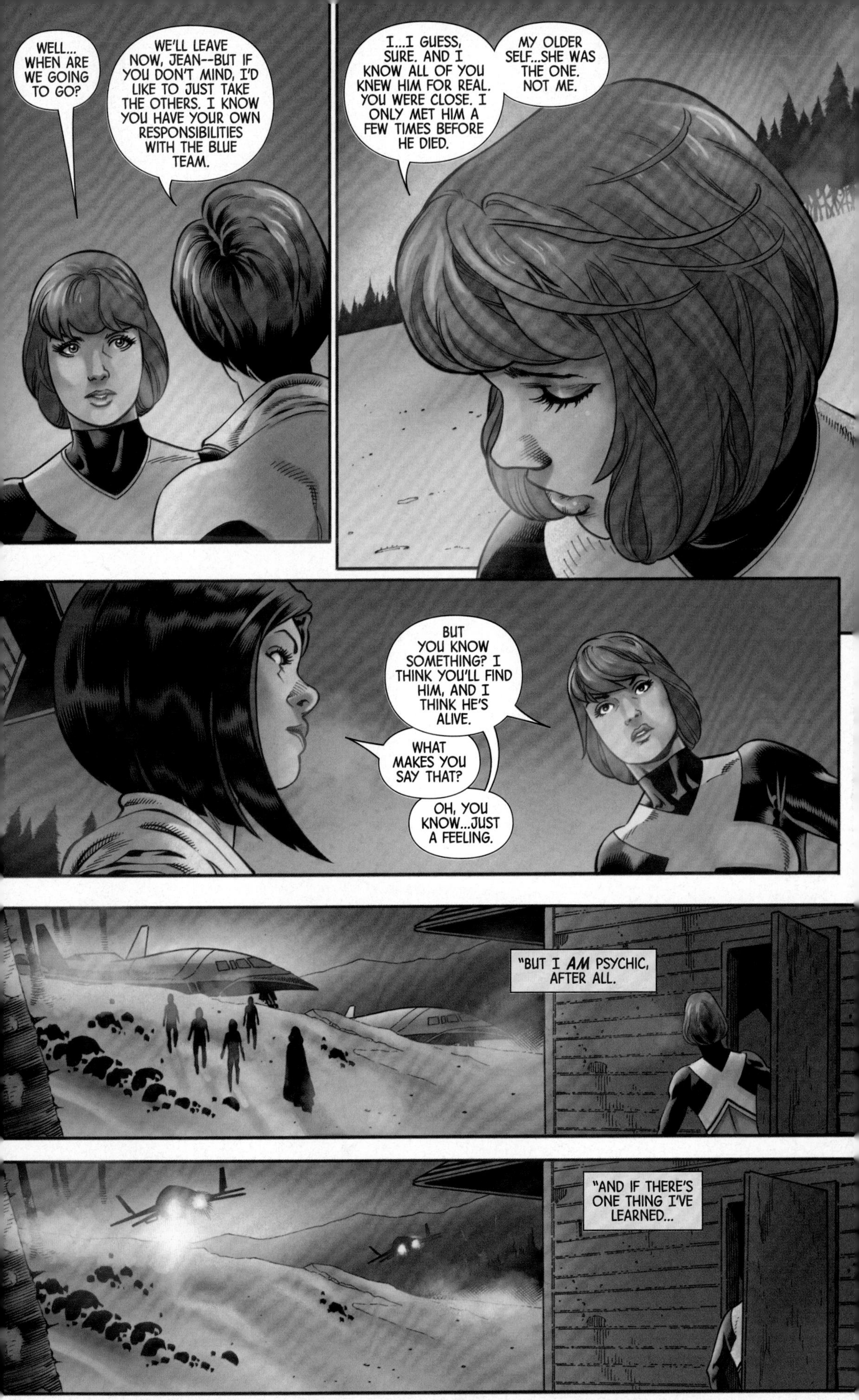
WELL... WHEN ARE WE GOING TO GO?
WE'LL LEAVE NOW, JEAN--BUT IF YOU DON'T MIND, I'D LIKE TO JUST TAKE THE OTHERS. I KNOW YOU HAVE YOUR OWN RESPONSIBILITIES WITH THE BLUE TEAM.
I...I GUESS, SURE. AND I KNOW ALL OF YOU KNEW HIM FOR REAL. YOU WERE CLOSE. I ONLY MET HIM A FEW TIMES BEFORE HE DIED.
MY OLDER SELF...SHE WAS THE ONE. NOT ME.
BUT YOU KNOW SOMETHING? I THINK YOU'LL FIND HIM, AND I THINK HE'S ALIVE.
WHAT MAKES YOU SAY THAT?
OH, YOU KNOW...JUST A FEELING.
"BUT I AM PSYCHIC, AFTER ALL.
"AND IF THERE'S ONE THING I'VE LEARNED...

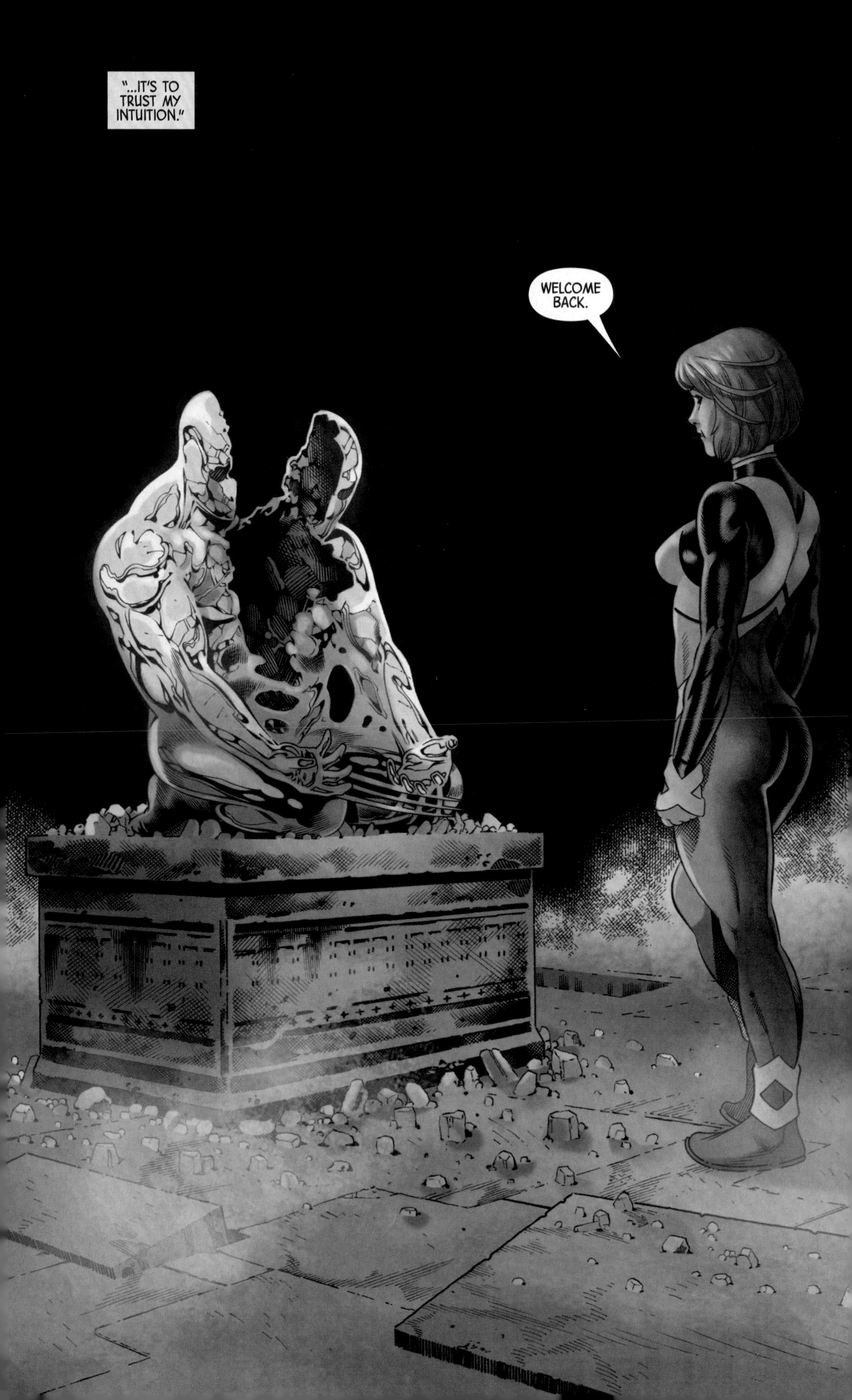
"...IT'S TO TRUST MY INTUITION."
WELCOME BACK.

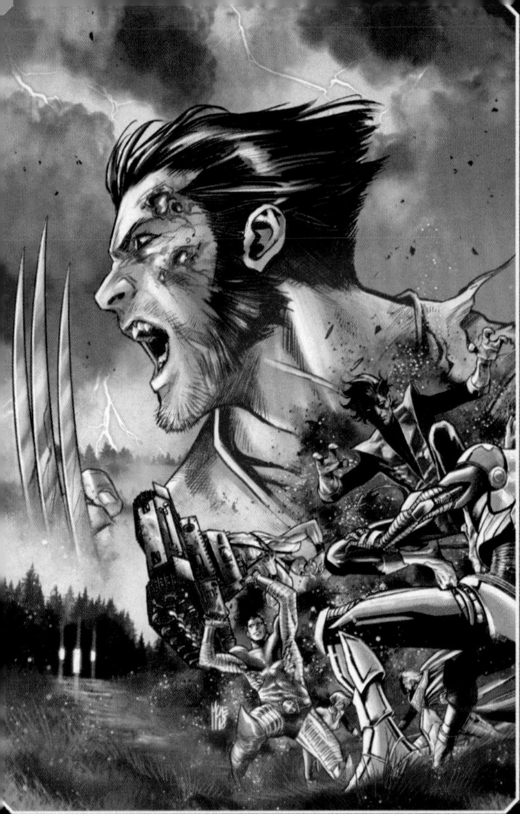

Marco Checchetto
HUNT FOR WOLVERINE #1 VARIANT

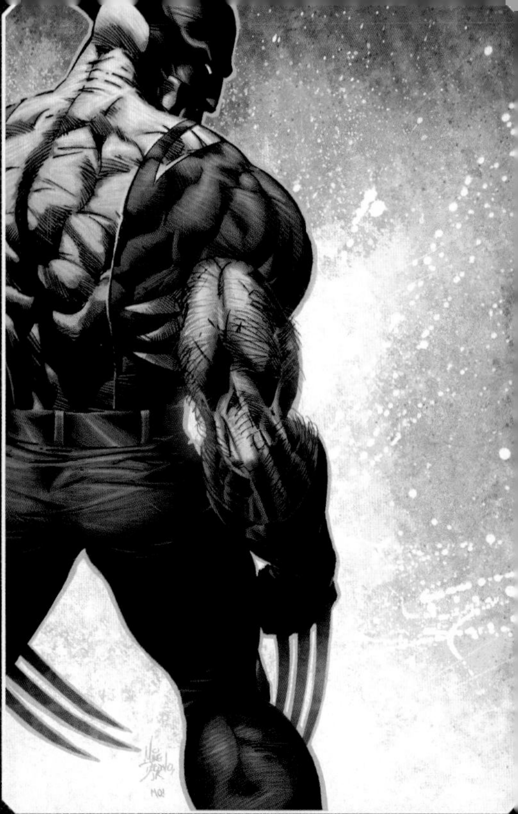

Mike Deodato Jr. & Morry Hollowell
HUNT FOR WOLVERINE #1 VARIANT

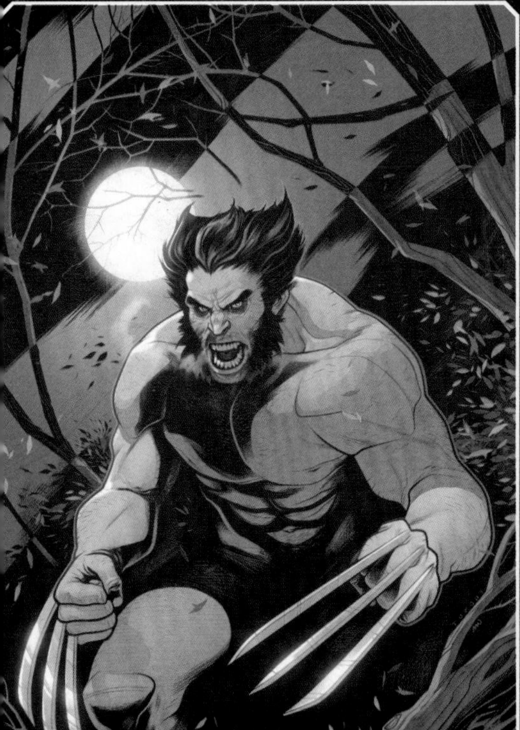

Elizabeth Torque & Nolan Woodard
HUNT FOR WOLVERINE #1 VARIANT

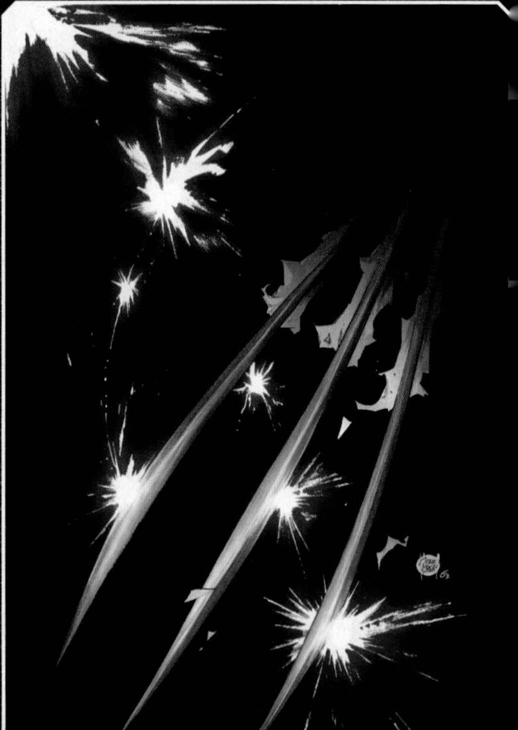

Adam Kubert & Dan Brown
HUNT FOR WOLVERINE #1 TEASER VARIANT

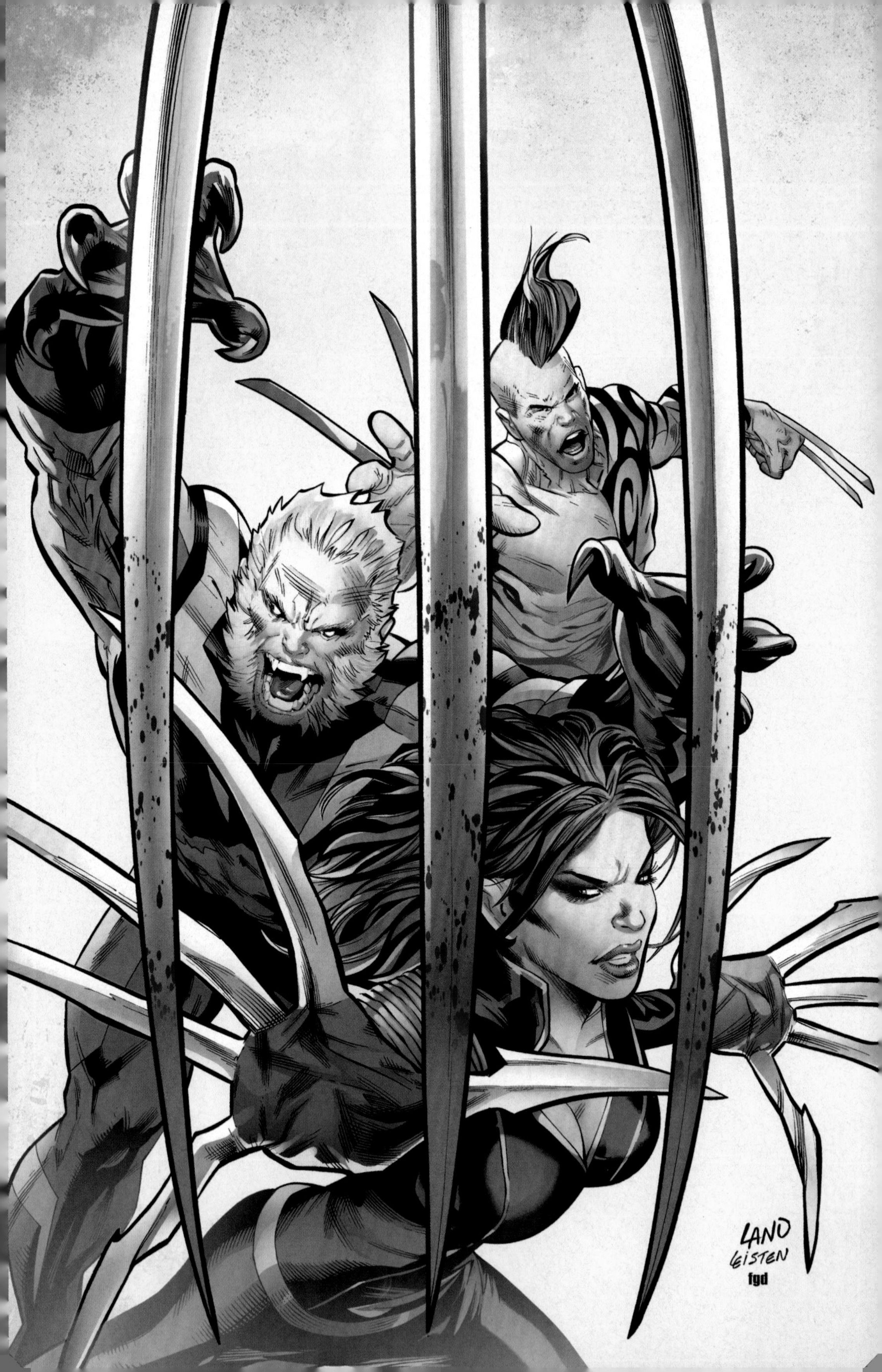
LAND
LEISTEN
fgd

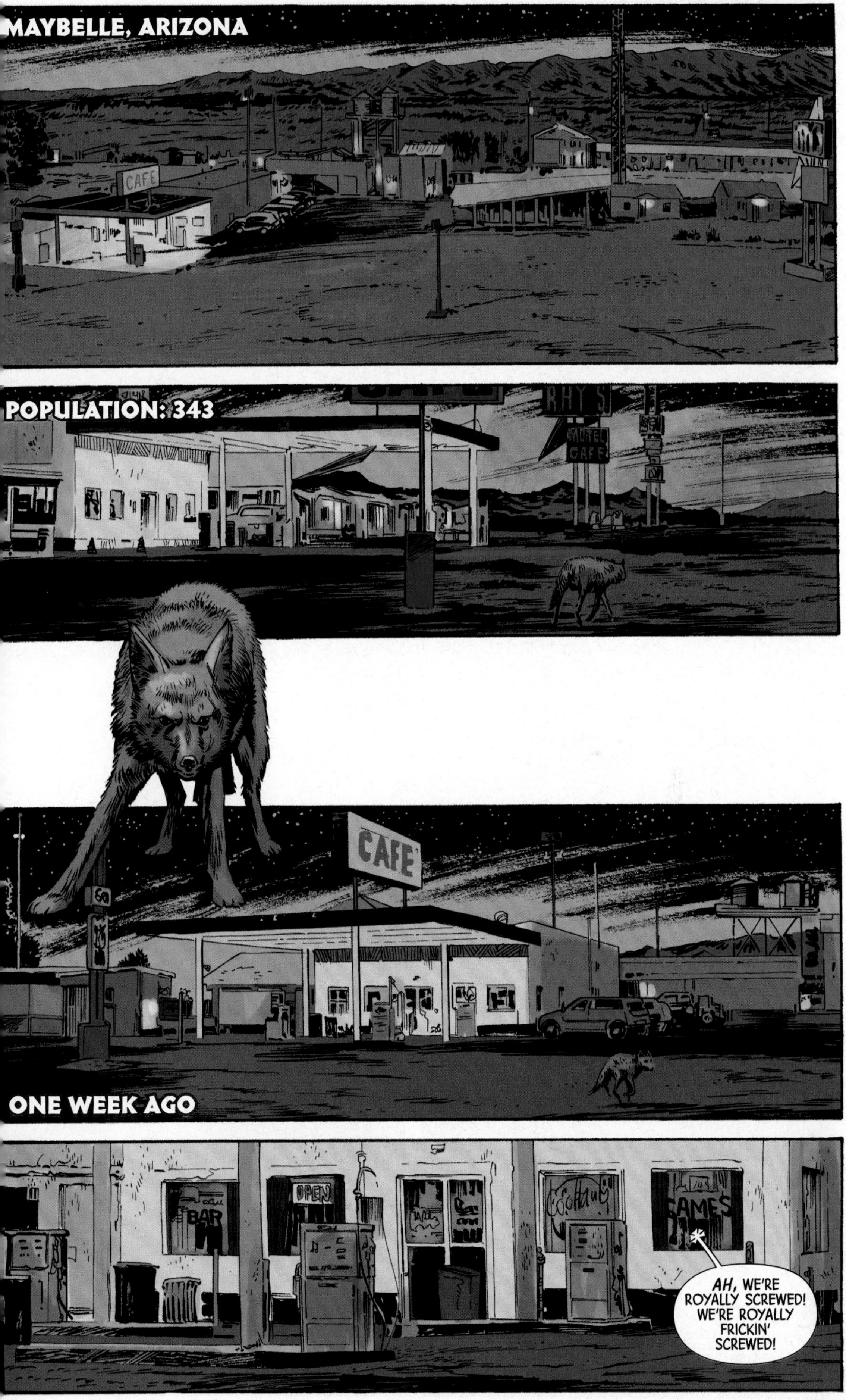
MAYBELLE, ARIZONA
CAFE
POPULATION: 343
MOTEL
CAFE
CAFE
ONE WEEK AGO
BAR
OPEN
GAMES
AH, WE'RE ROYALLY SCREWED! WE'RE ROYALLY FRICKIN' SCREWED!

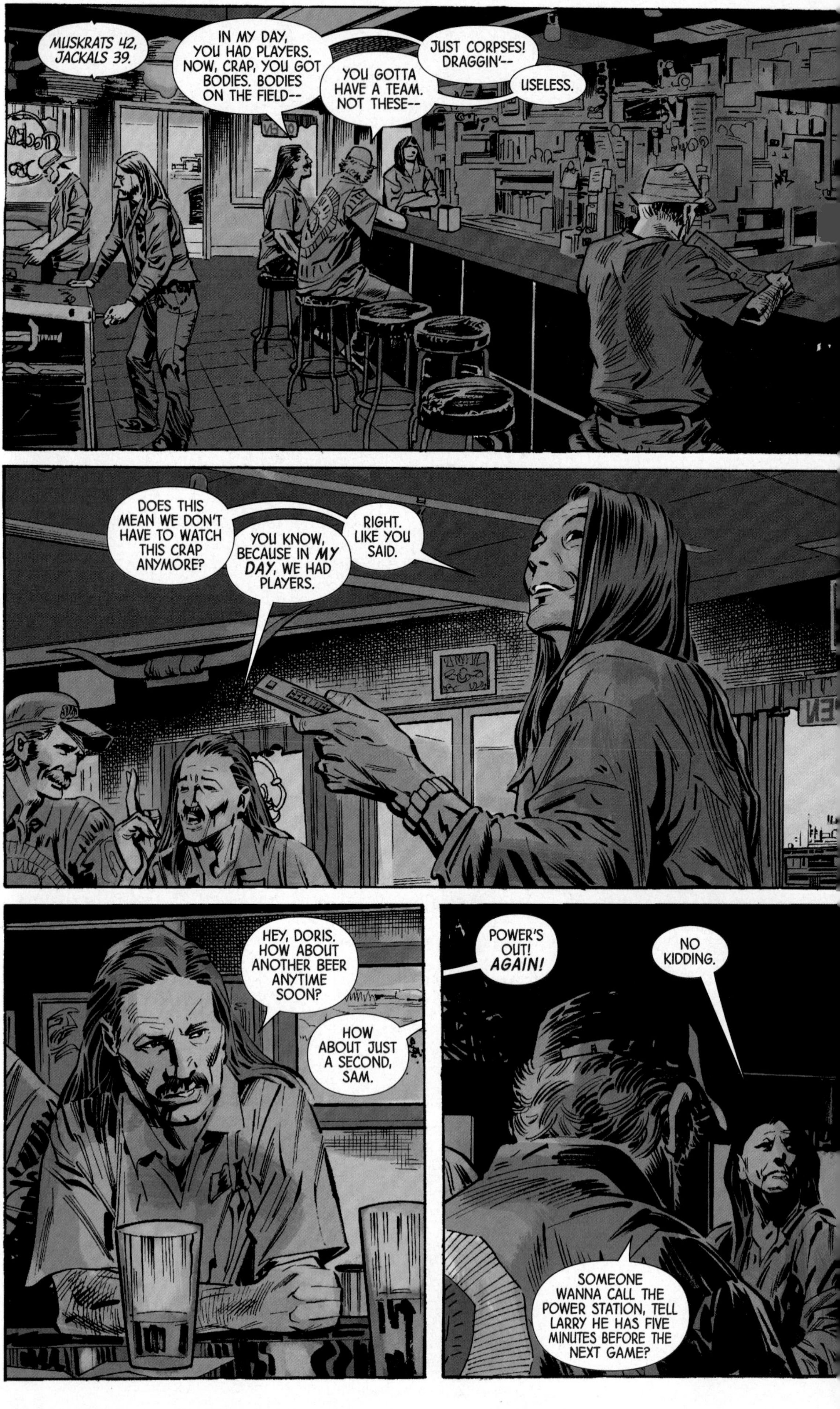
MUSKRATS 42, JACKALS 39.
IN MY DAY, YOU HAD PLAYERS. NOW, CRAP, YOU GOT BODIES. BODIES ON THE FIELD--
JUST CORPSES! DRAGGIN'--
YOU GOTTA HAVE A TEAM. NOT THESE--
USELESS.
DOES THIS MEAN WE DON'T HAVE TO WATCH THIS CRAP ANYMORE?
RIGHT. LIKE YOU SAID.
YOU KNOW, BECAUSE IN *MY DAY*, WE HAD PLAYERS.
HEY, DORIS. HOW ABOUT ANOTHER BEER ANYTIME SOON?
HOW ABOUT JUST A SECOND, SAM.
POWER'S OUT! ***AGAIN!***
NO KIDDING.
SOMEONE WANNA CALL THE POWER STATION, TELL LARRY HE HAS FIVE MINUTES BEFORE THE NEXT GAME?

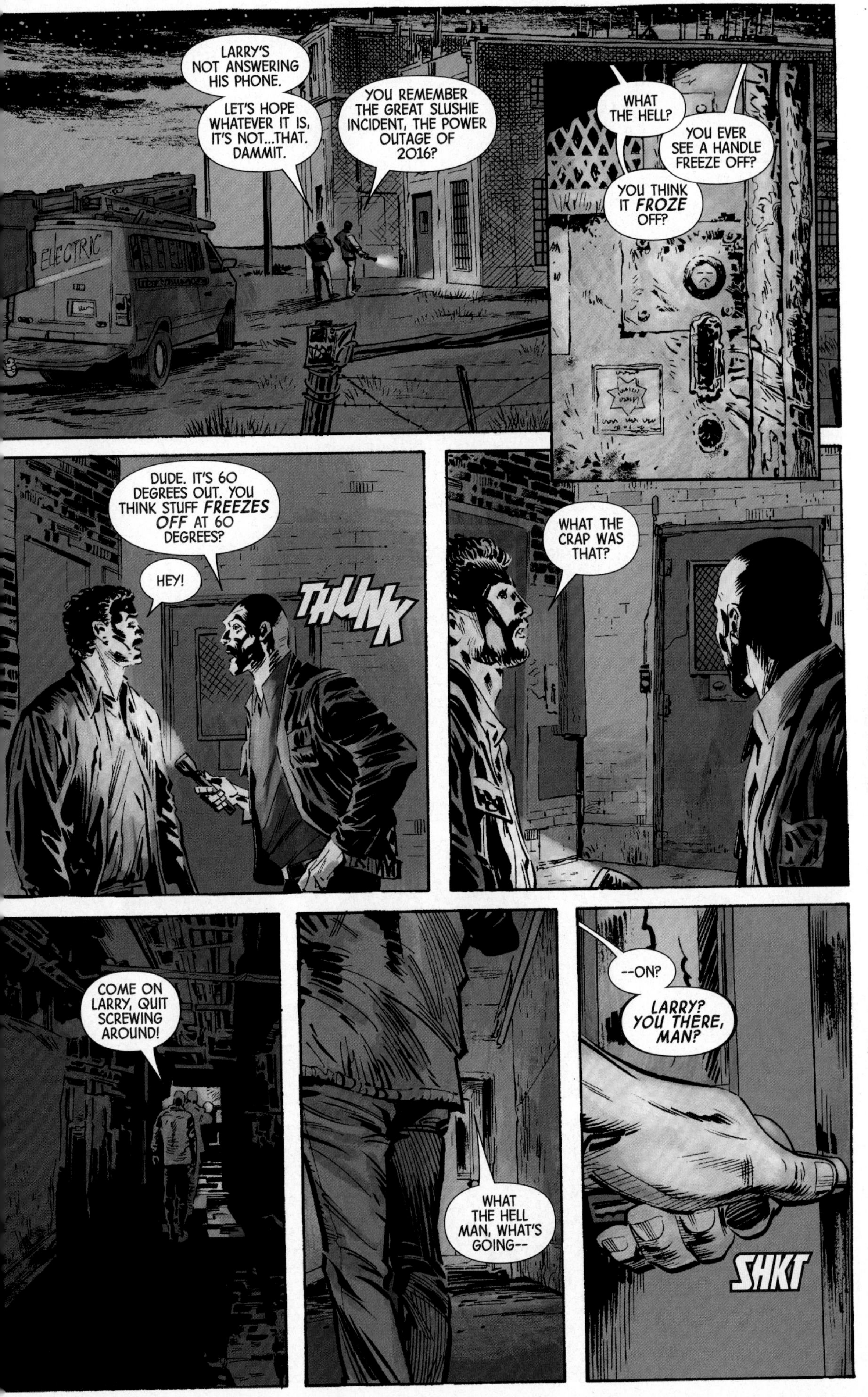

LARRY'S NOT ANSWERING HIS PHONE.
LET'S HOPE WHATEVER IT IS, IT'S NOT...THAT. DAMMIT.
YOU REMEMBER THE GREAT SLUSHIE INCIDENT, THE POWER OUTAGE OF 2016?
ELECTRIC
WHAT THE HELL?
YOU EVER SEE A HANDLE FREEZE OFF?
YOU THINK IT FROZE OFF?
DUDE. IT'S 60 DEGREES OUT. YOU THINK STUFF FREEZES OFF AT 60 DEGREES?
HEY!
THUNK
WHAT THE CRAP WAS THAT?
COME ON LARRY, QUIT SCREWING AROUND!
WHAT THE HELL MAN, WHAT'S GOING--
--ON?
LARRY? YOU THERE, MAN?
SHKT

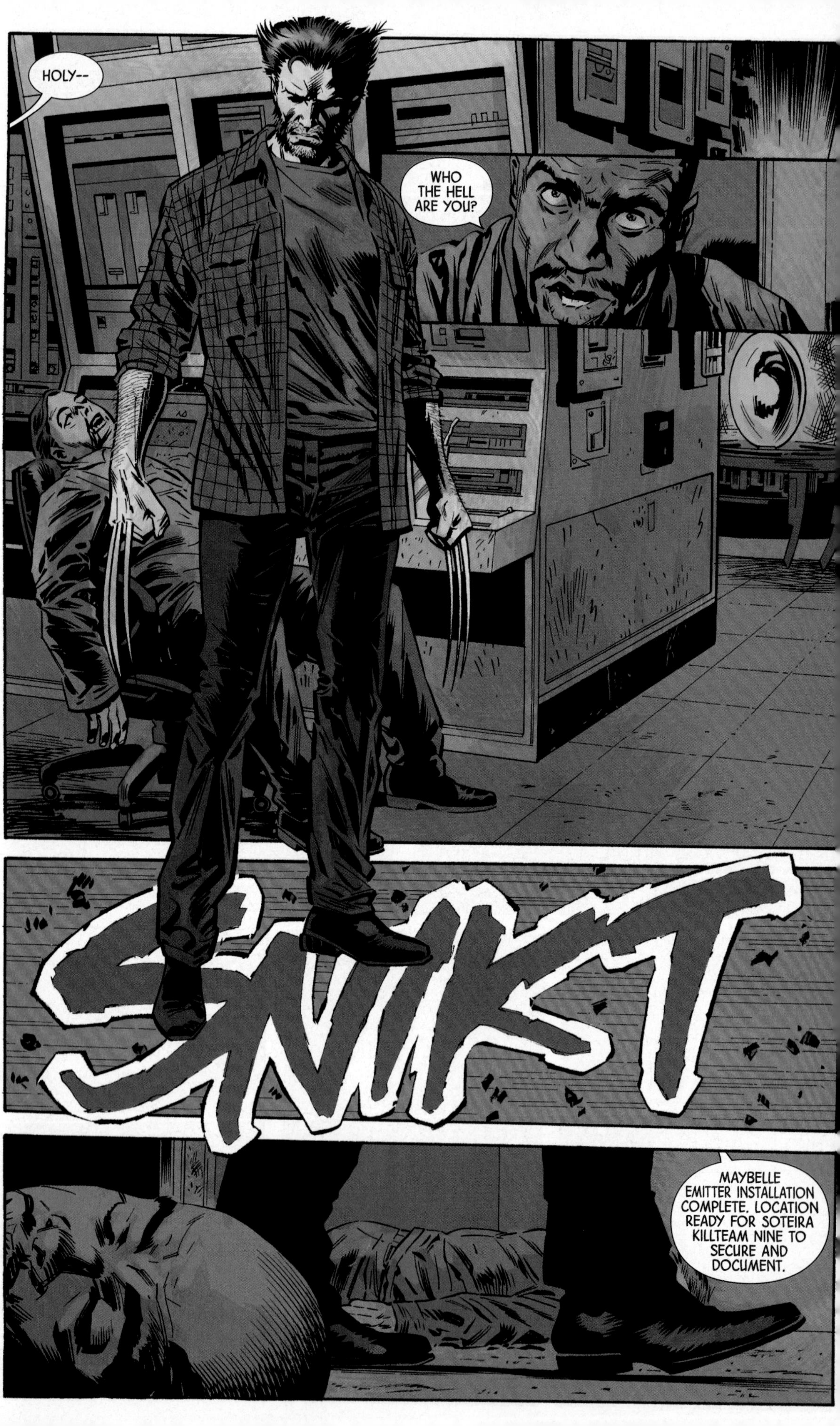
HOLY--
WHO THE HELL ARE YOU?
SNIKT
MAYBELLE EMITTER INSTALLATION COMPLETE. LOCATION READY FOR SOTEIRA KILLTEAM NINE TO SECURE AND DOCUMENT.

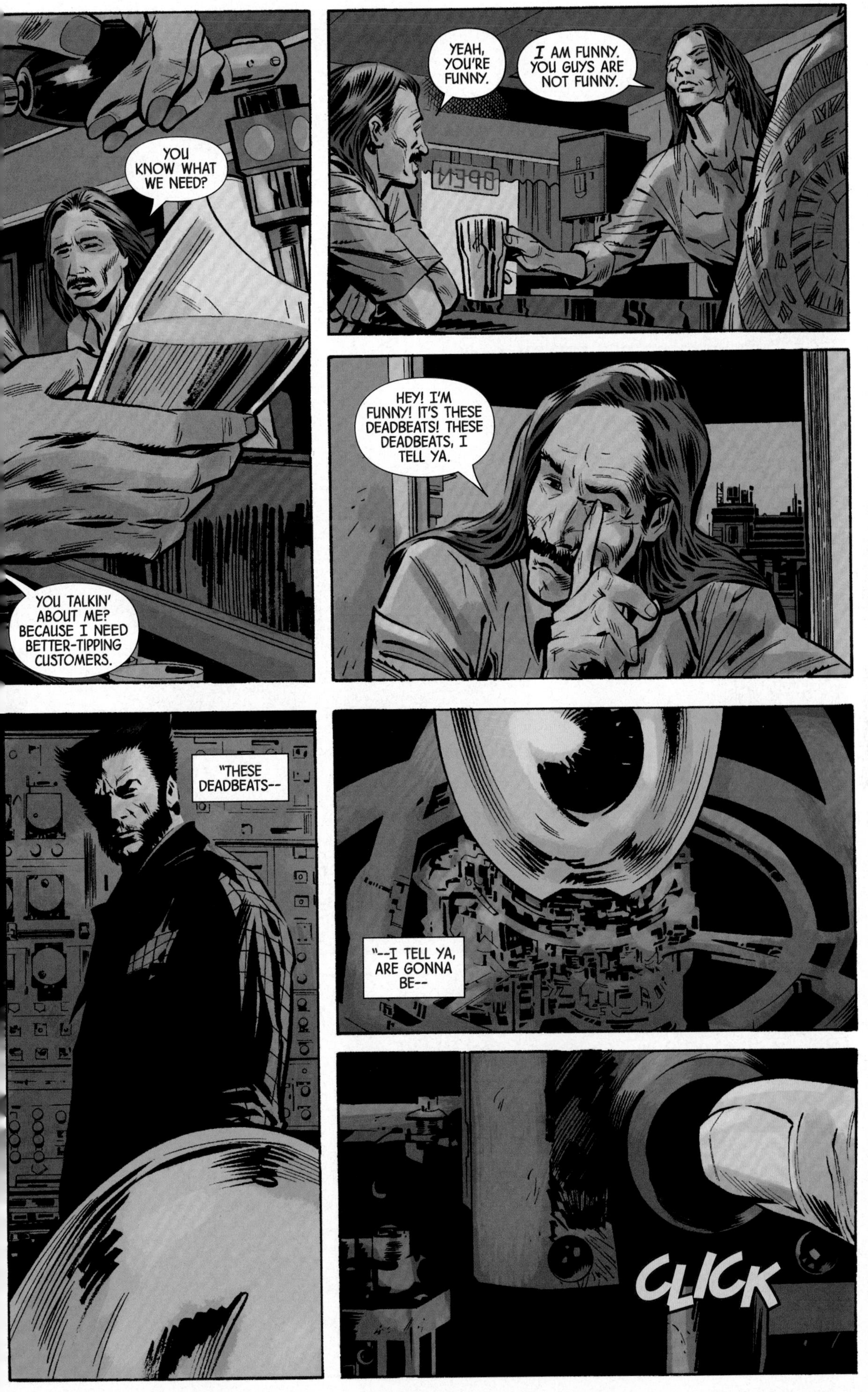
YOU KNOW WHAT WE NEED?
YOU TALKIN' ABOUT ME? BECAUSE I NEED BETTER-TIPPING CUSTOMERS.
YEAH, YOU'RE FUNNY.
I AM FUNNY. YOU GUYS ARE NOT FUNNY.
OPEN
HEY! I'M FUNNY! IT'S THESE DEADBEATS! THESE DEADBEATS, I TELL YA.
"THESE DEADBEATS--
"--I TELL YA, ARE GONNA BE--
CLICK

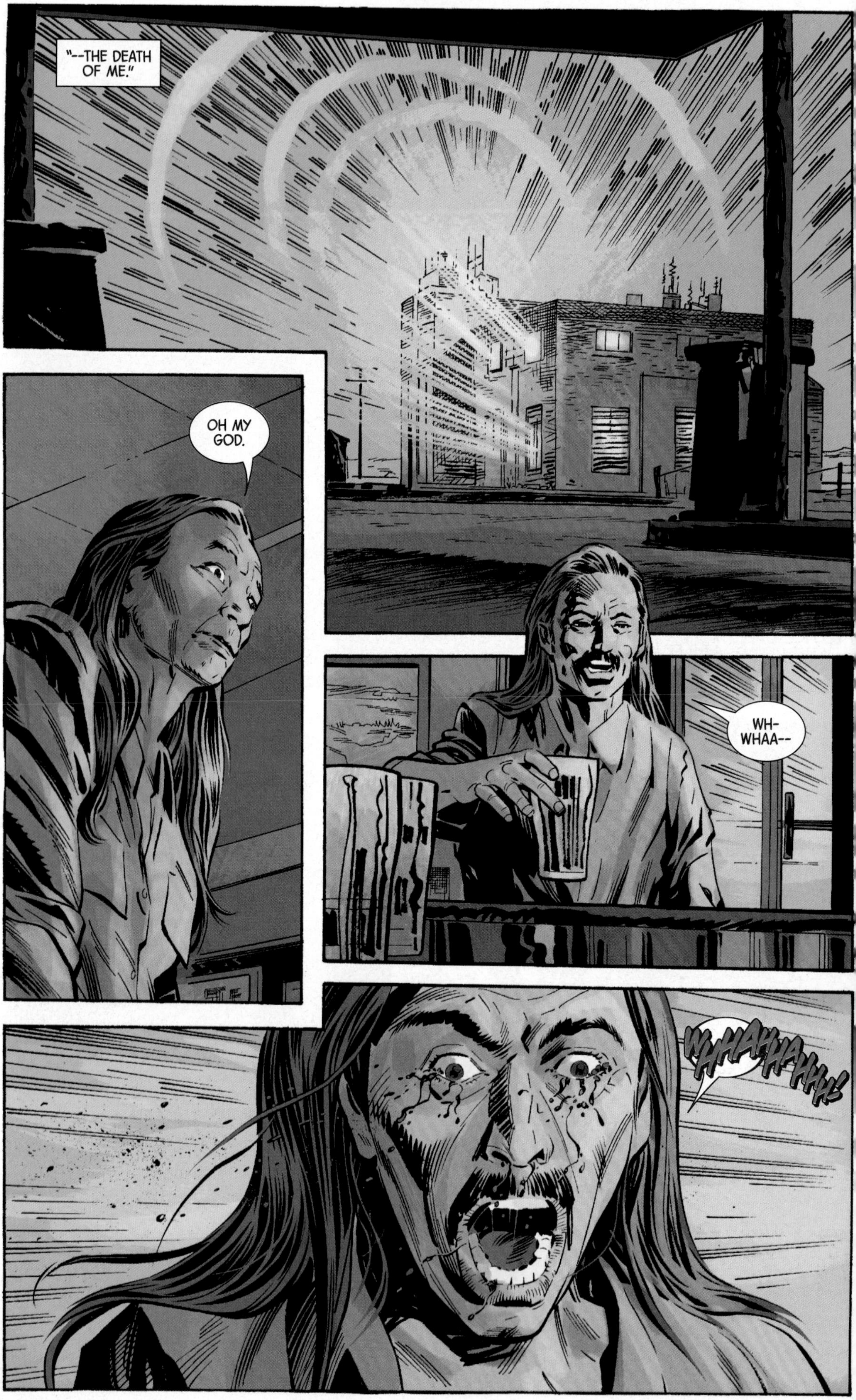
"--THE DEATH OF ME."
OH MY GOD.
WH- WHAA--
WHHAHHAHHH!

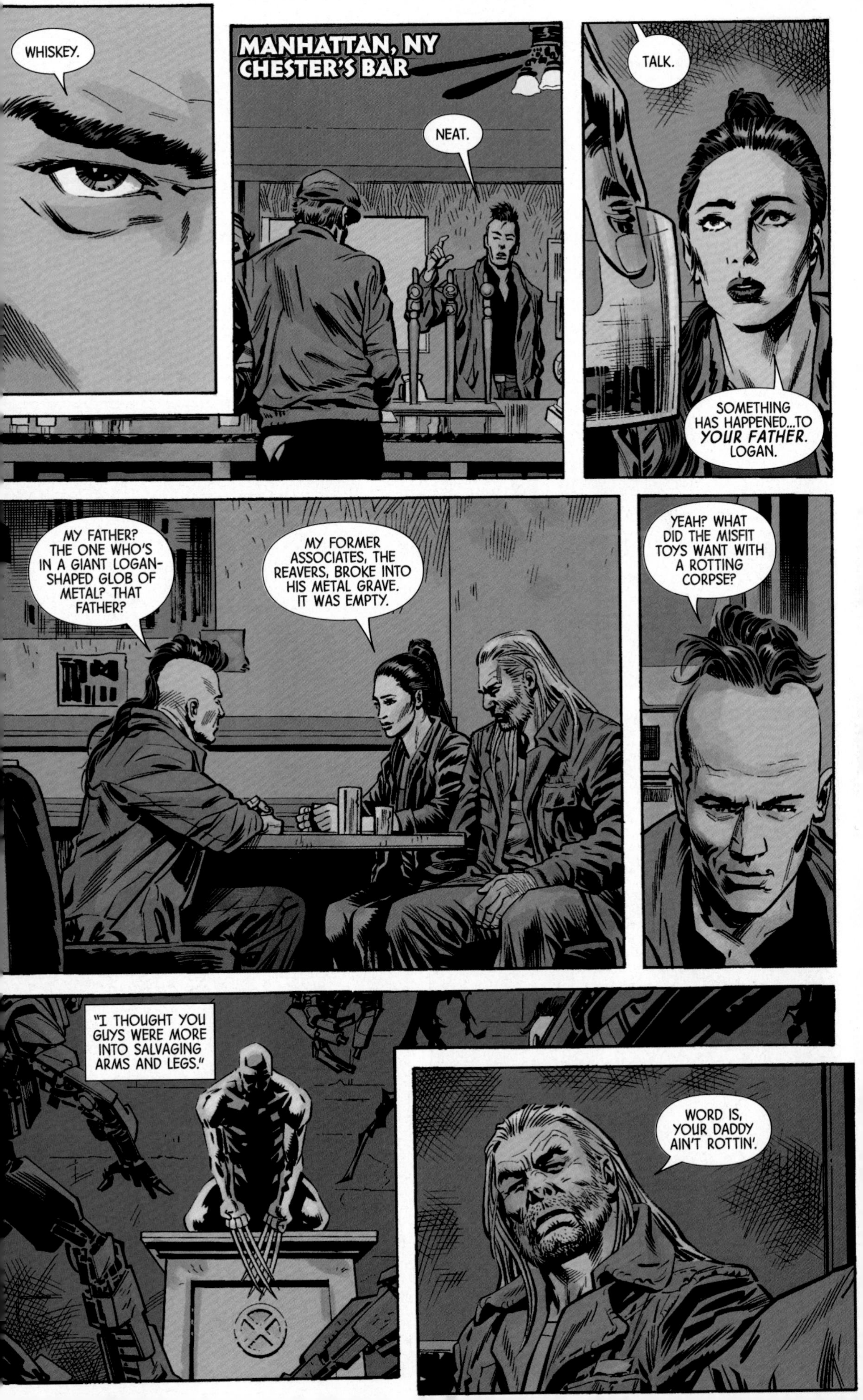
WHISKEY.
MANHATTAN, NY CHESTER'S BAR
NEAT.
TALK.
SOMETHING HAS HAPPENED...TO YOUR FATHER. LOGAN.
MY FATHER? THE ONE WHO'S IN A GIANT LOGAN-SHAPED GLOB OF METAL? THAT FATHER?
MY FORMER ASSOCIATES, THE REAVERS, BROKE INTO HIS METAL GRAVE. IT WAS EMPTY.
YEAH? WHAT DID THE MISFIT TOYS WANT WITH A ROTTING CORPSE?
"I THOUGHT YOU GUYS WERE MORE INTO SALVAGING ARMS AND LEGS."
WORD IS, YOUR DADDY AIN'T ROTTIN'.

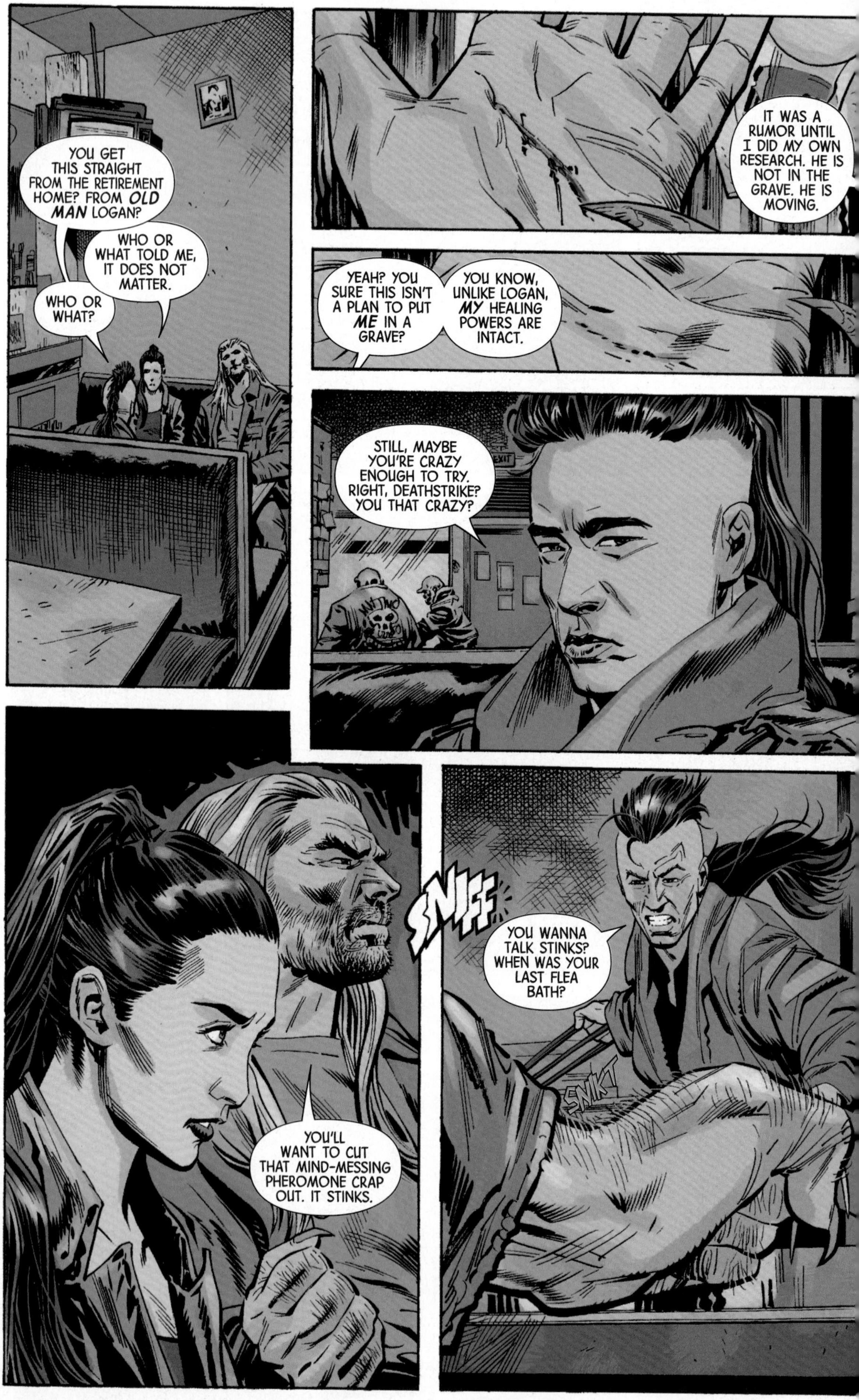
YOU GET THIS STRAIGHT FROM THE RETIREMENT HOME? FROM OLD MAN LOGAN?
WHO OR WHAT TOLD ME, IT DOES NOT MATTER.
WHO OR WHAT?
IT WAS A RUMOR UNTIL I DID MY OWN RESEARCH. HE IS NOT IN THE GRAVE. HE IS MOVING.
YEAH? YOU SURE THIS ISN'T A PLAN TO PUT ME IN A GRAVE?
YOU KNOW, UNLIKE LOGAN, MY HEALING POWERS ARE INTACT.
STILL, MAYBE YOU'RE CRAZY ENOUGH TO TRY. RIGHT, DEATHSTRIKE? YOU THAT CRAZY?
EXIT
YOU'LL WANT TO CUT THAT MIND-MESSING PHEROMONE CRAP OUT. IT STINKS.
SNIFF
YOU WANNA TALK STINKS? WHEN WAS YOUR LAST FLEA BATH?
SNIKT

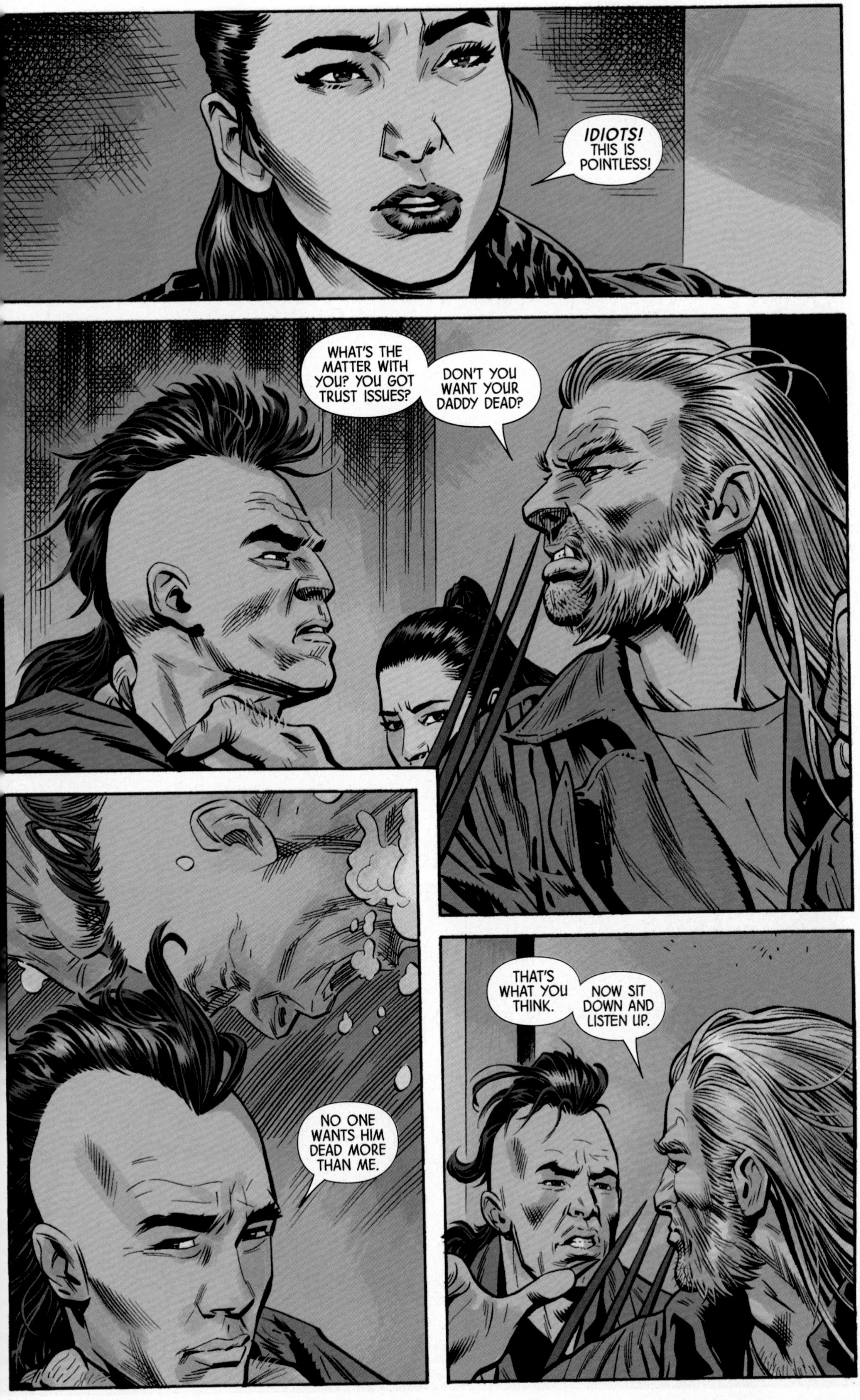
IDIOTS! THIS IS POINTLESS!
WHAT'S THE MATTER WITH YOU? YOU GOT TRUST ISSUES?
DON'T YOU WANT YOUR DADDY DEAD?
NO ONE WANTS HIM DEAD MORE THAN ME.
THAT'S WHAT YOU THINK.
NOW SIT DOWN AND LISTEN UP.

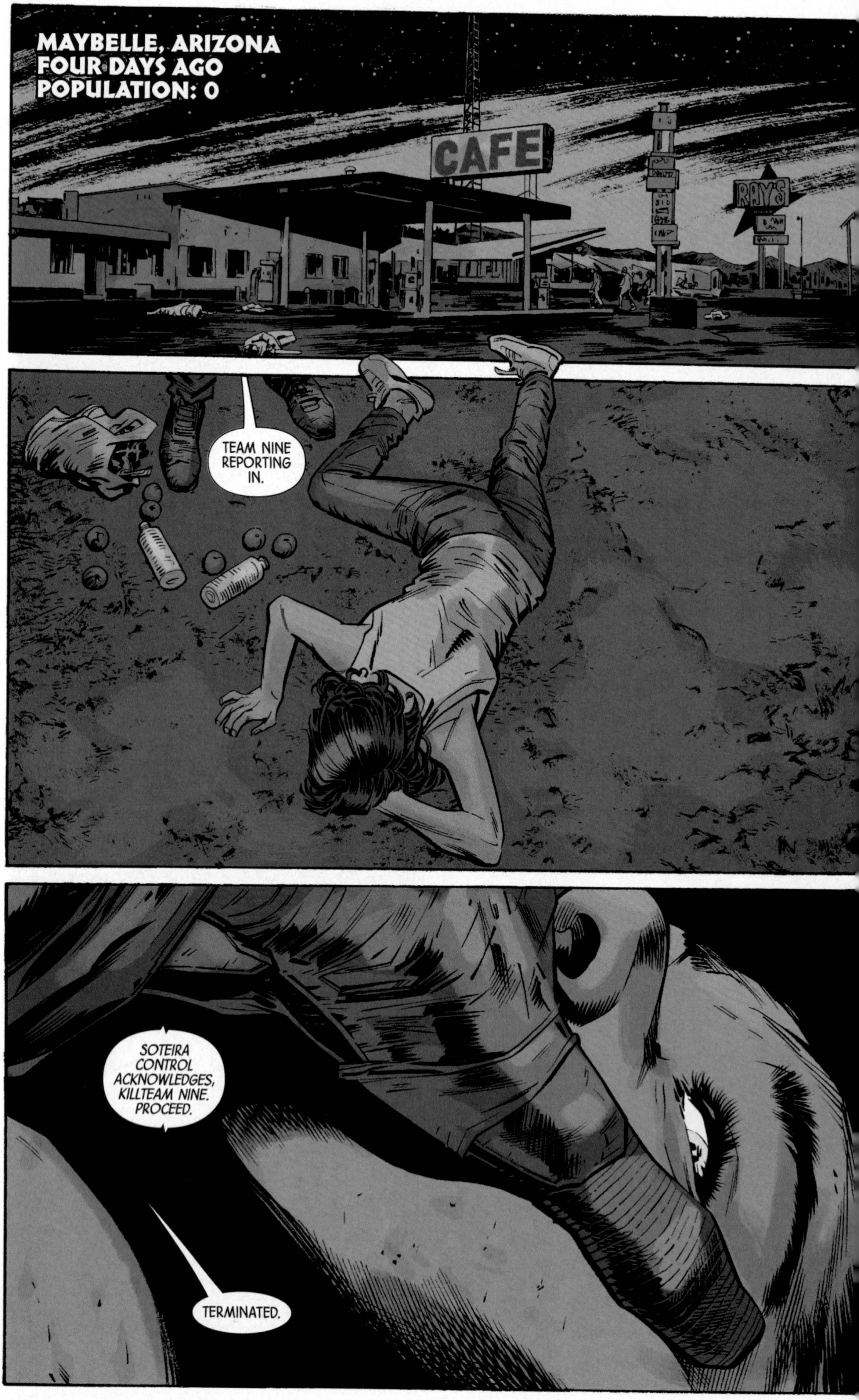
MAYBELLE, ARIZONA
FOUR DAYS AGO
POPULATION: 0
CAFE
RAY'S
TEAM NINE REPORTING IN.
SOTEIRA CONTROL ACKNOWLEDGES, KILLTEAM NINE. PROCEED.
TERMINATED.

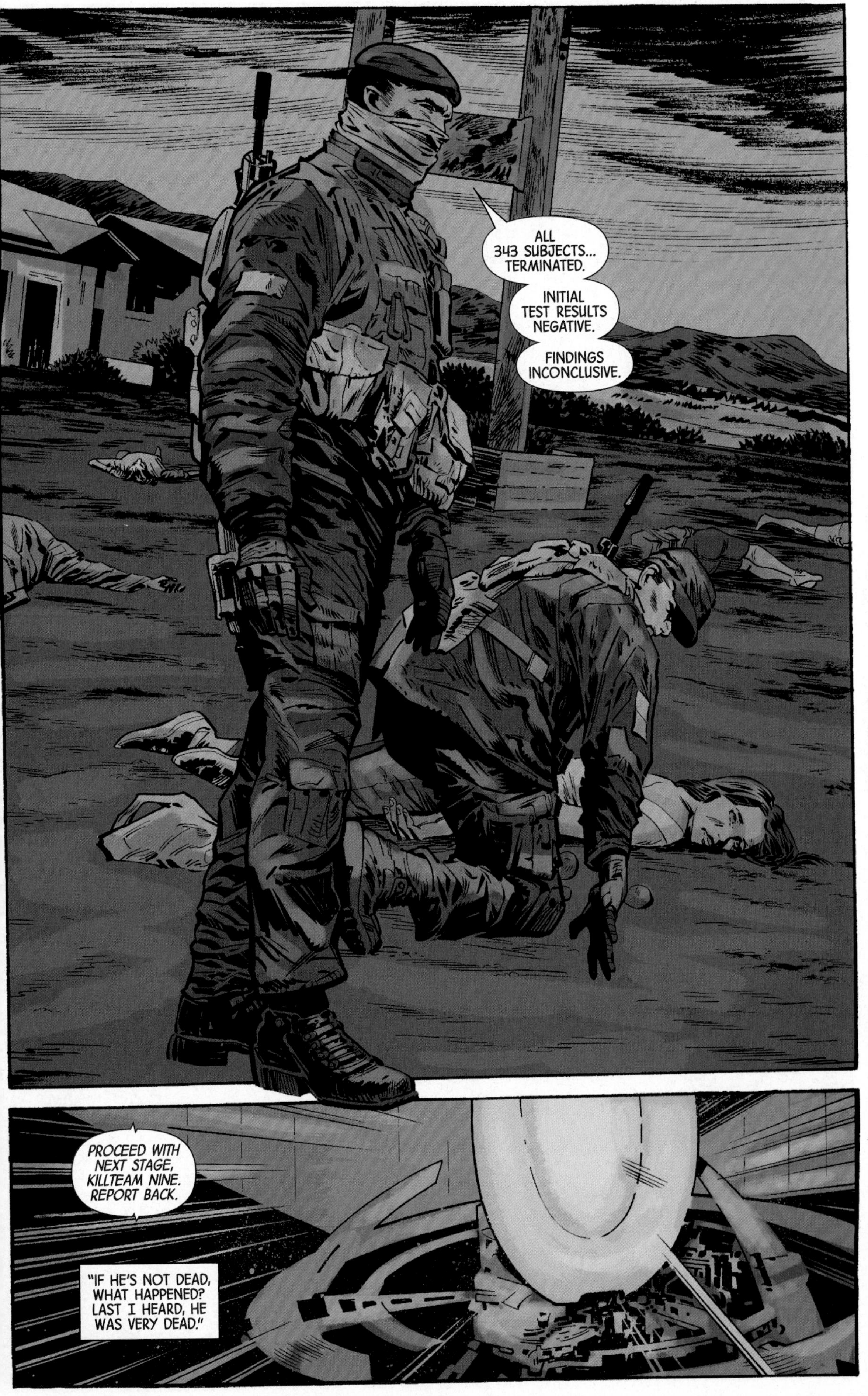
ALL 343 SUBJECTS... TERMINATED.
INITIAL TEST RESULTS NEGATIVE.
FINDINGS INCONCLUSIVE.
PROCEED WITH NEXT STAGE, KILLTEAM NINE. REPORT BACK.
"IF HE'S NOT DEAD, WHAT HAPPENED? LAST I HEARD, HE WAS VERY DEAD."

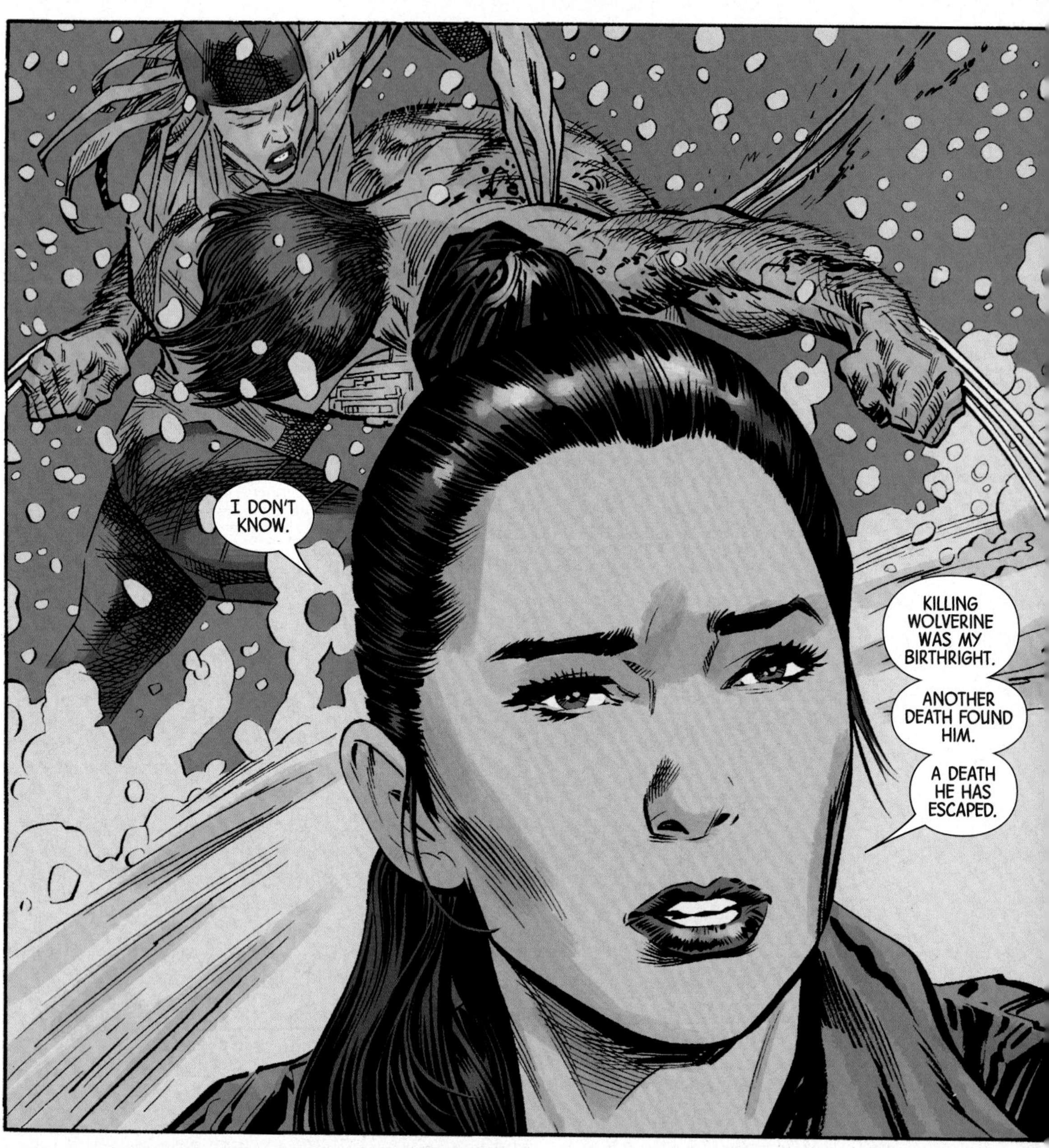
I DON'T KNOW.
KILLING WOLVERINE WAS MY BIRTHRIGHT.
ANOTHER DEATH FOUND HIM.
A DEATH HE HAS ESCAPED.

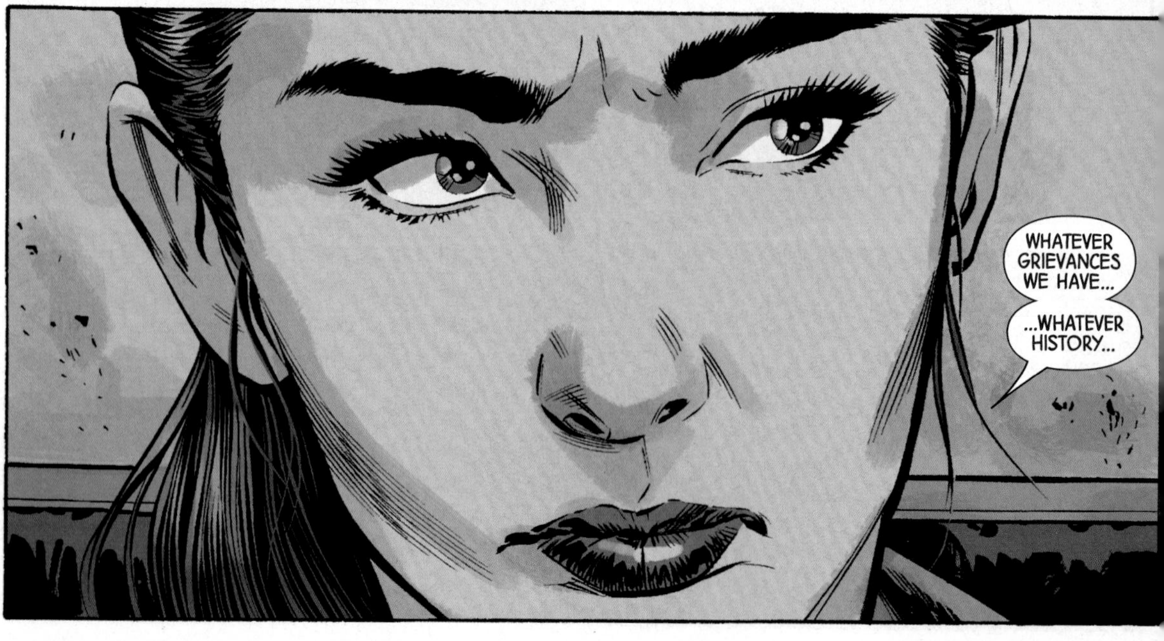
WHATEVER GRIEVANCES WE HAVE...
...WHATEVER HISTORY...

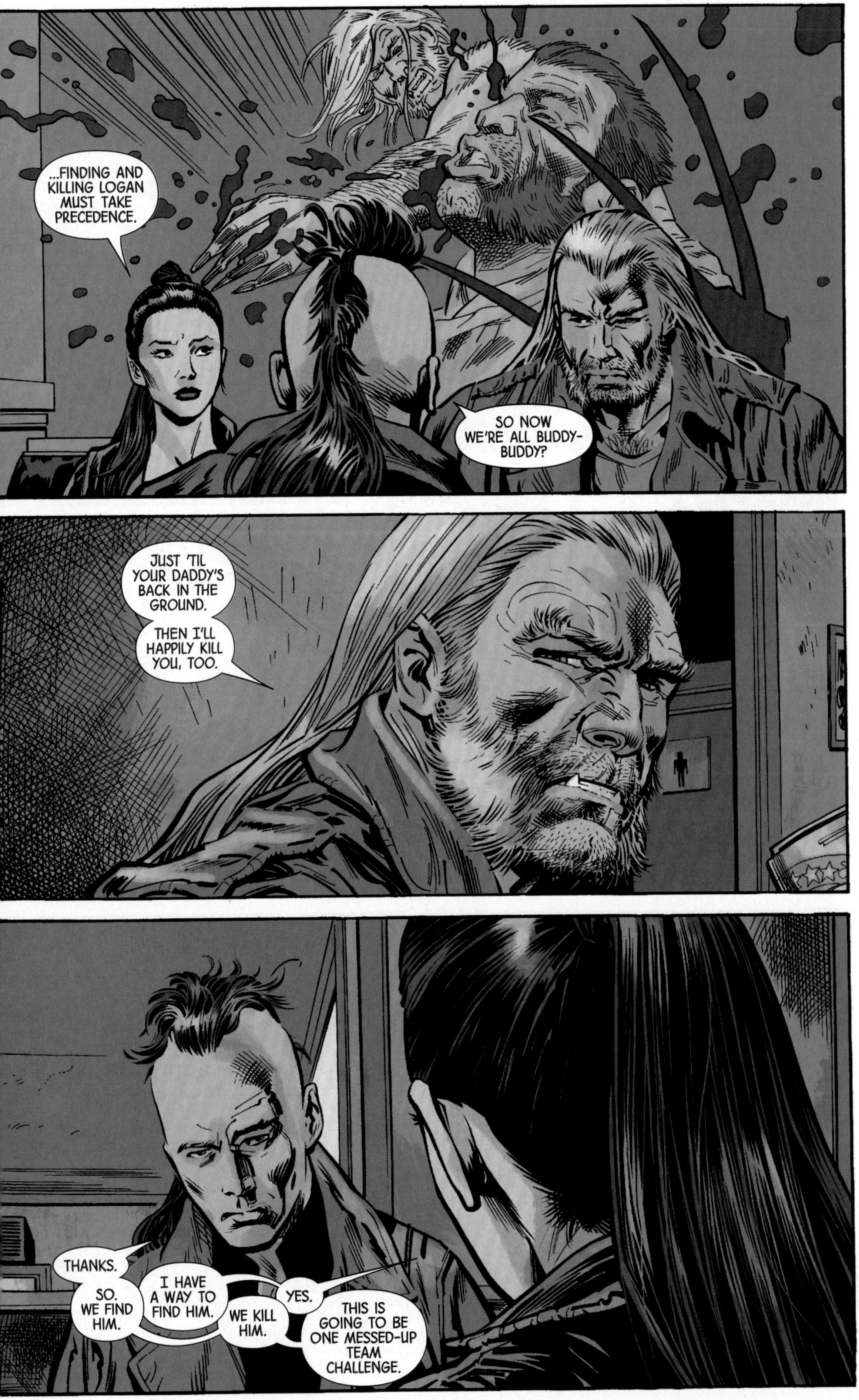
...FINDING AND KILLING LOGAN MUST TAKE PRECEDENCE.
SO NOW WE'RE ALL BUDDY-BUDDY?
JUST 'TIL YOUR DADDY'S BACK IN THE GROUND.
THEN I'LL HAPPILY KILL YOU, TOO.
THANKS.
SO. WE FIND HIM.
I HAVE A WAY TO FIND HIM.
YES.
WE KILL HIM.
THIS IS GOING TO BE ONE MESSED-UP TEAM CHALLENGE.

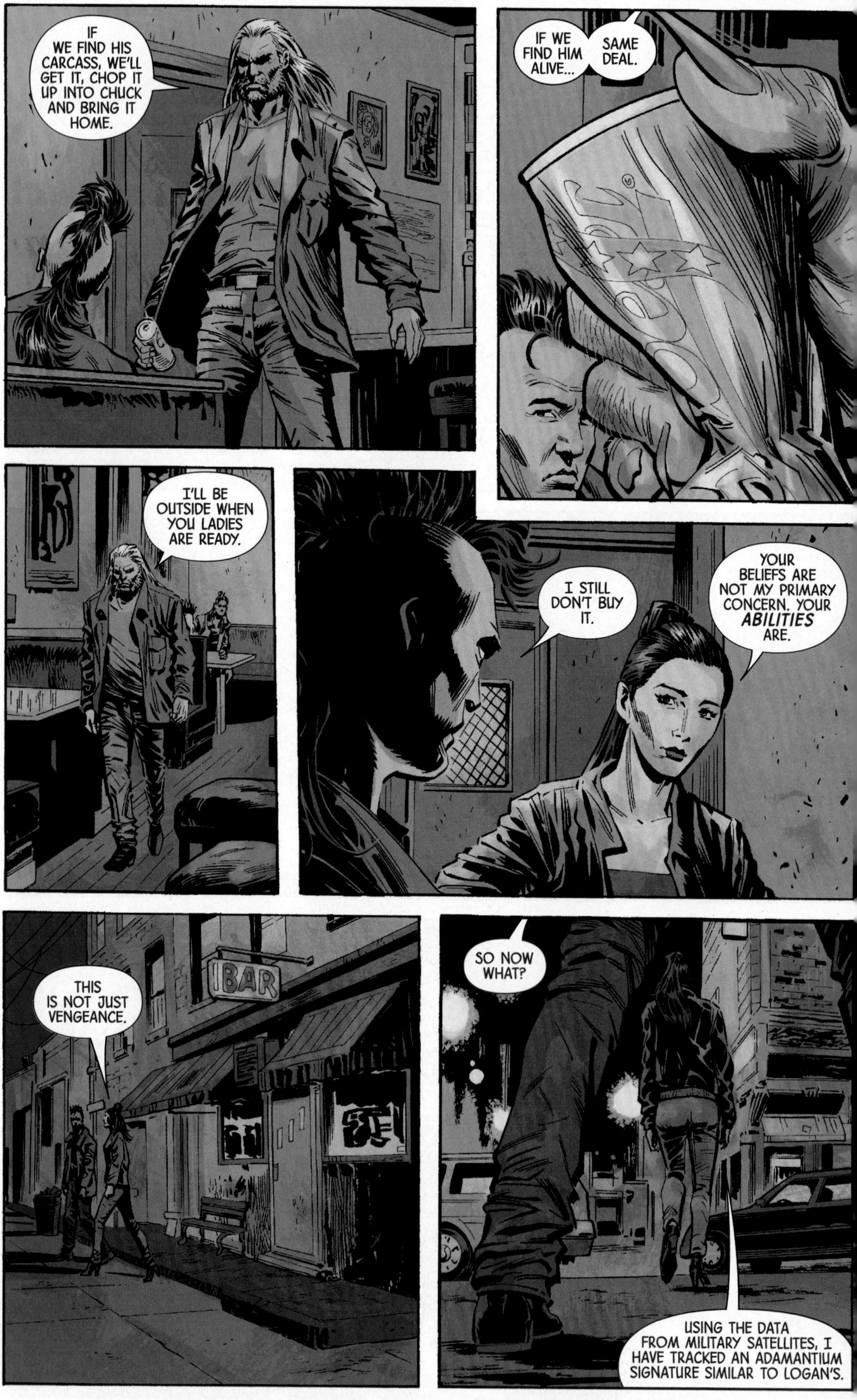
IF WE FIND HIS CARCASS, WE'LL GET IT, CHOP IT UP INTO CHUCK AND BRING IT HOME.
IF WE FIND HIM ALIVE...
SAME DEAL.
I'LL BE OUTSIDE WHEN YOU LADIES ARE READY.
I STILL DON'T BUY IT.
YOUR BELIEFS ARE NOT MY PRIMARY CONCERN. YOUR *ABILITIES* ARE.
BAR
THIS IS NOT JUST VENGEANCE.
SO NOW WHAT?
USING THE DATA FROM MILITARY SATELLITES, I HAVE TRACKED AN ADAMANTIUM SIGNATURE SIMILAR TO LOGAN'S.

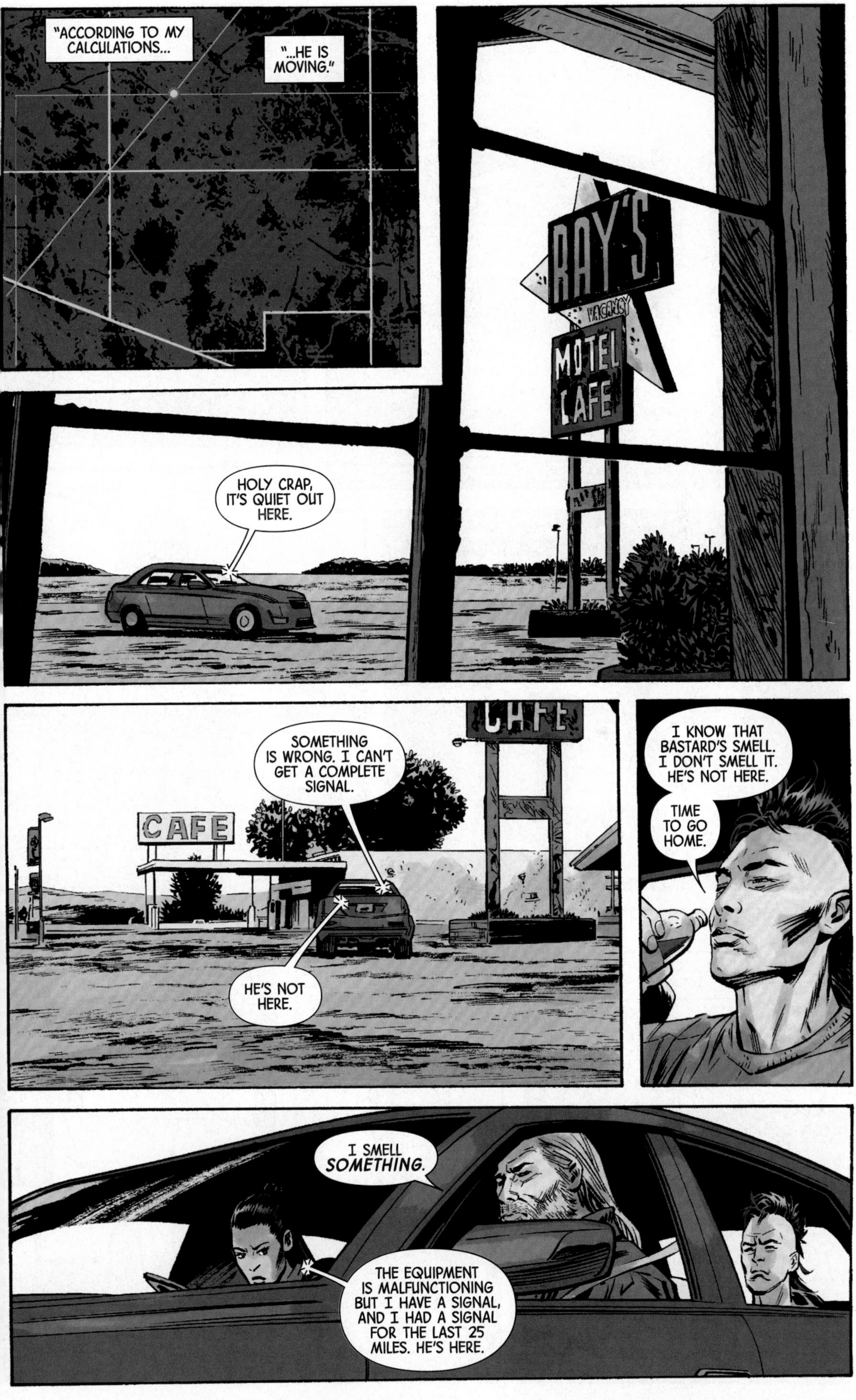
"ACCORDING TO MY CALCULATIONS...
"...HE IS MOVING."
RAY'S
VACANCY
MOTEL
CAFE
HOLY CRAP, IT'S QUIET OUT HERE.
CAFE
CAFE
SOMETHING IS WRONG. I CAN'T GET A COMPLETE SIGNAL.
HE'S NOT HERE.
I KNOW THAT BASTARD'S SMELL. I DON'T SMELL IT. HE'S NOT HERE.
TIME TO GO HOME.
I SMELL *SOMETHING*.
THE EQUIPMENT IS MALFUNCTIONING BUT I HAVE A SIGNAL, AND I HAD A SIGNAL FOR THE LAST 25 MILES. HE'S HERE.

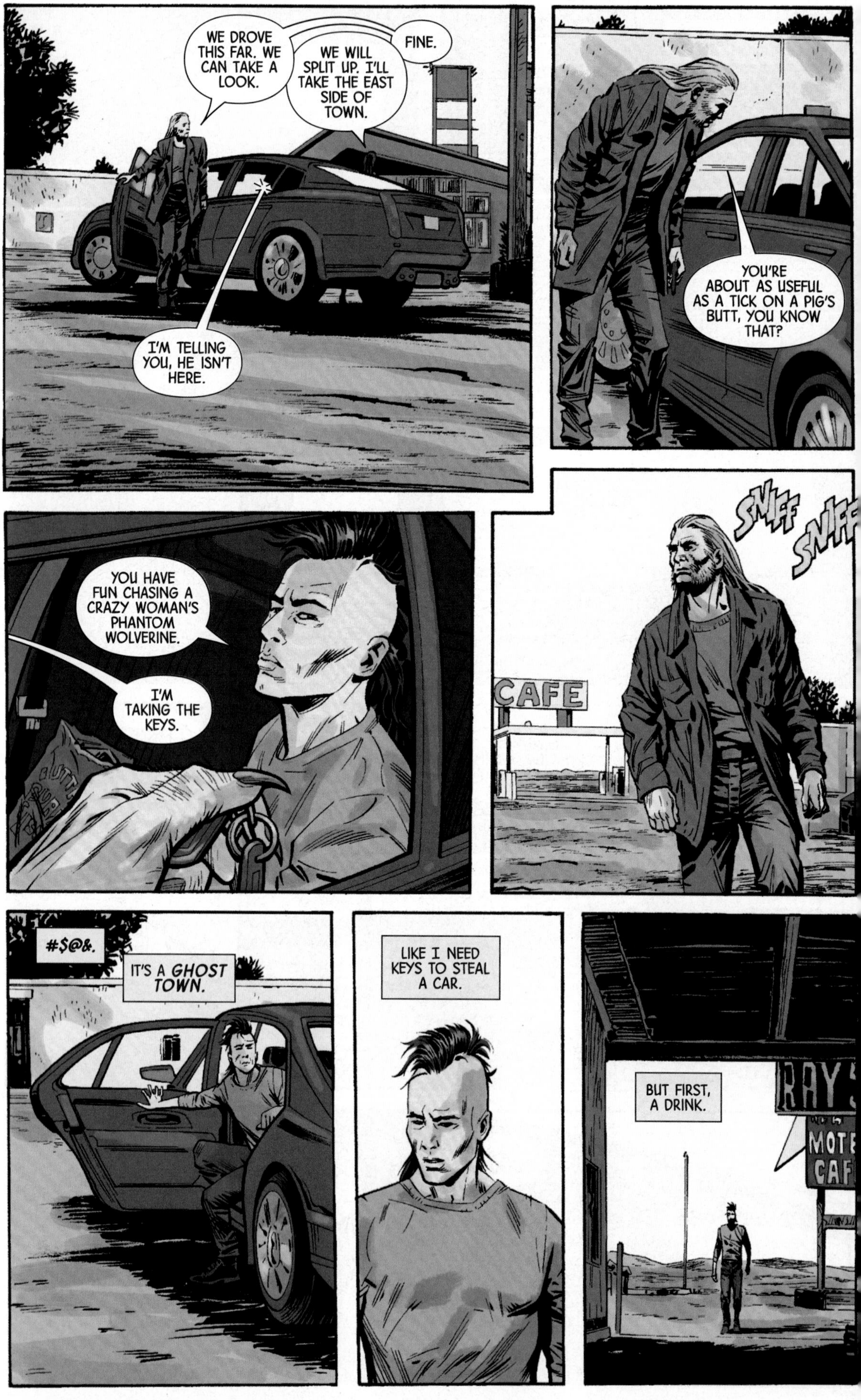
WE DROVE THIS FAR. WE CAN TAKE A LOOK.
WE WILL SPLIT UP. I'LL TAKE THE EAST SIDE OF TOWN.
FINE.
I'M TELLING YOU, HE ISN'T HERE.
YOU'RE ABOUT AS USEFUL AS A TICK ON A PIG'S BUTT, YOU KNOW THAT?
YOU HAVE FUN CHASING A CRAZY WOMAN'S PHANTOM WOLVERINE.
I'M TAKING THE KEYS.
SNIFF
SNIFF
CAFE
#$@&.
IT'S A GHOST TOWN.
LIKE I NEED KEYS TO STEAL A CAR.
BUT FIRST, A DRINK.
MOTE
CAF

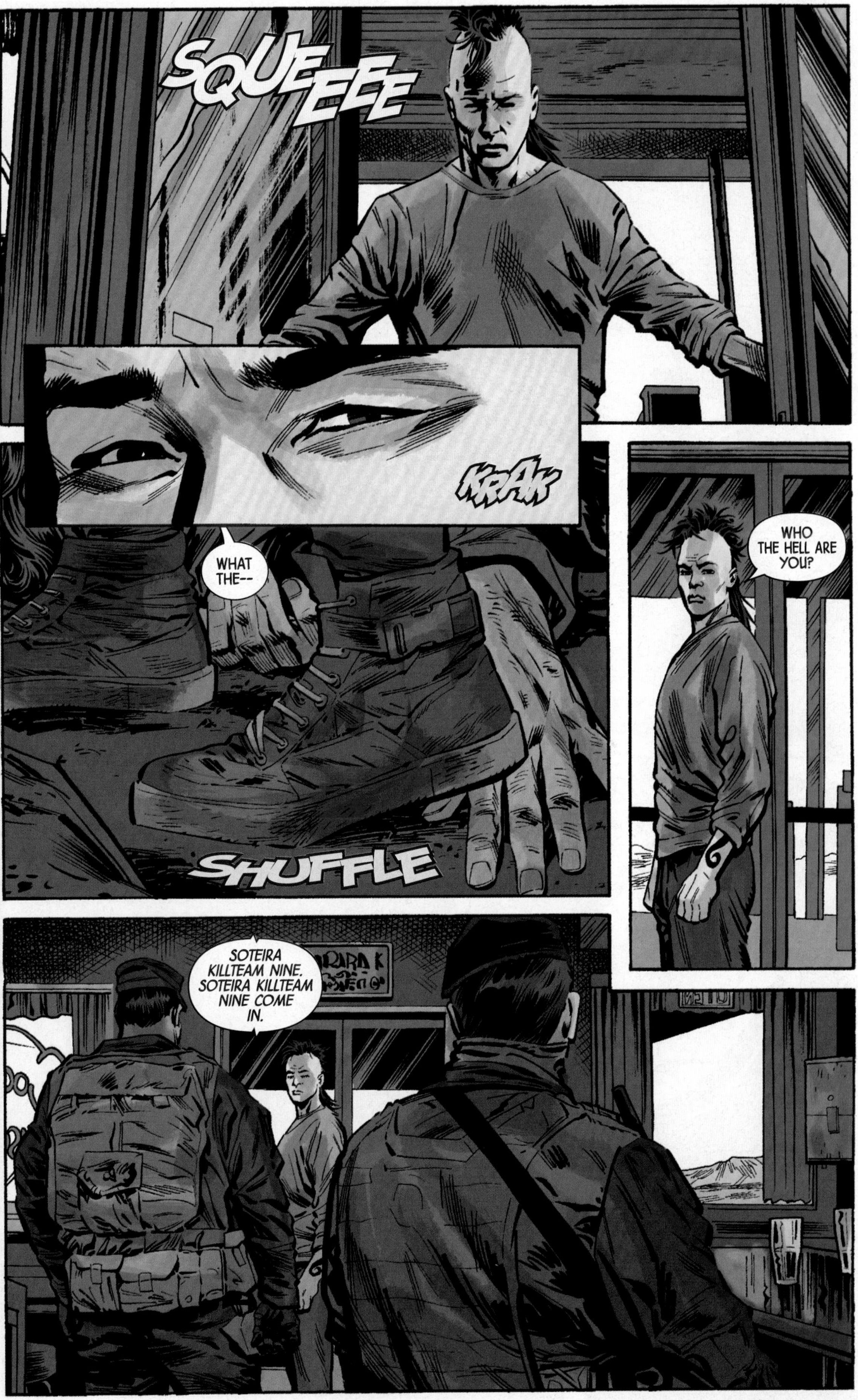
SQUEEEE
KRAK
WHAT THE--
SHUFFLE
WHO THE HELL ARE YOU?
SOTEIRA KILLTEAM NINE. SOTEIRA KILLTEAM NINE COME IN.

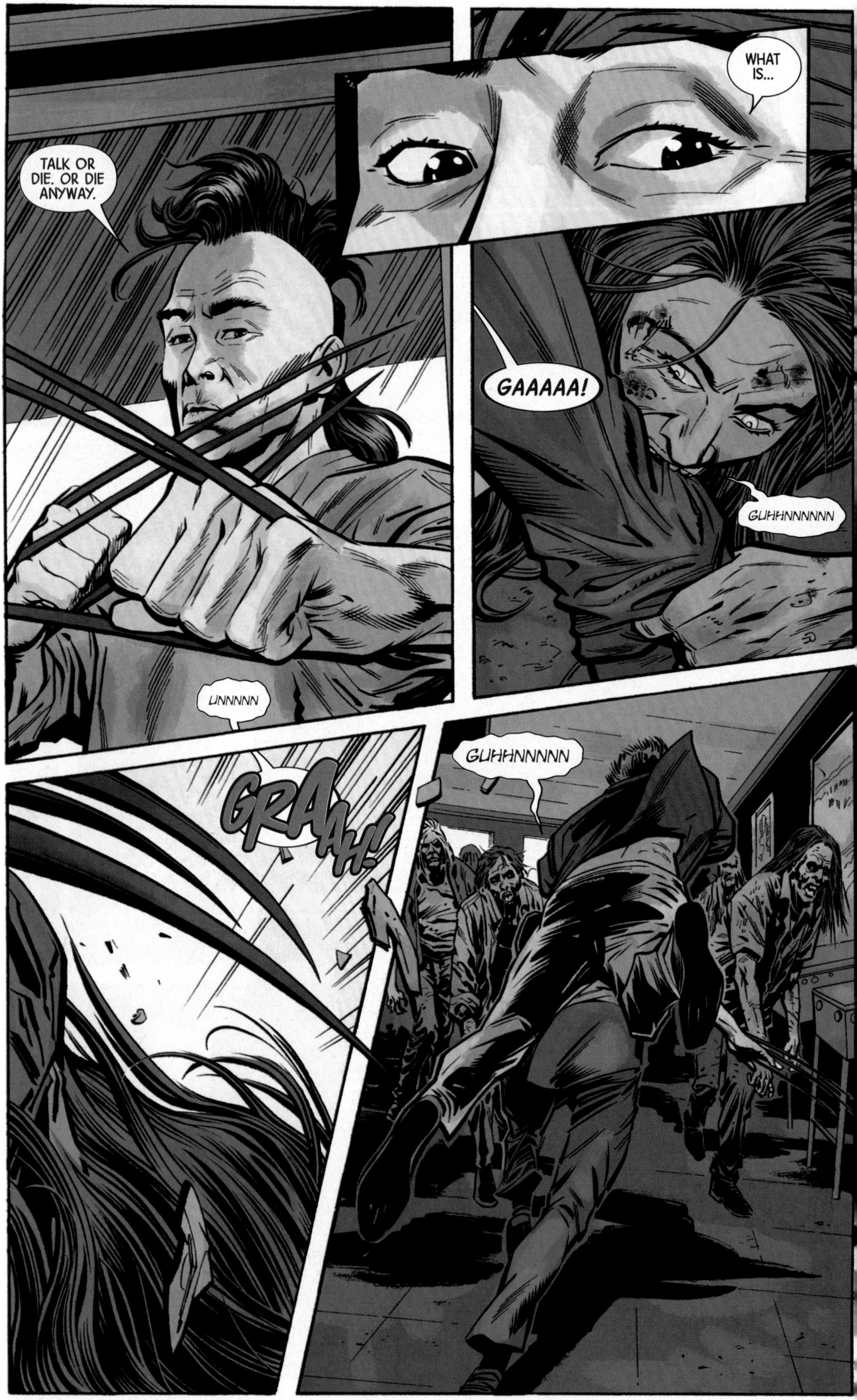
TALK OR DIE. OR DIE ANYWAY.
WHAT IS...
GAAAAA!
GUHHNNNNNN
UNNNNN
GRAAAH!
GUHHNNNNN

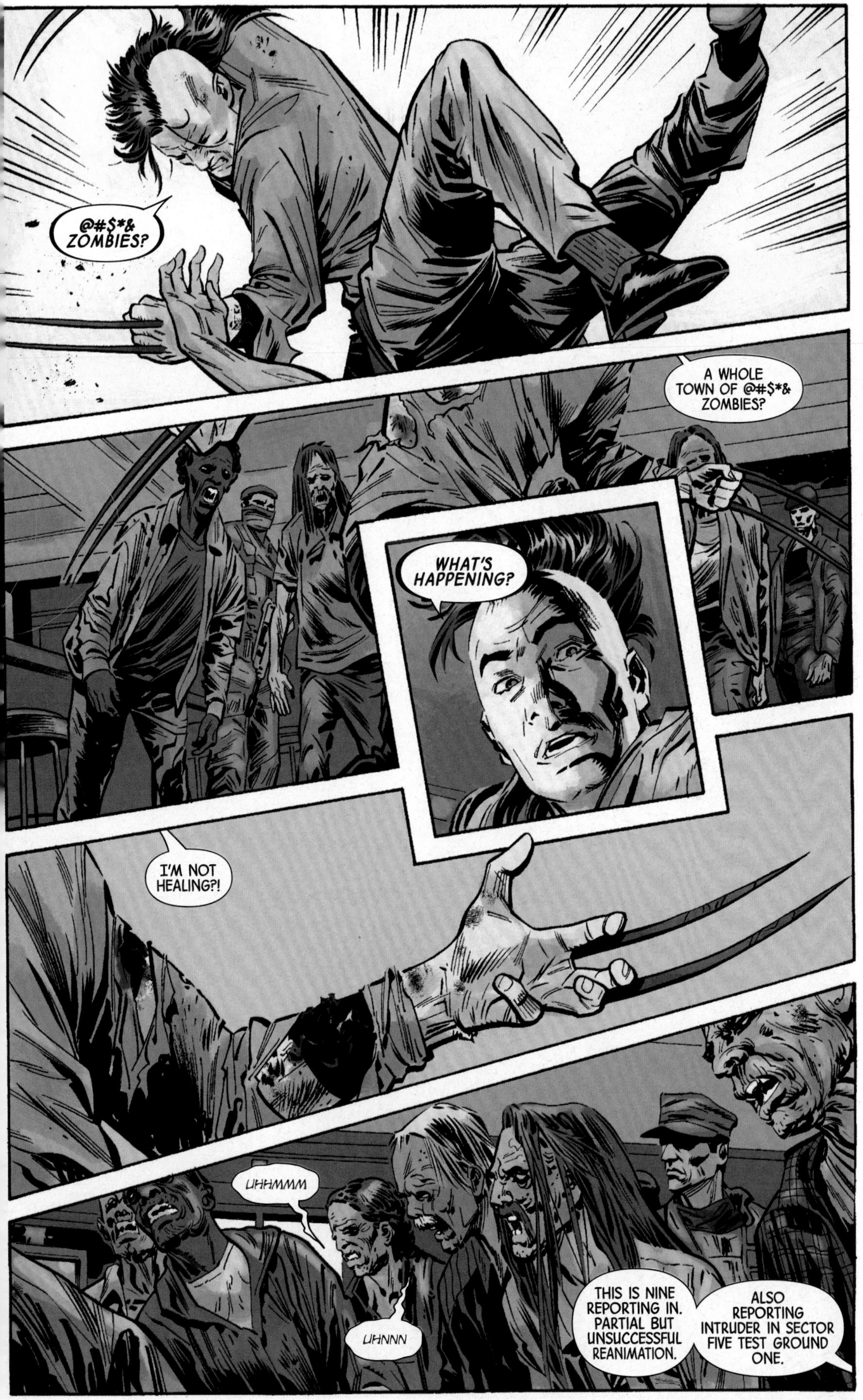
@#$*& ZOMBIES?
A WHOLE TOWN OF @#$*& ZOMBIES?
WHAT'S HAPPENING?
I'M NOT HEALING?!
UHHMMM
UHNNN
THIS IS NINE REPORTING IN. PARTIAL BUT UNSUCCESSFUL REANIMATION.
ALSO REPORTING INTRUDER IN SECTOR FIVE TEST GROUND ONE.

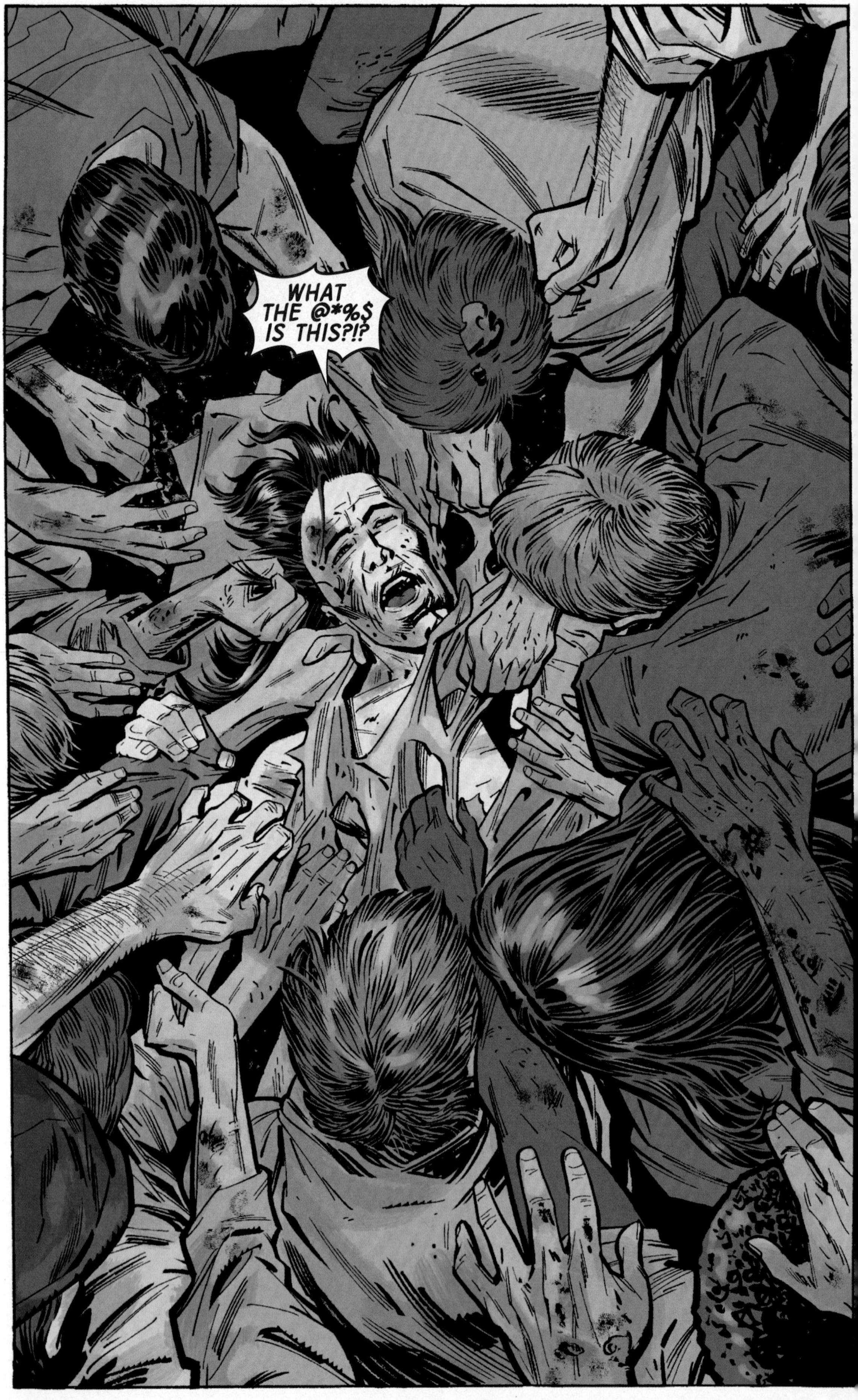
WHAT THE @*%$ IS THIS?!?

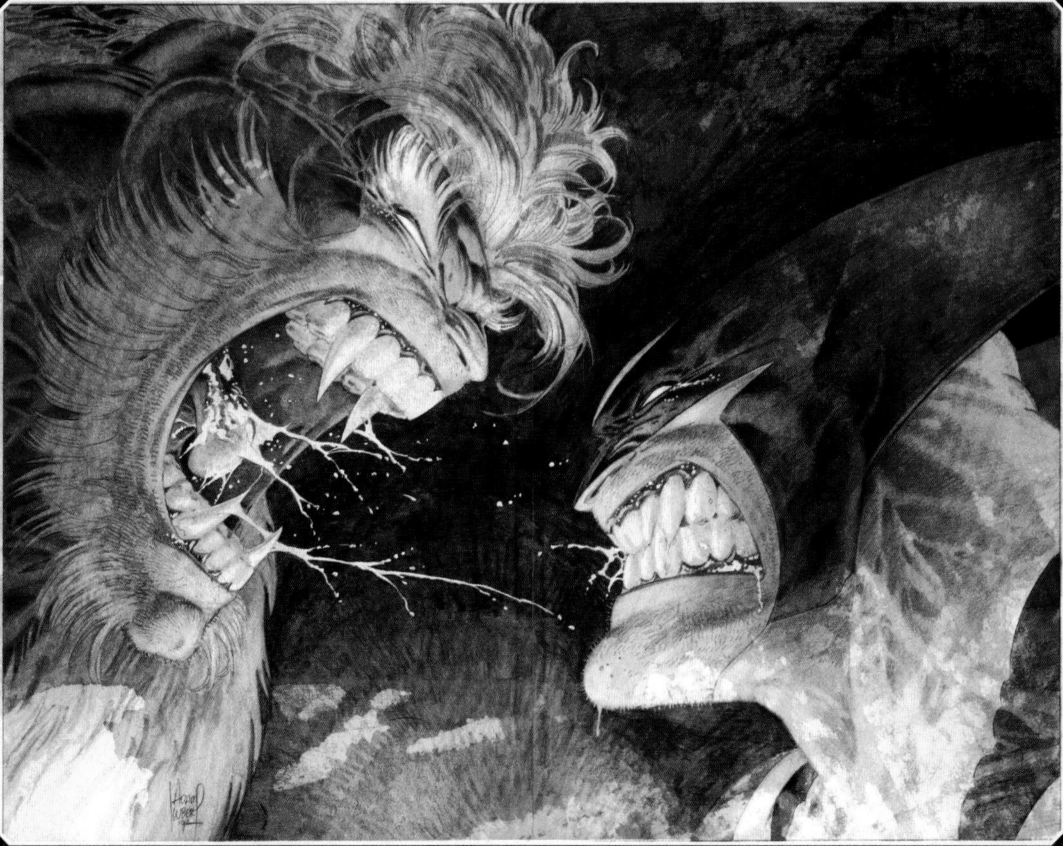

Adam Kubert & Dan Brown
HUNT FOR WOLVERINE #1 REMASTERED VARIANT

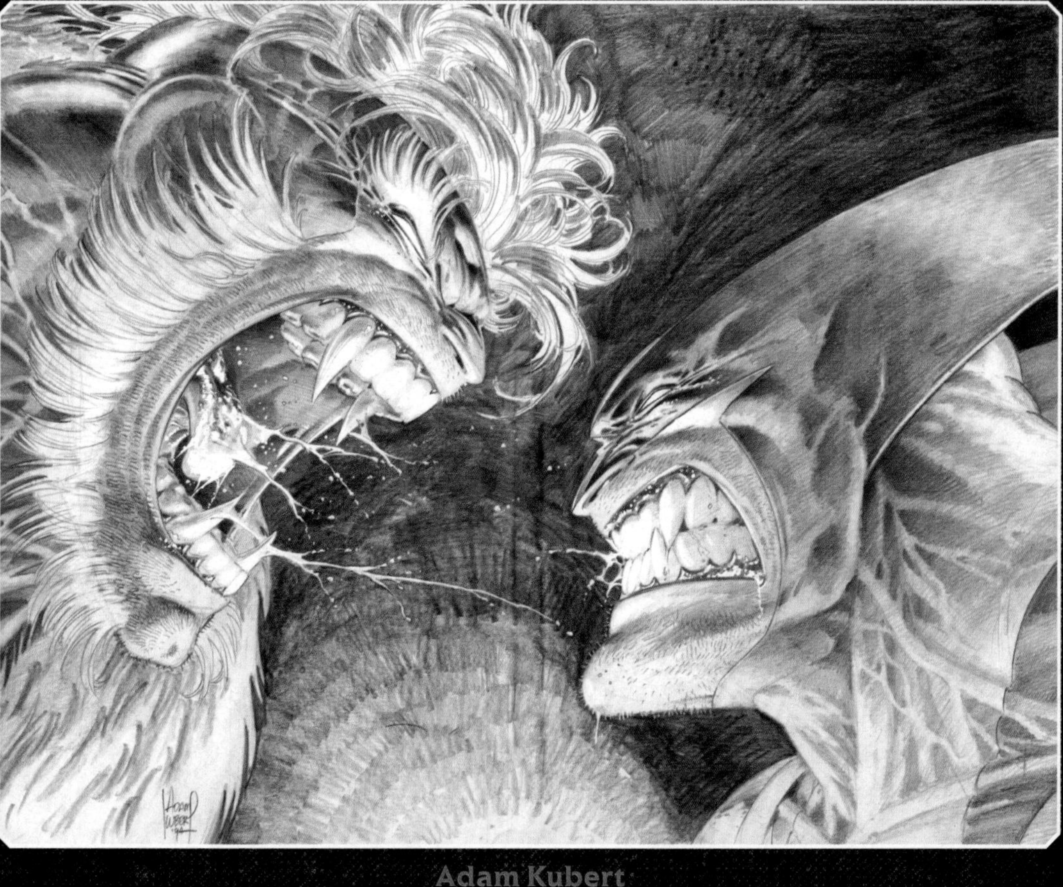

Adam Kubert
HUNT FOR WOLVERINE #1 REMASTERED BLACK & WHITE VARIANT

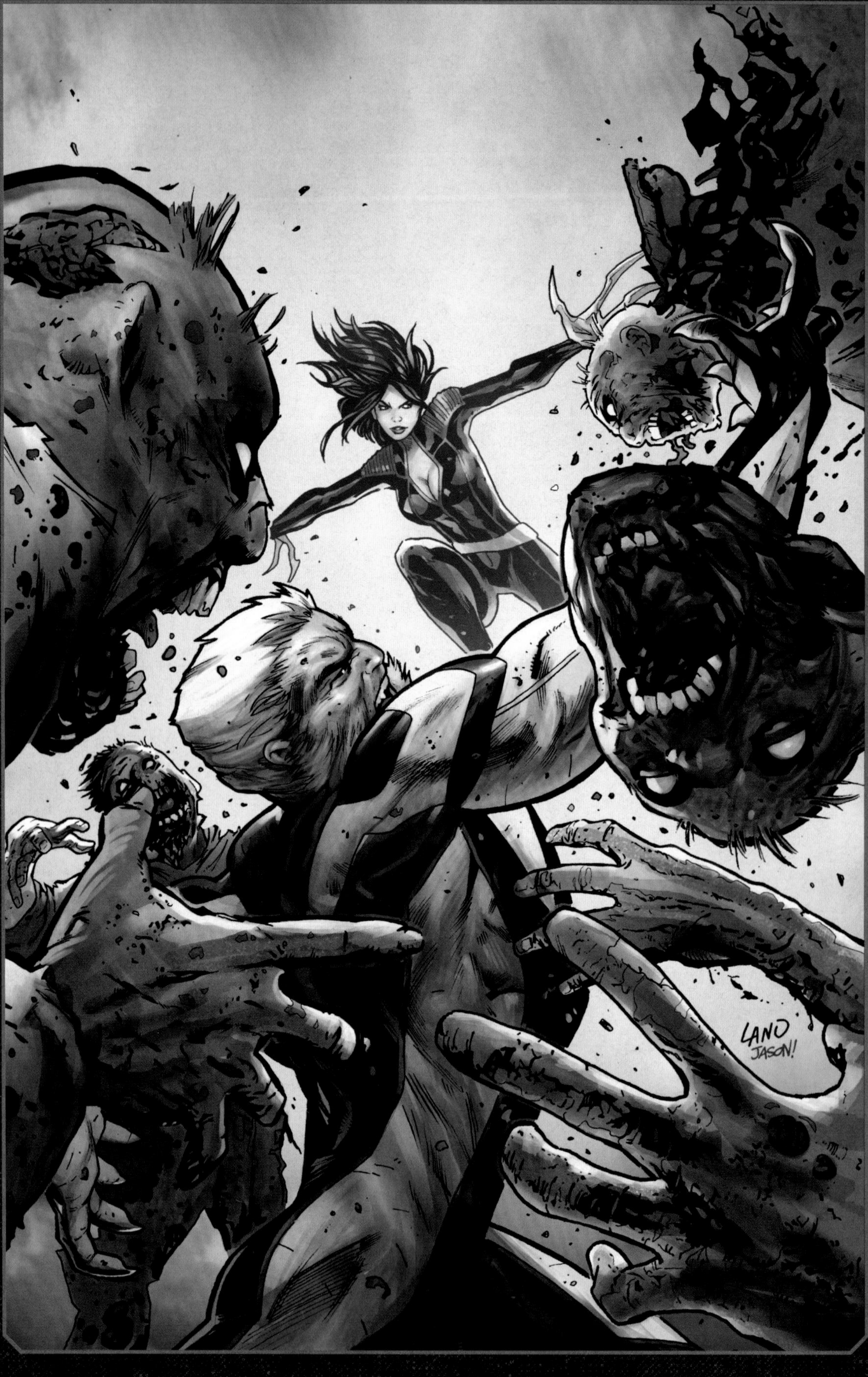
LAND
JASON!

CLAWS OF A KILLER 2

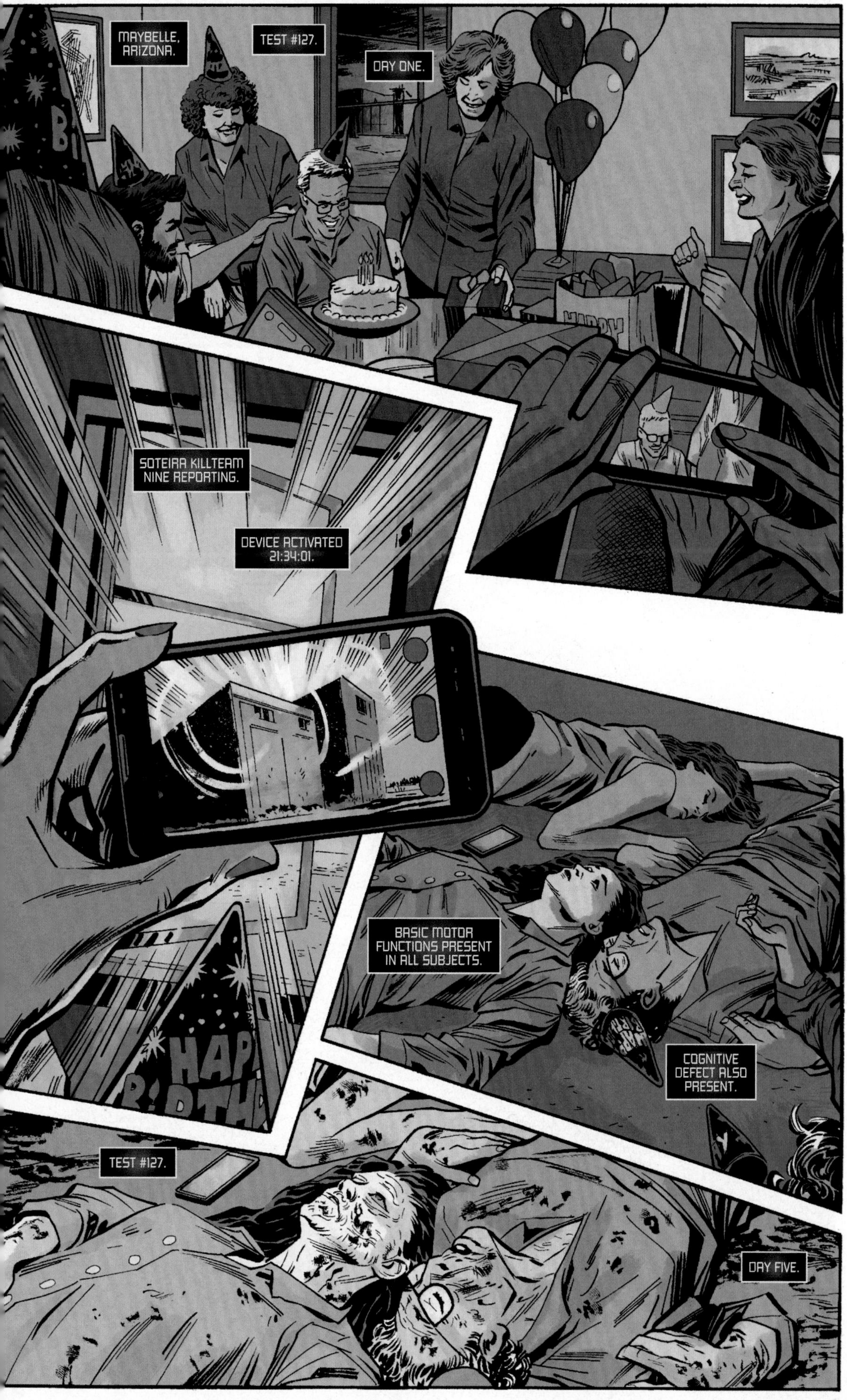
MAYBELLE, ARIZONA.
TEST #127.
DAY ONE.
HAPPY
SOTEIRA KILLTEAM NINE REPORTING.
DEVICE ACTIVATED 21:34:01.
BASIC MOTOR FUNCTIONS PRESENT IN ALL SUBJECTS.
COGNITIVE DEFECT ALSO PRESENT.
TEST #127.
DAY FIVE.

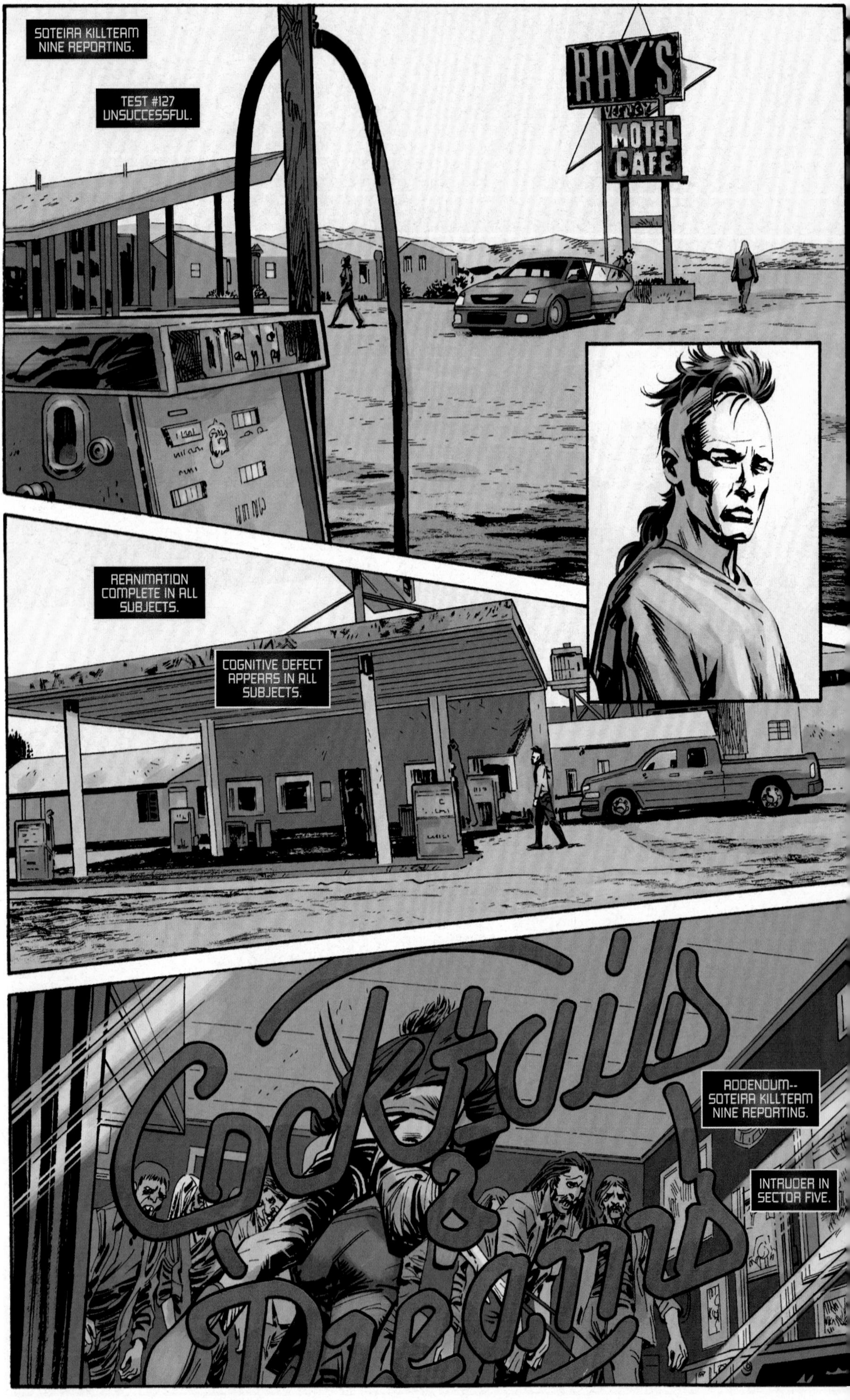
SOTEIRA KILLTEAM NINE REPORTING.
TEST #127 UNSUCCESSFUL.
RAY'S
MOTEL
CAFE
REANIMATION COMPLETE IN ALL SUBJECTS.
COGNITIVE DEFECT APPEARS IN ALL SUBJECTS.
Cocktails & Dreams
ADDENDUM-- SOTEIRA KILLTEAM NINE REPORTING.
INTRUDER IN SECTOR FIVE.

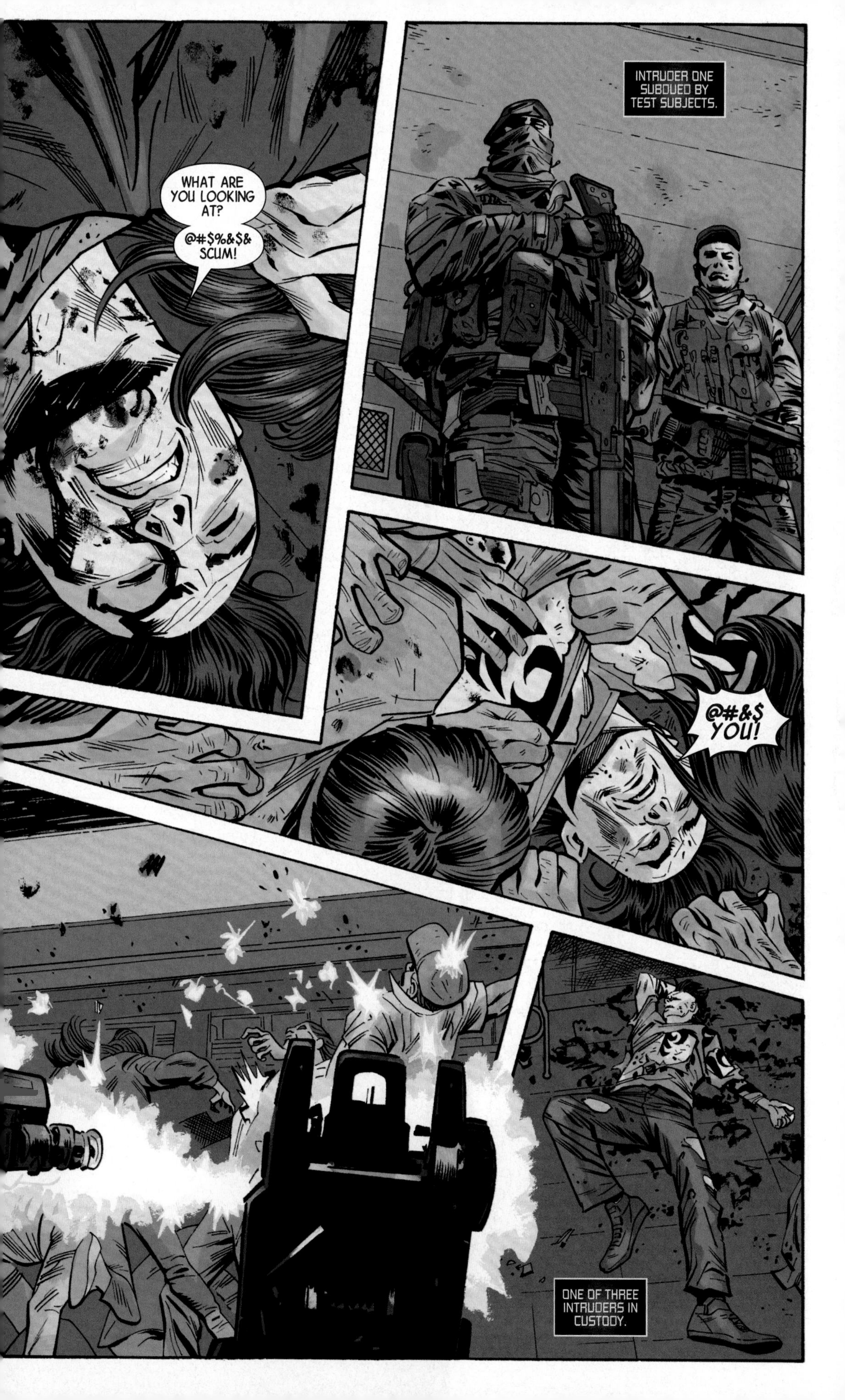
WHAT ARE YOU LOOKING AT?
@#$%&$& SCUM!
INTRUDER ONE SUBDUED BY TEST SUBJECTS.
@#&$ YOU!
ONE OF THREE INTRUDERS IN CUSTODY.

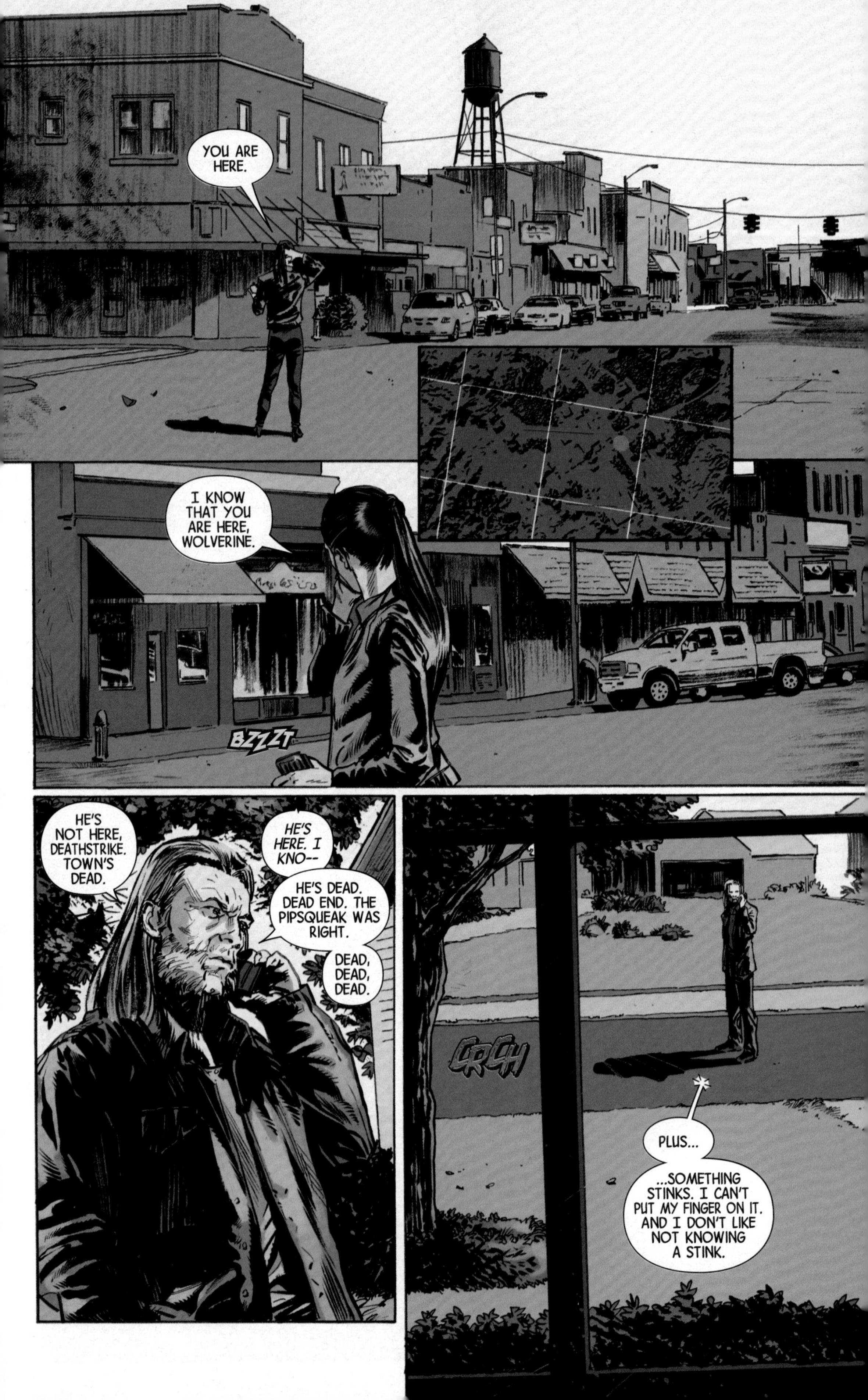
YOU ARE HERE.
I KNOW THAT YOU ARE HERE, WOLVERINE.
BZZZT
HE'S NOT HERE, DEATHSTRIKE. TOWN'S DEAD.
HE'S HERE. I KNO--
HE'S DEAD. DEAD END. THE PIPSQUEAK WAS RIGHT.
DEAD, DEAD, DEAD.
CRCH
PLUS...
...SOMETHING STINKS. I CAN'T PUT MY FINGER ON IT. AND I DON'T LIKE NOT KNOWING A STINK.

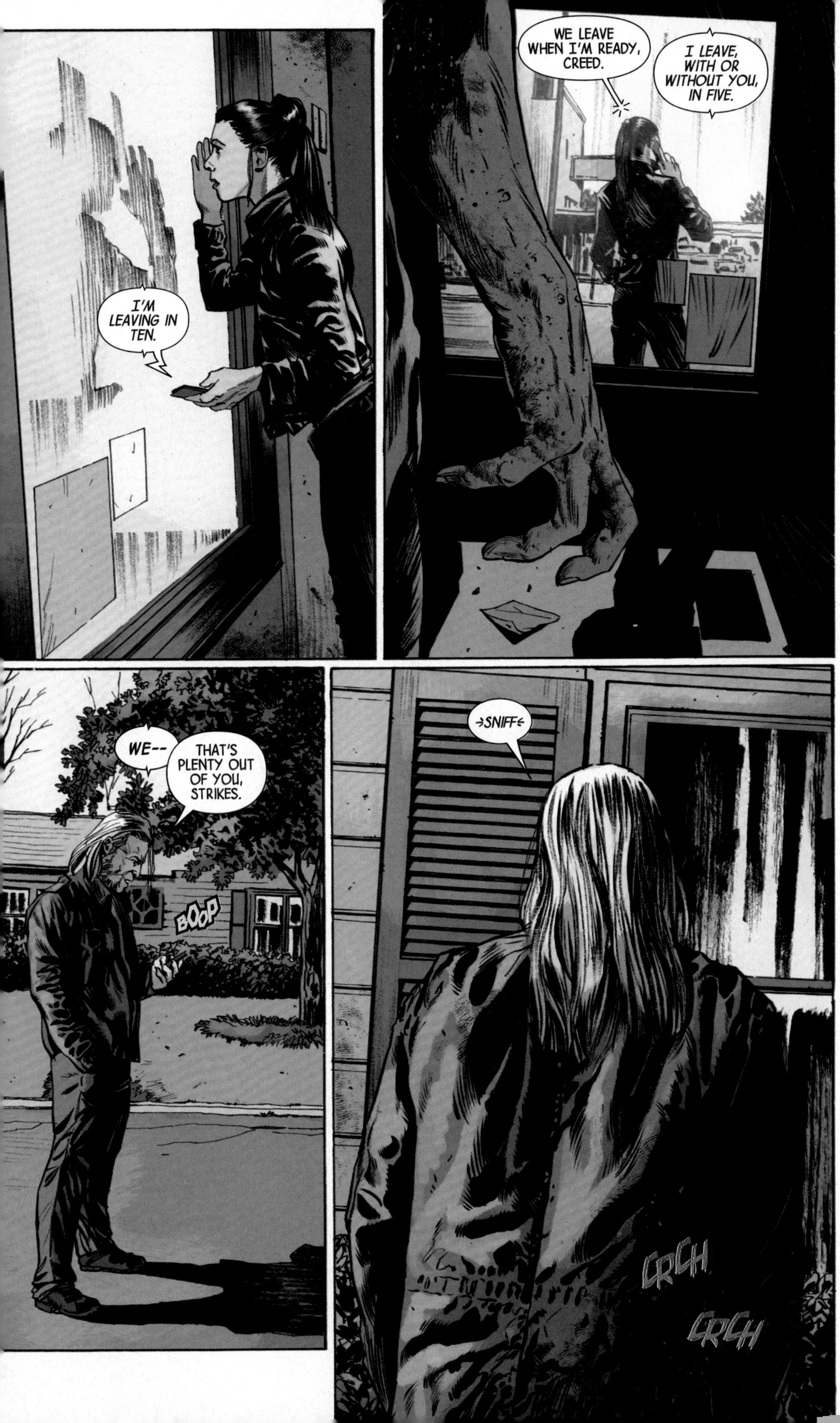
I'M LEAVING IN TEN.
WE LEAVE WHEN I'M READY, CREED.
I LEAVE, WITH OR WITHOUT YOU, IN FIVE.
WE--
THAT'S PLENTY OUT OF YOU, STRIKES.
BOOP
SNIFF
CRCH
CRCH

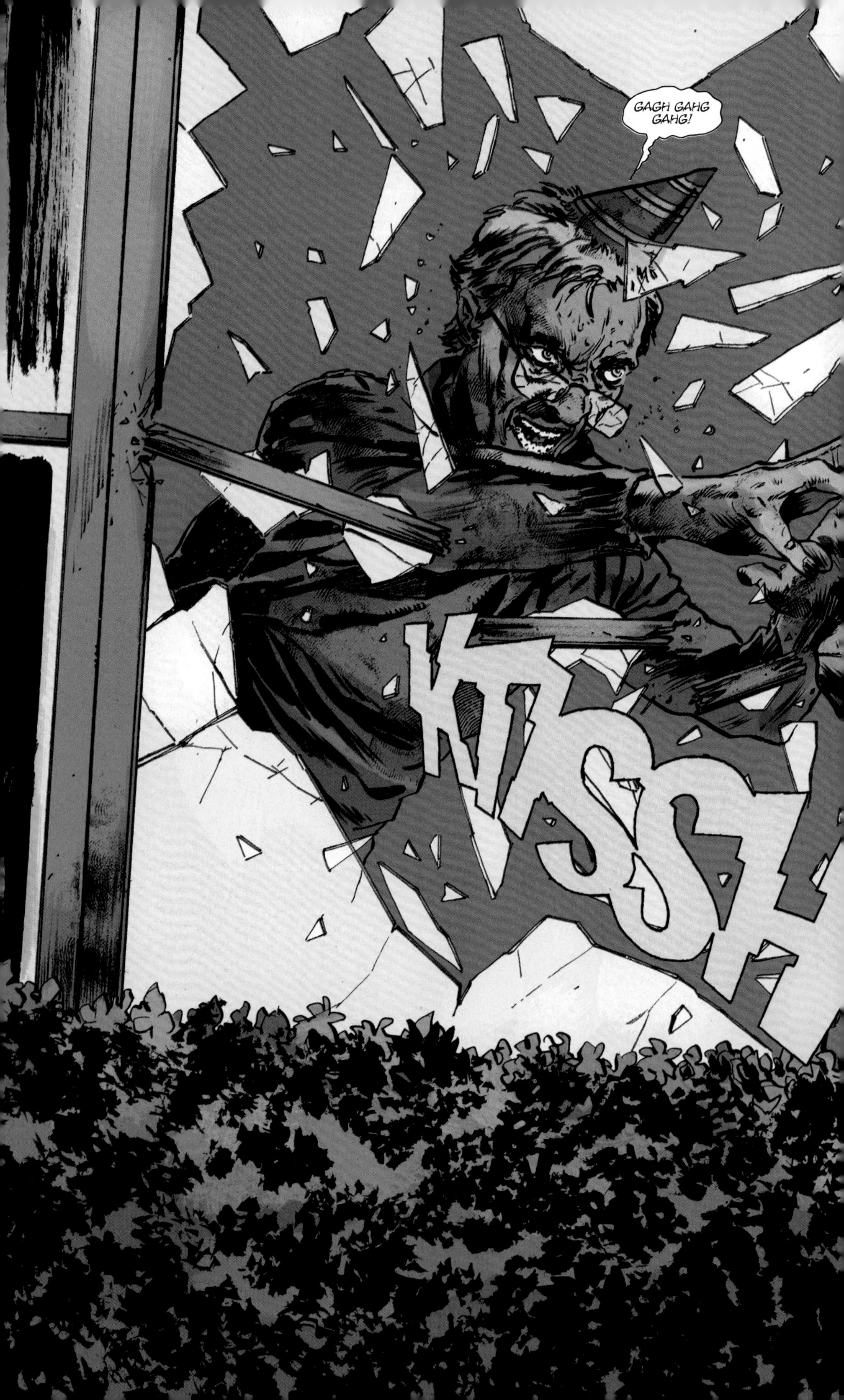
GAGH GAHG GAHG!
KSSH

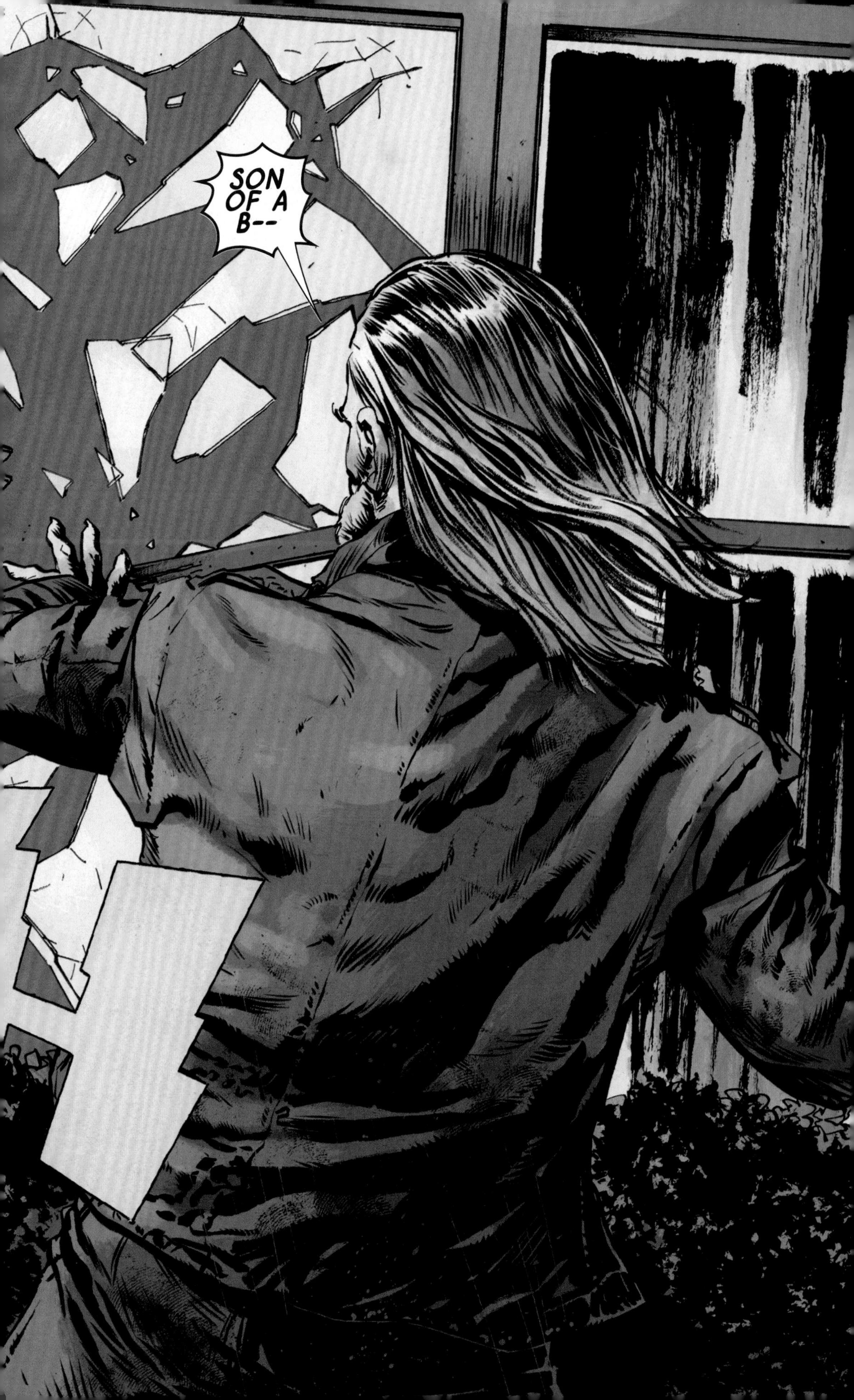
SON OF A B--

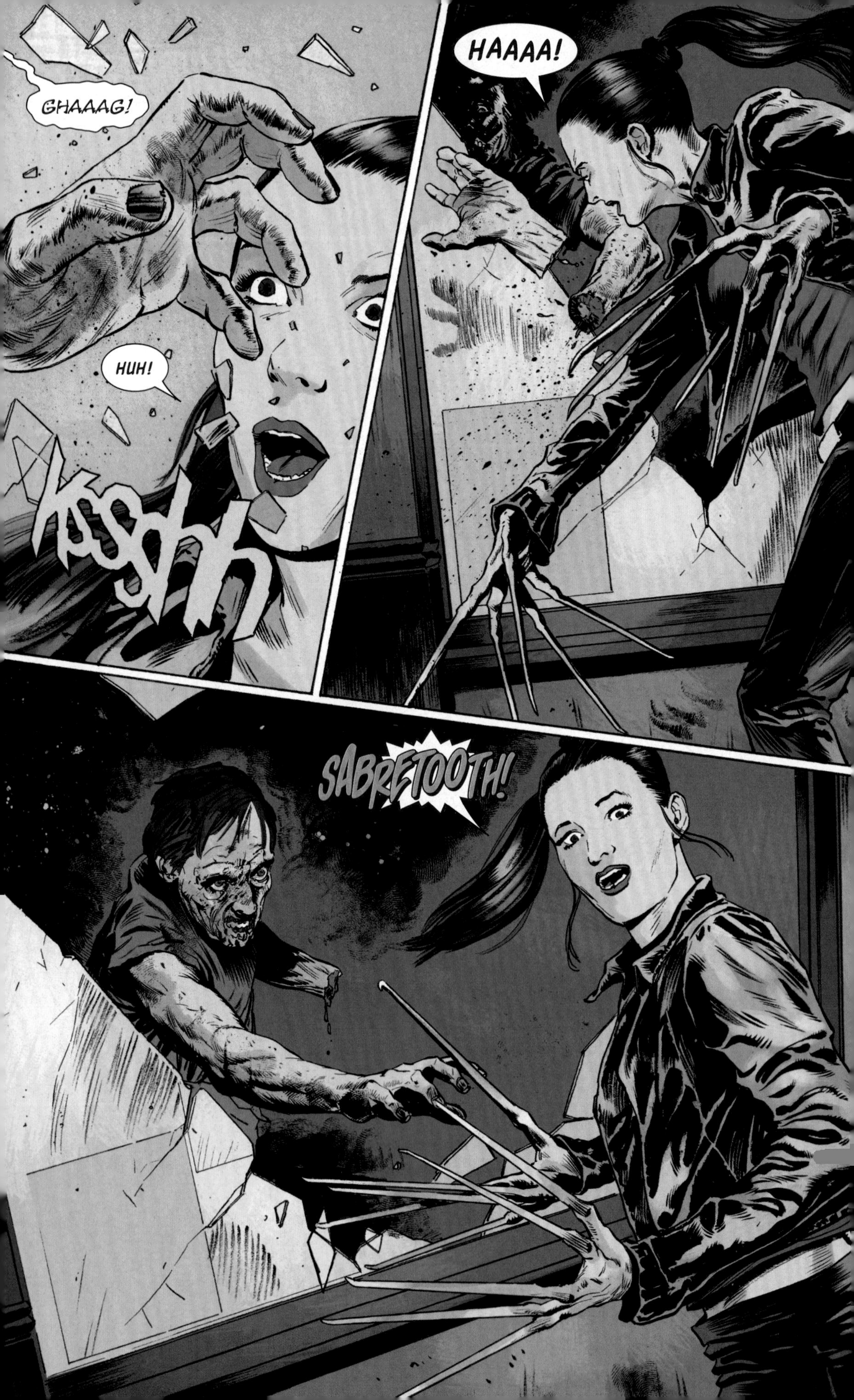
GHAAAG!
HUH!
KSSSH
HAAAA!
SABRETOOTH!

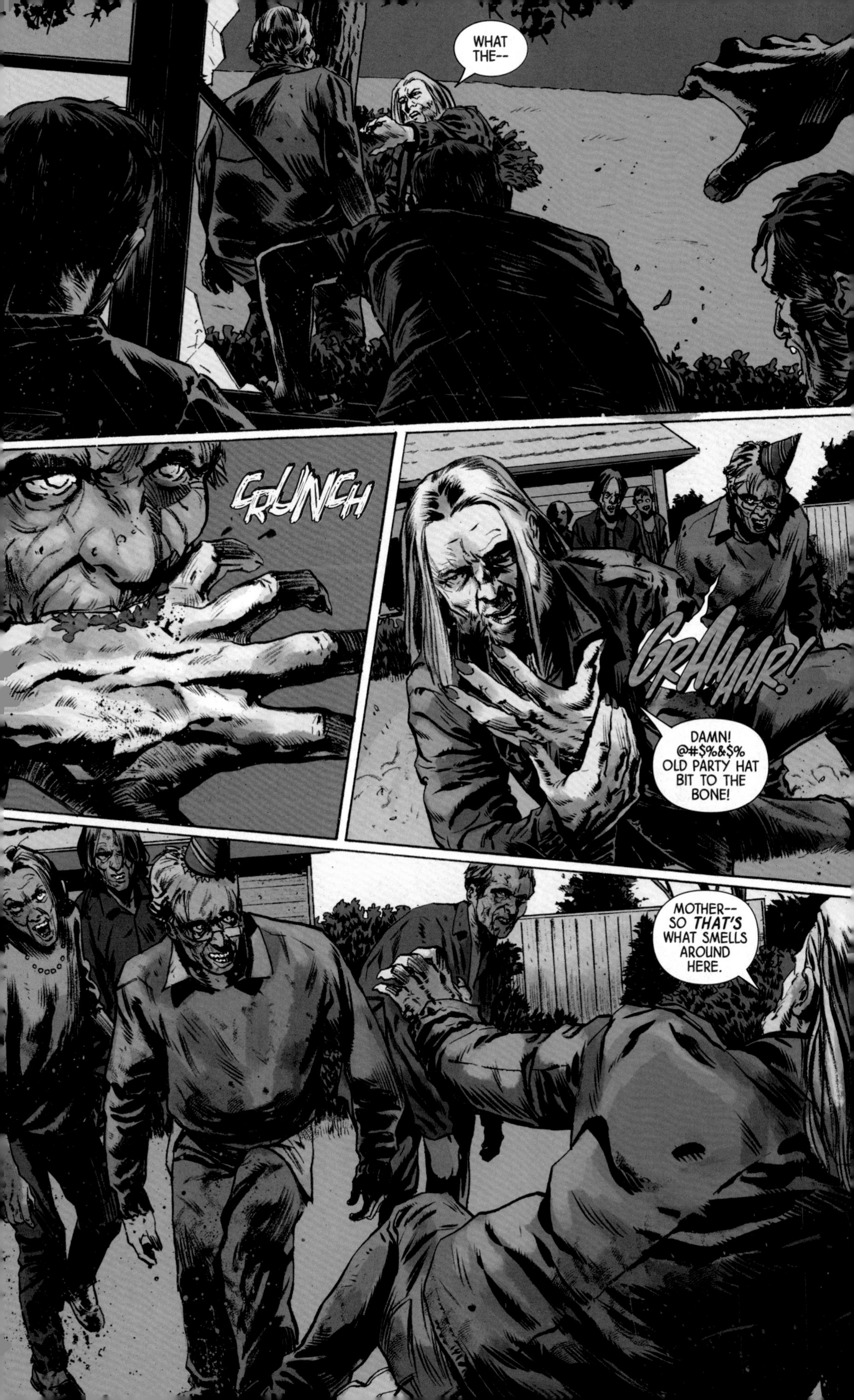
WHAT THE--
CRUNCH
GRAAAAR!
DAMN! @#$%&$% OLD PARTY HAT BIT TO THE BONE!
MOTHER-- SO *THAT'S* WHAT SMELLS AROUND HERE.

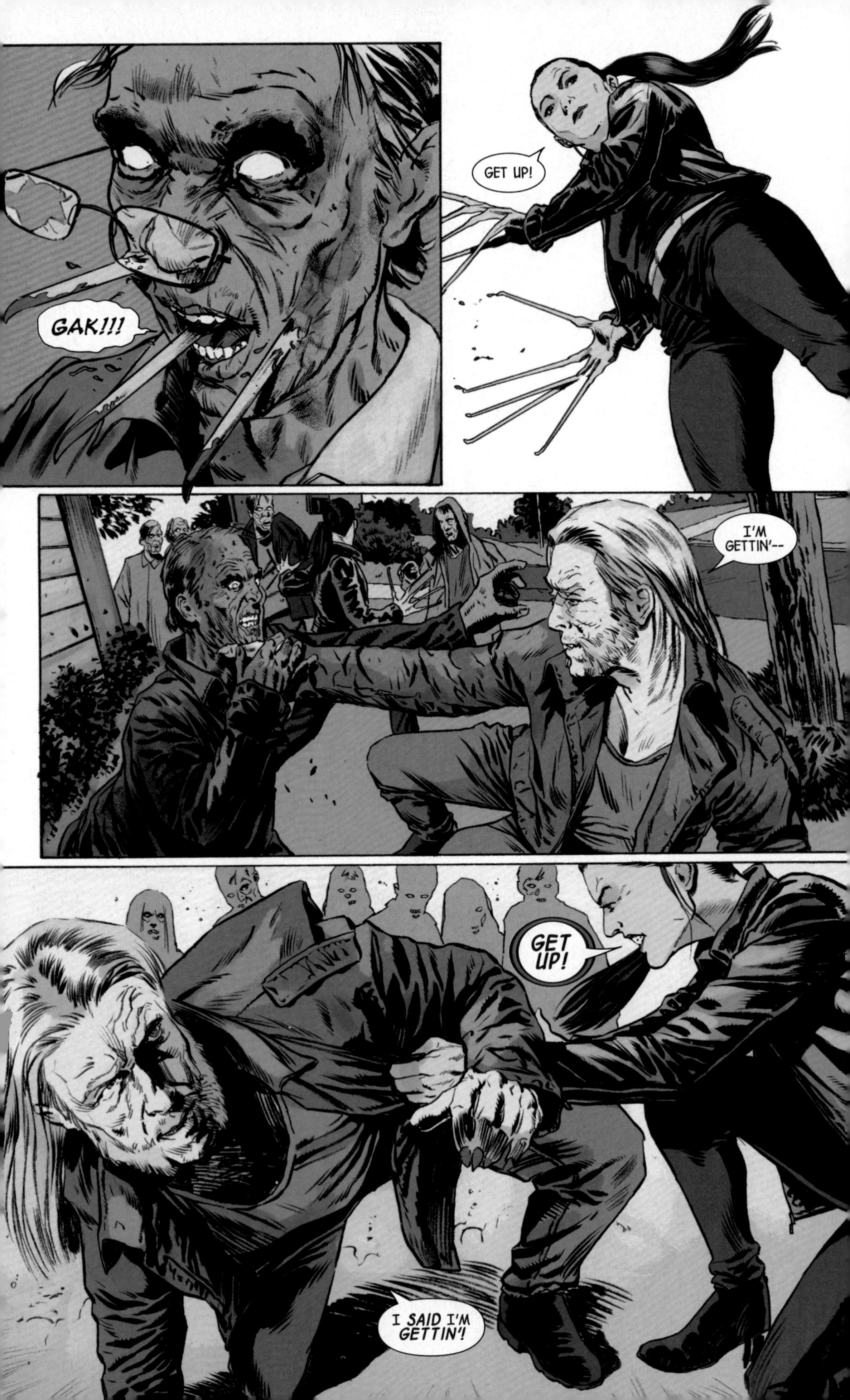
GAK!!!
GET UP!
I'M GETTIN'--
GET UP!
I SAID I'M GETTIN'!

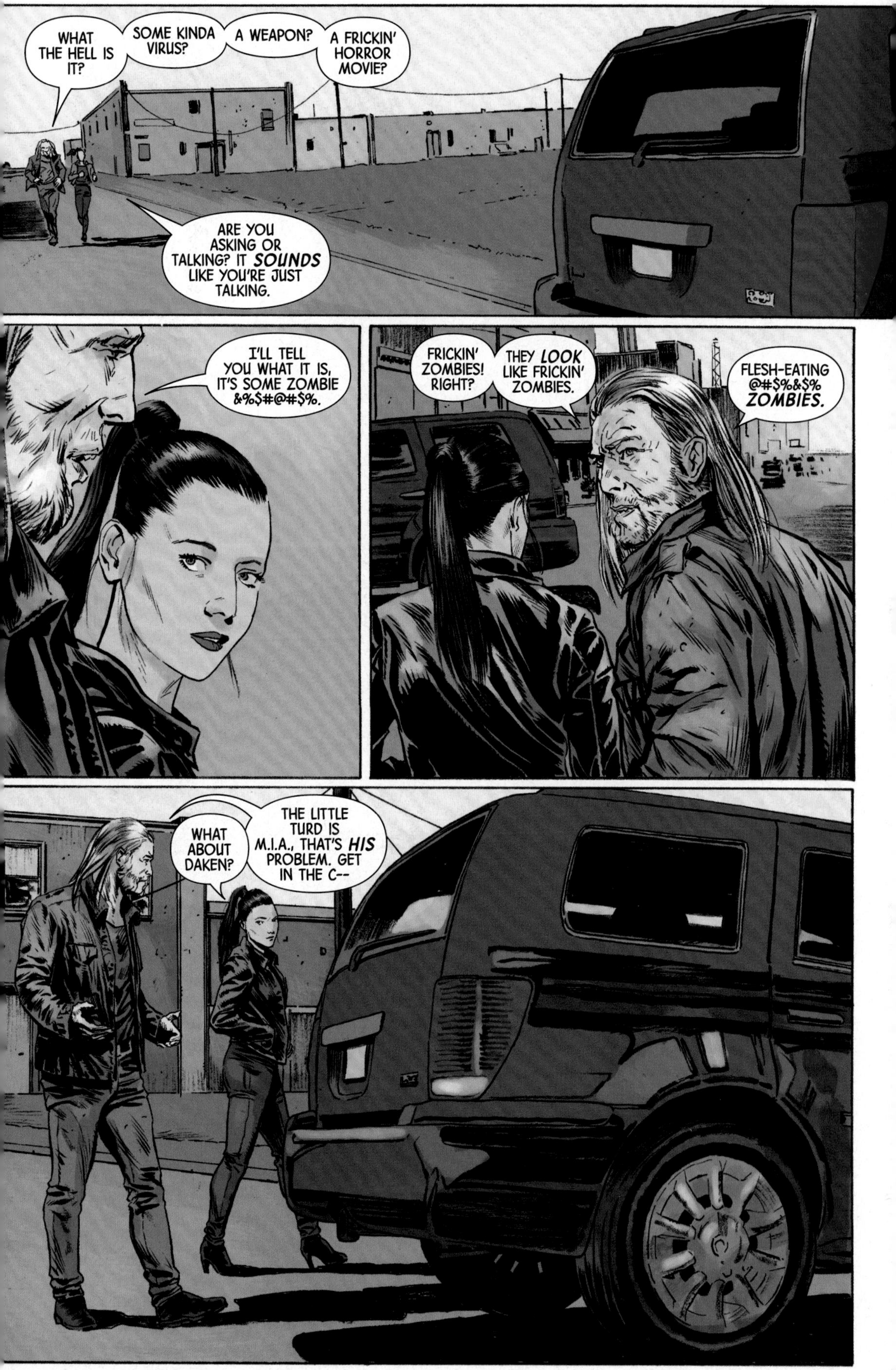
WHAT THE HELL IS IT?
SOME KINDA VIRUS?
A WEAPON?
A FRICKIN' HORROR MOVIE?
ARE YOU ASKING OR TALKING? IT SOUNDS LIKE YOU'RE JUST TALKING.
I'LL TELL YOU WHAT IT IS, IT'S SOME ZOMBIE &%$#@#$%.
FRICKIN' ZOMBIES! RIGHT?
THEY LOOK LIKE FRICKIN' ZOMBIES.
FLESH-EATING @#$%&$% ZOMBIES.
WHAT ABOUT DAKEN?
THE LITTLE TURD IS M.I.A., THAT'S HIS PROBLEM. GET IN THE C--

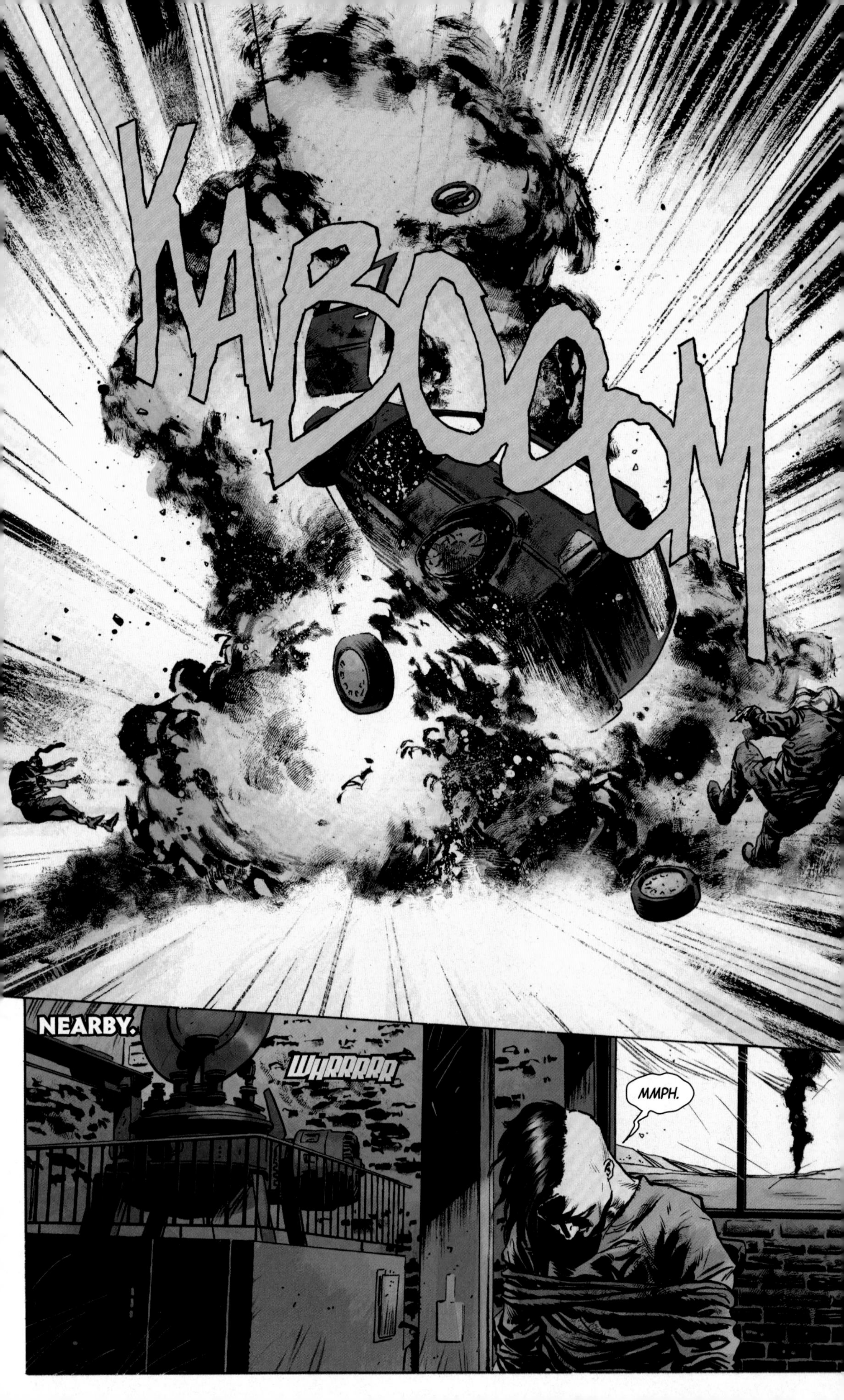
KABOOOM
NEARBY.
WHRRRRR
MMPH.

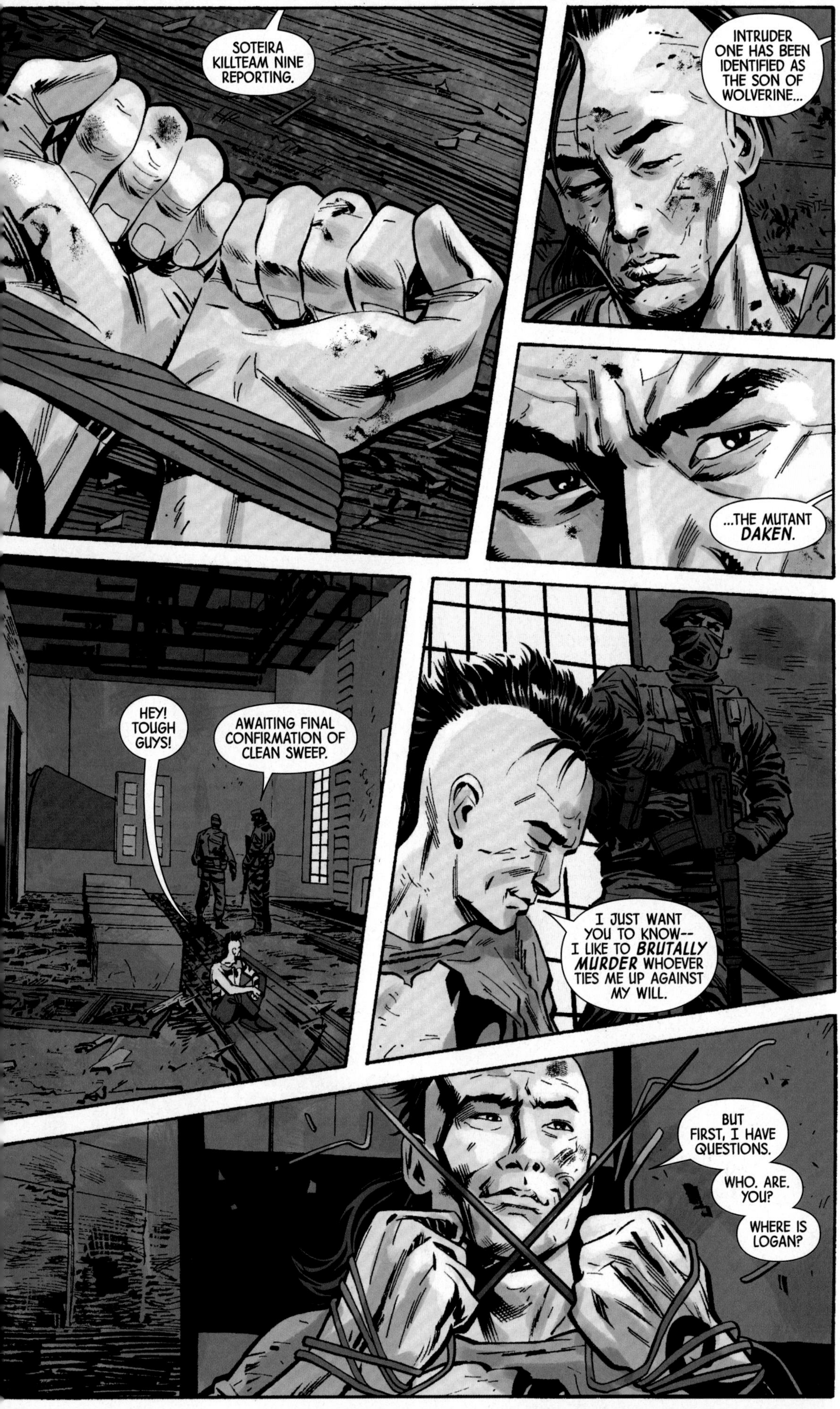
SOTEIRA KILLTEAM NINE REPORTING.
INTRUDER ONE HAS BEEN IDENTIFIED AS THE SON OF WOLVERINE...
...THE MUTANT DAKEN.
HEY! TOUGH GUYS!
AWAITING FINAL CONFIRMATION OF CLEAN SWEEP.
I JUST WANT YOU TO KNOW-- I LIKE TO BRUTALLY MURDER WHOEVER TIES ME UP AGAINST MY WILL.
BUT FIRST, I HAVE QUESTIONS.
WHO. ARE. YOU?
WHERE IS LOGAN?

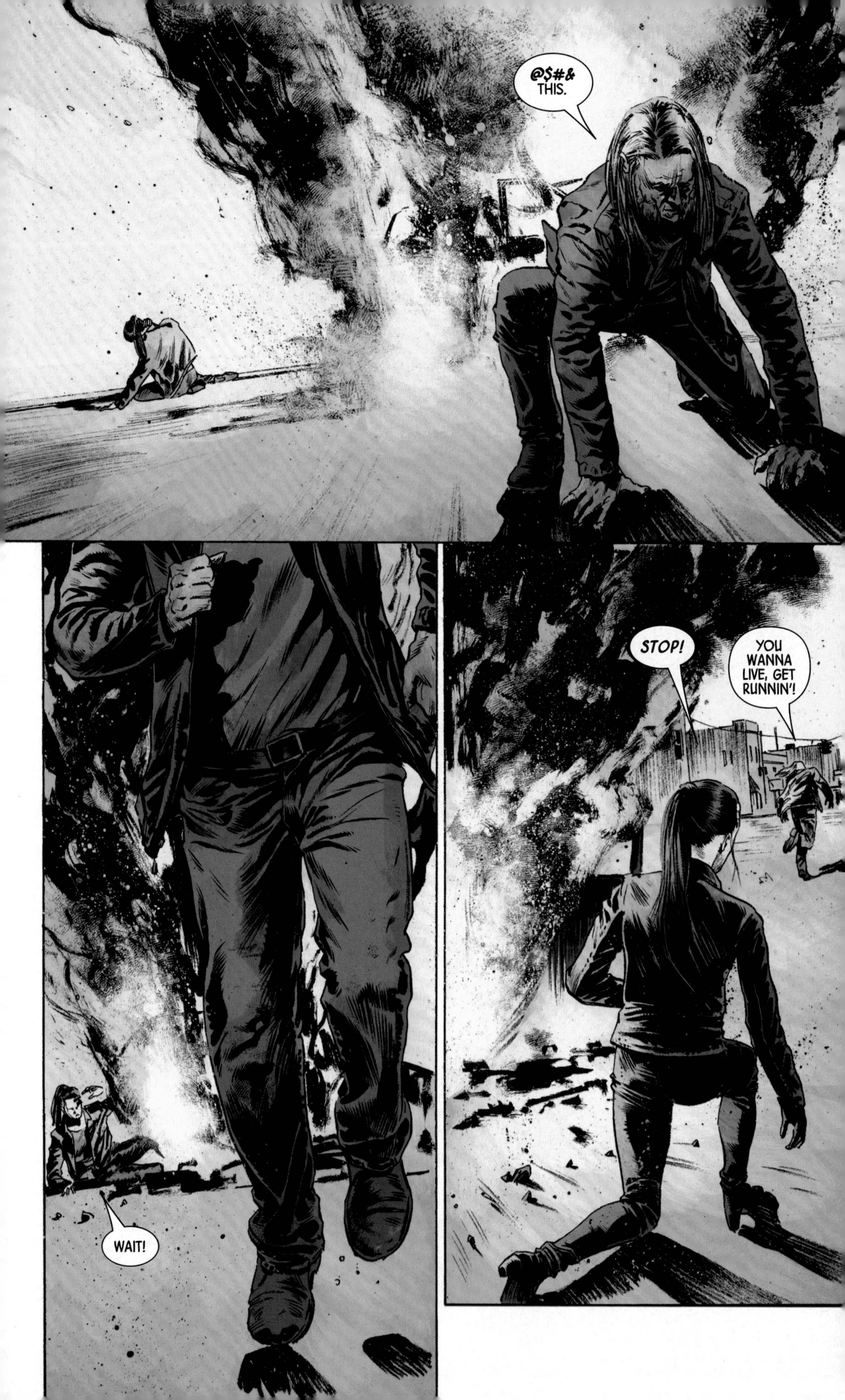
@$#&
THIS.
WAIT!
STOP!
YOU WANNA LIVE, GET RUNNIN'!

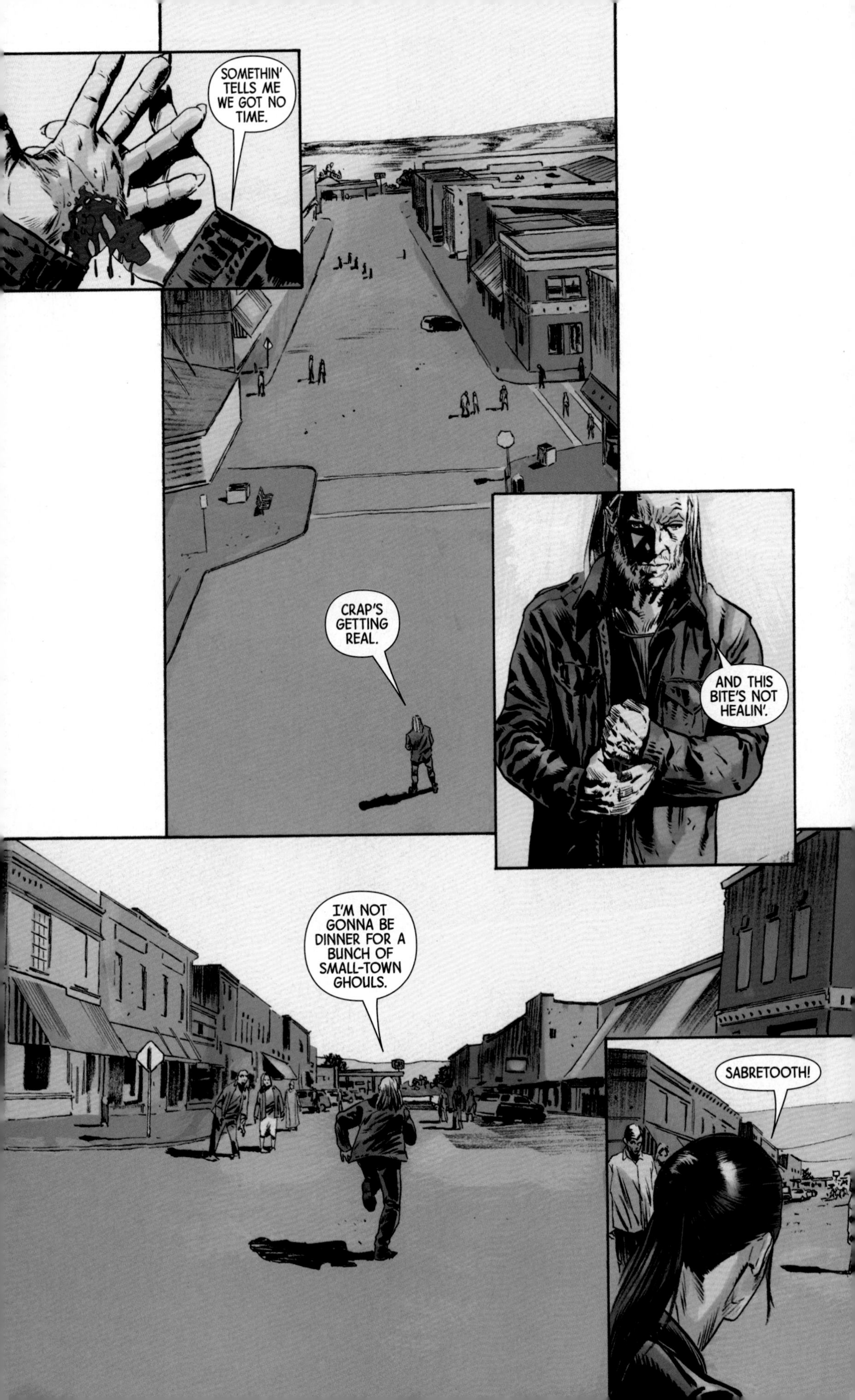
SOMETHIN' TELLS ME WE GOT NO TIME.
CRAP'S GETTING REAL.
AND THIS BITE'S NOT HEALIN'.
I'M NOT GONNA BE DINNER FOR A BUNCH OF SMALL-TOWN GHOULS.
SABRETOOTH!

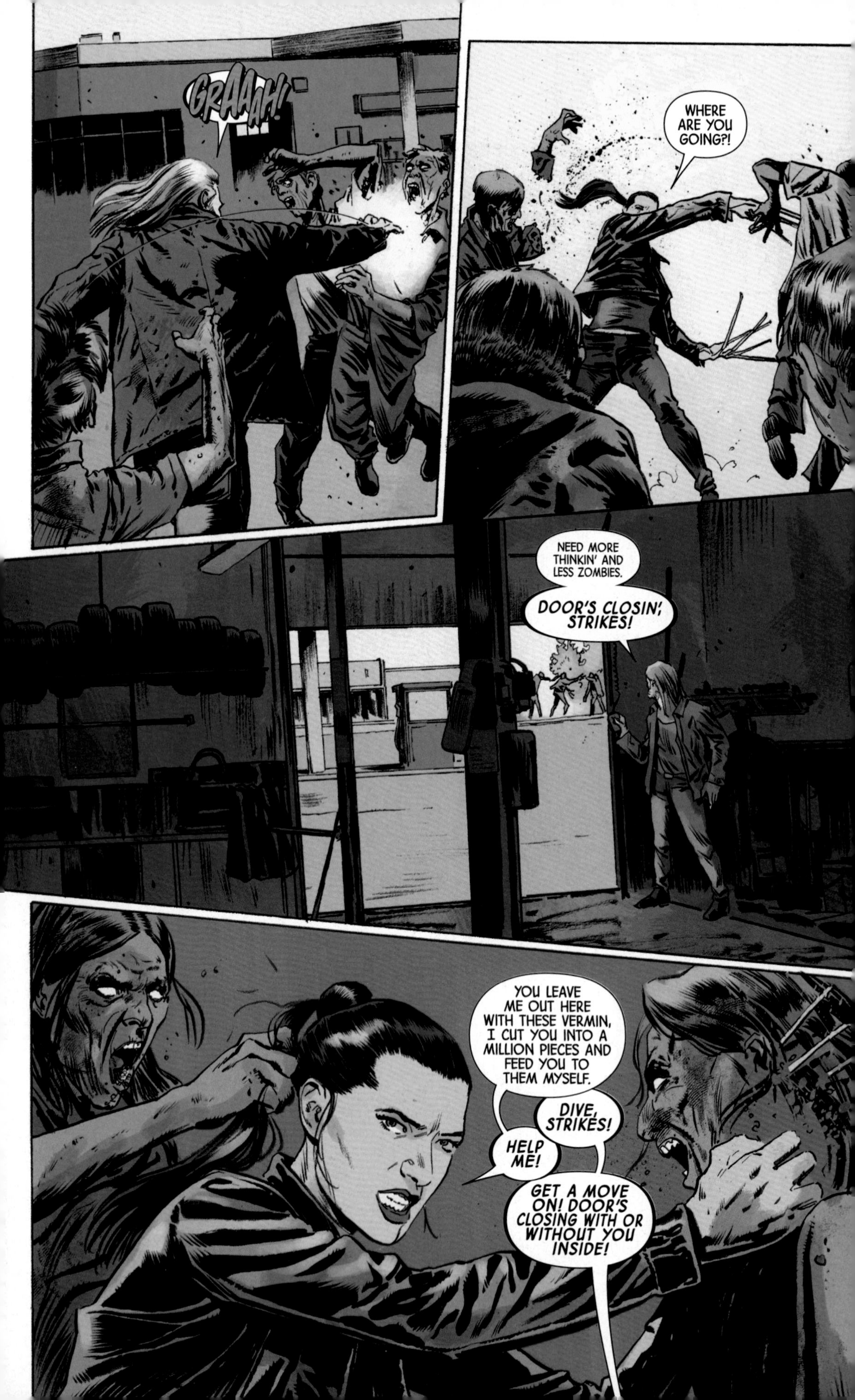
GRAAAH!
WHERE ARE YOU GOING?!
NEED MORE THINKIN' AND LESS ZOMBIES.
DOOR'S CLOSIN', STRIKES!
YOU LEAVE ME OUT HERE WITH THESE VERMIN, I CUT YOU INTO A MILLION PIECES AND FEED YOU TO THEM MYSELF.
DIVE, STRIKES!
HELP ME!
GET A MOVE ON! DOOR'S CLOSING WITH OR WITHOUT YOU INSIDE!

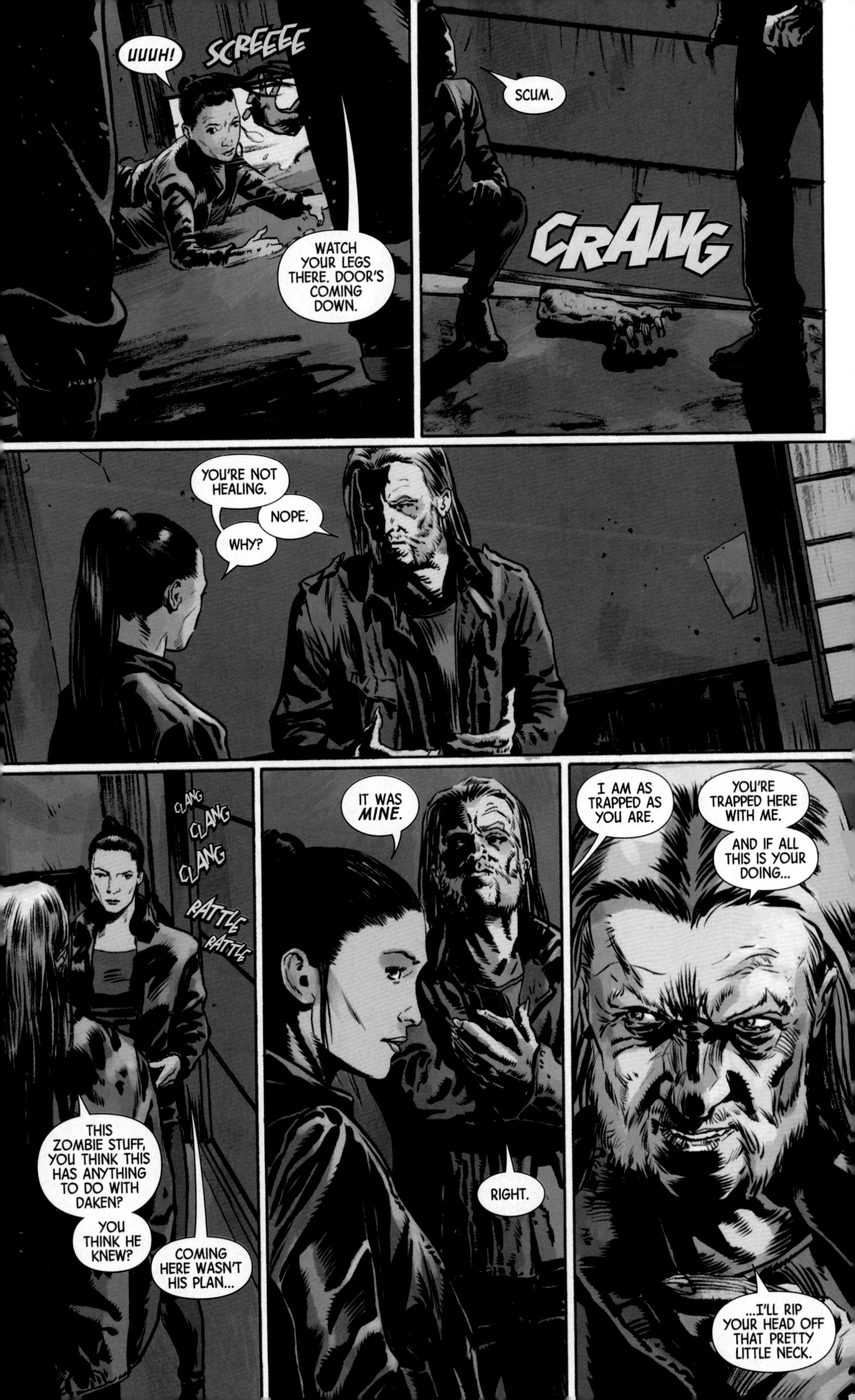
UUUH!
SCREEEE
WATCH YOUR LEGS THERE. DOOR'S COMING DOWN.
SCUM.
CRANG
YOU'RE NOT HEALING.
NOPE.
WHY?
CLANG
CLANG
CLANG
RATTLE
RATTLE
THIS ZOMBIE STUFF, YOU THINK THIS HAS ANYTHING TO DO WITH DAKEN?
YOU THINK HE KNEW?
COMING HERE WASN'T HIS PLAN...
IT WAS *MINE*.
RIGHT.
I AM AS TRAPPED AS YOU ARE.
YOU'RE TRAPPED HERE WITH ME.
AND IF ALL THIS IS YOUR DOING...
...I'LL RIP YOUR HEAD OFF THAT PRETTY LITTLE NECK.

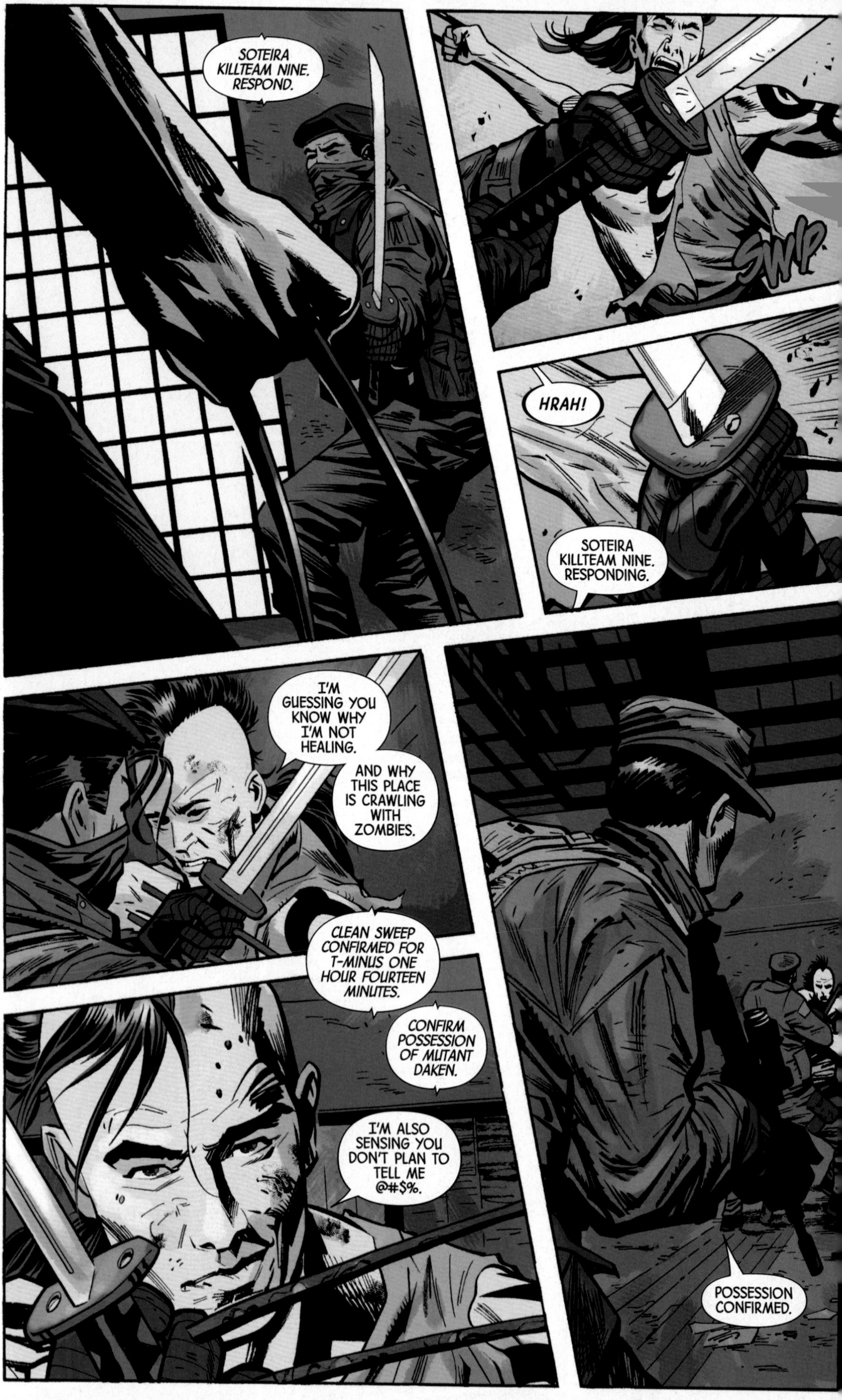
SOTEIRA KILLTEAM NINE. RESPOND.
SWIP
HRAH!
SOTEIRA KILLTEAM NINE. RESPONDING.
I'M GUESSING YOU KNOW WHY I'M NOT HEALING.
AND WHY THIS PLACE IS CRAWLING WITH ZOMBIES.
CLEAN SWEEP CONFIRMED FOR T-MINUS ONE HOUR FOURTEEN MINUTES.
CONFIRM POSSESSION OF MUTANT DAKEN.
I'M ALSO SENSING YOU DON'T PLAN TO TELL ME @#$%.
POSSESSION CONFIRMED.

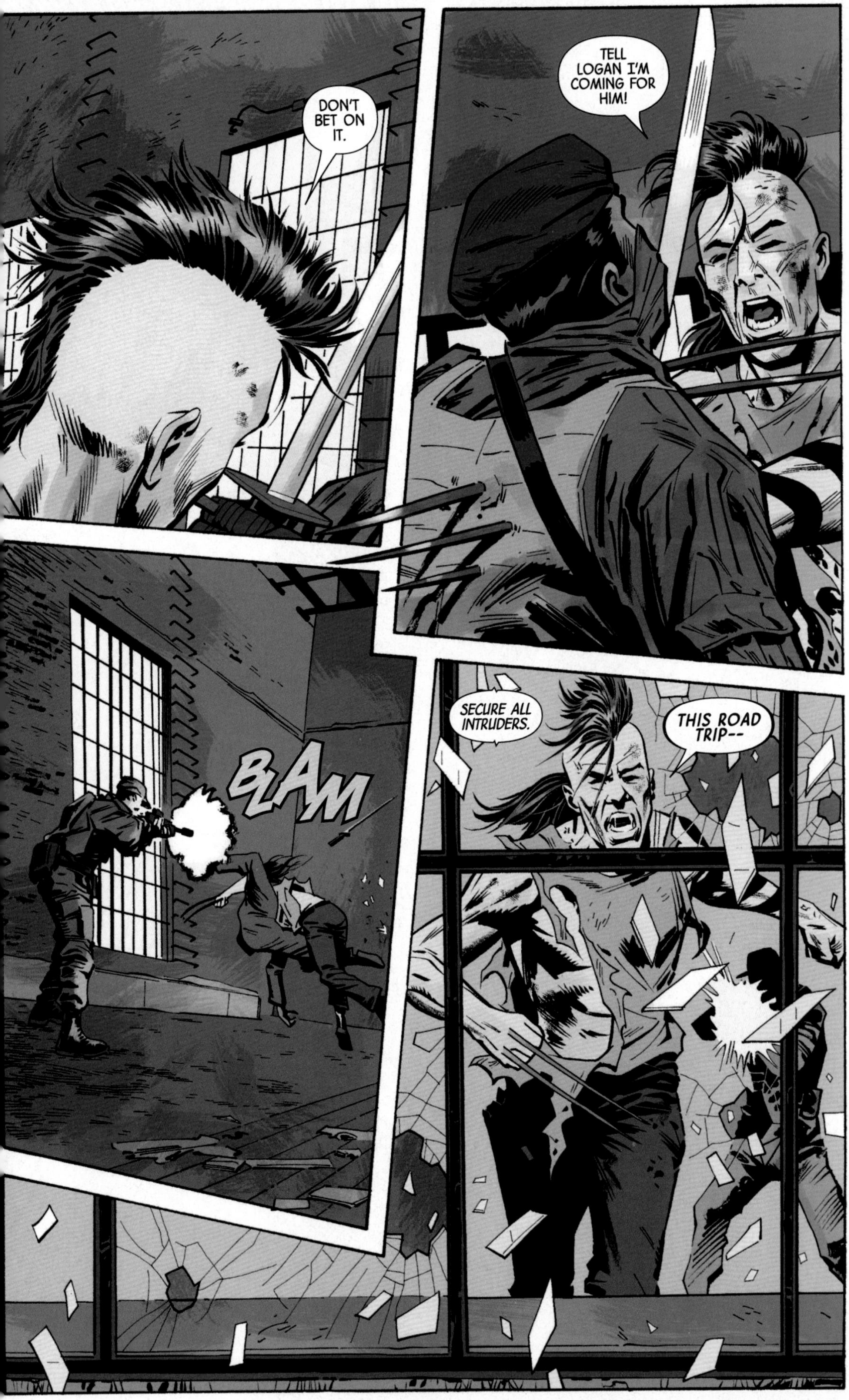
DON'T BET ON IT.
TELL LOGAN I'M COMING FOR HIM!
BLAM
SECURE ALL INTRUDERS.
THIS ROAD TRIP--

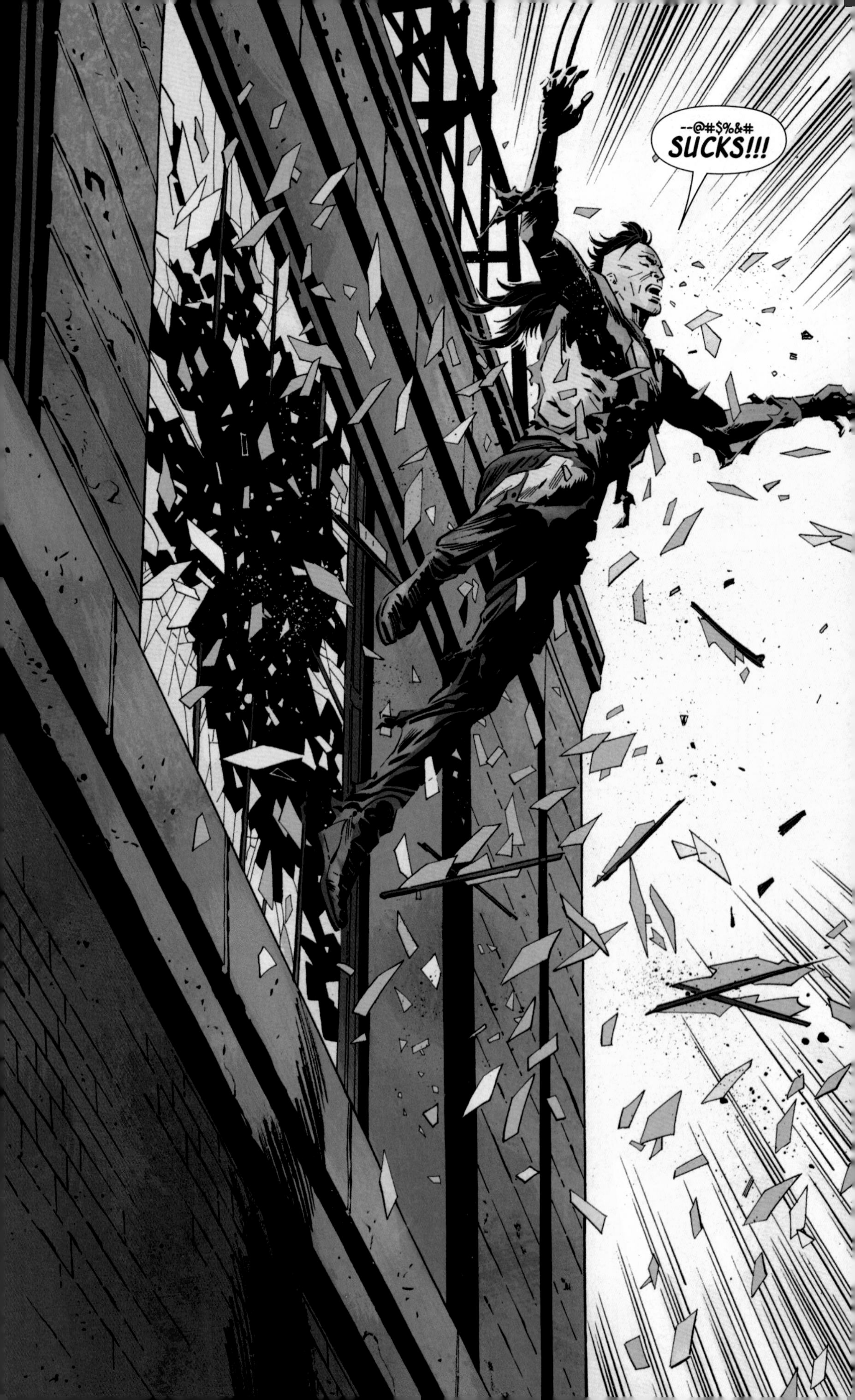
--@#$%&# SUCKS!!!

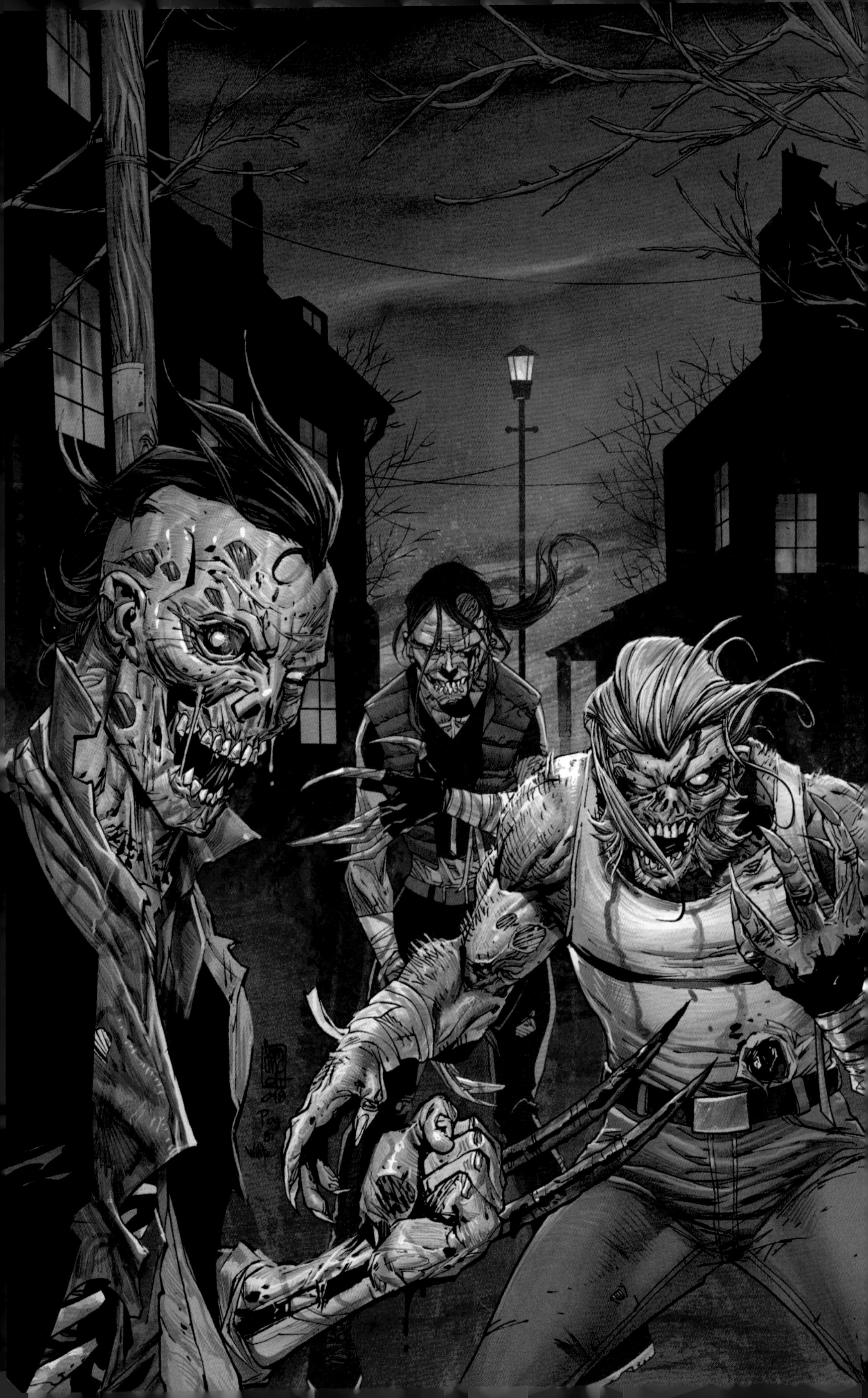

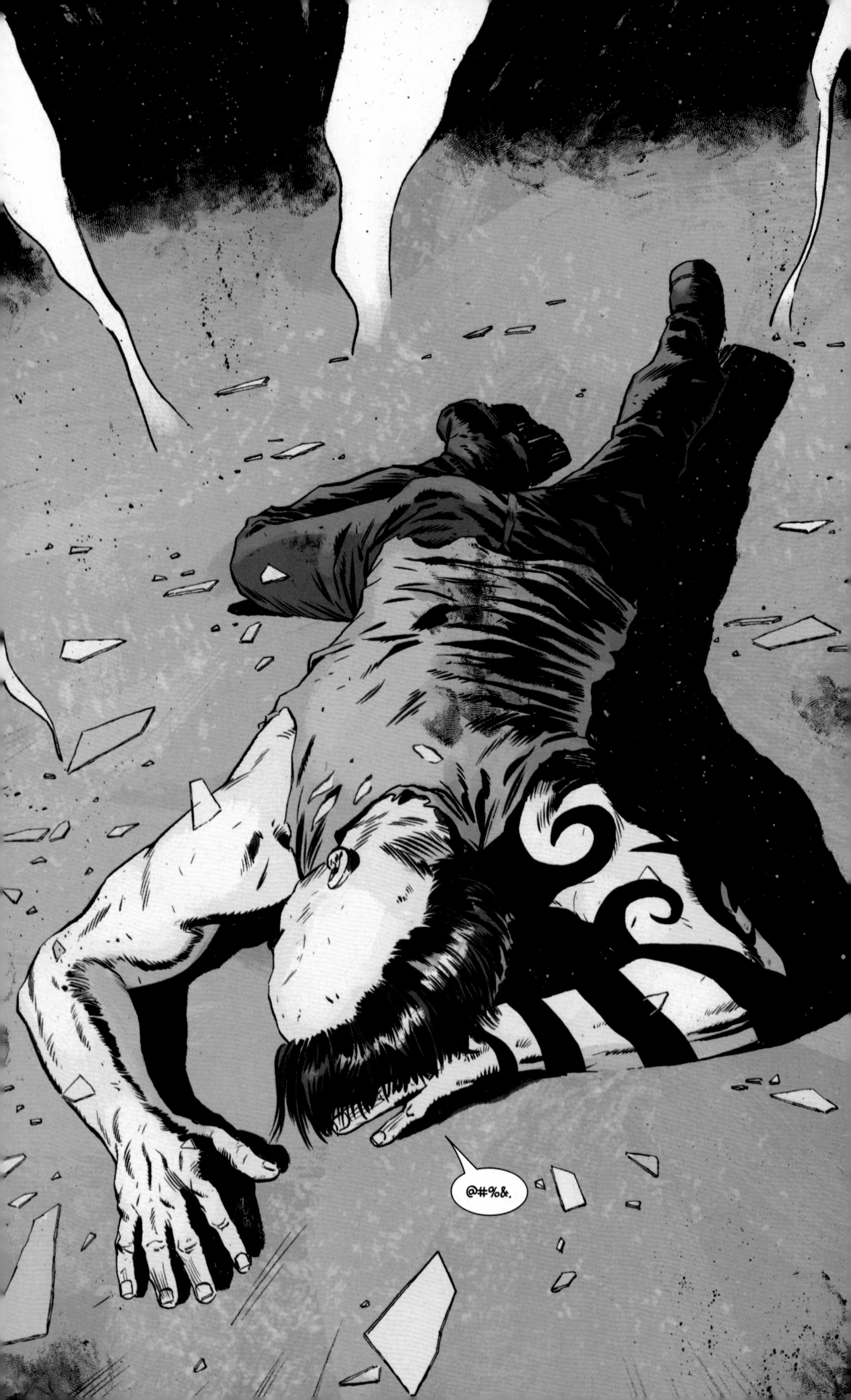
@#%&.

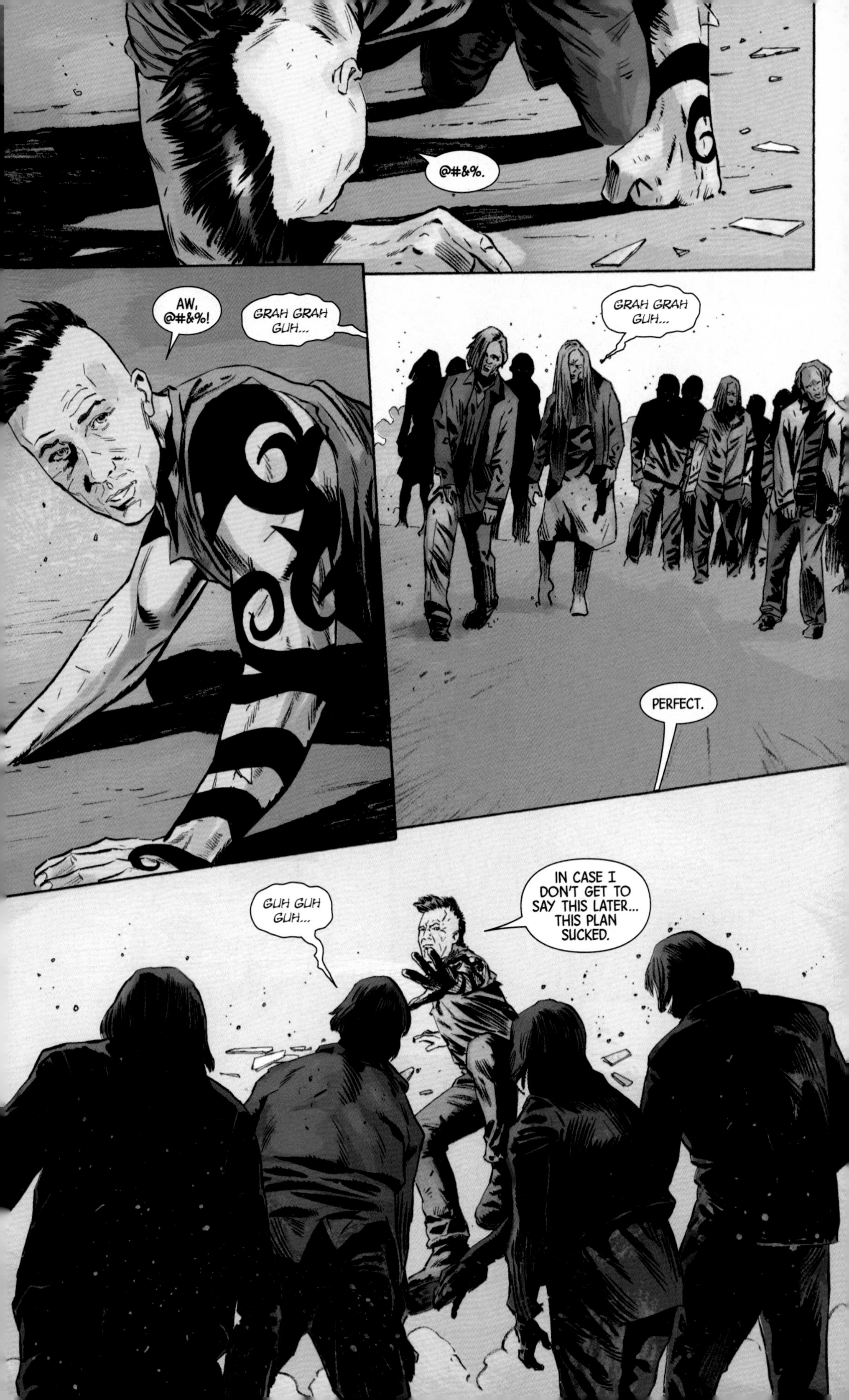
@#&%.
AW, @#&%!
GRAH GRAH GUH...
GRAH GRAH GUH...
PERFECT.
GUH GUH GUH...
IN CASE I DON'T GET TO SAY THIS LATER... THIS PLAN SUCKED.

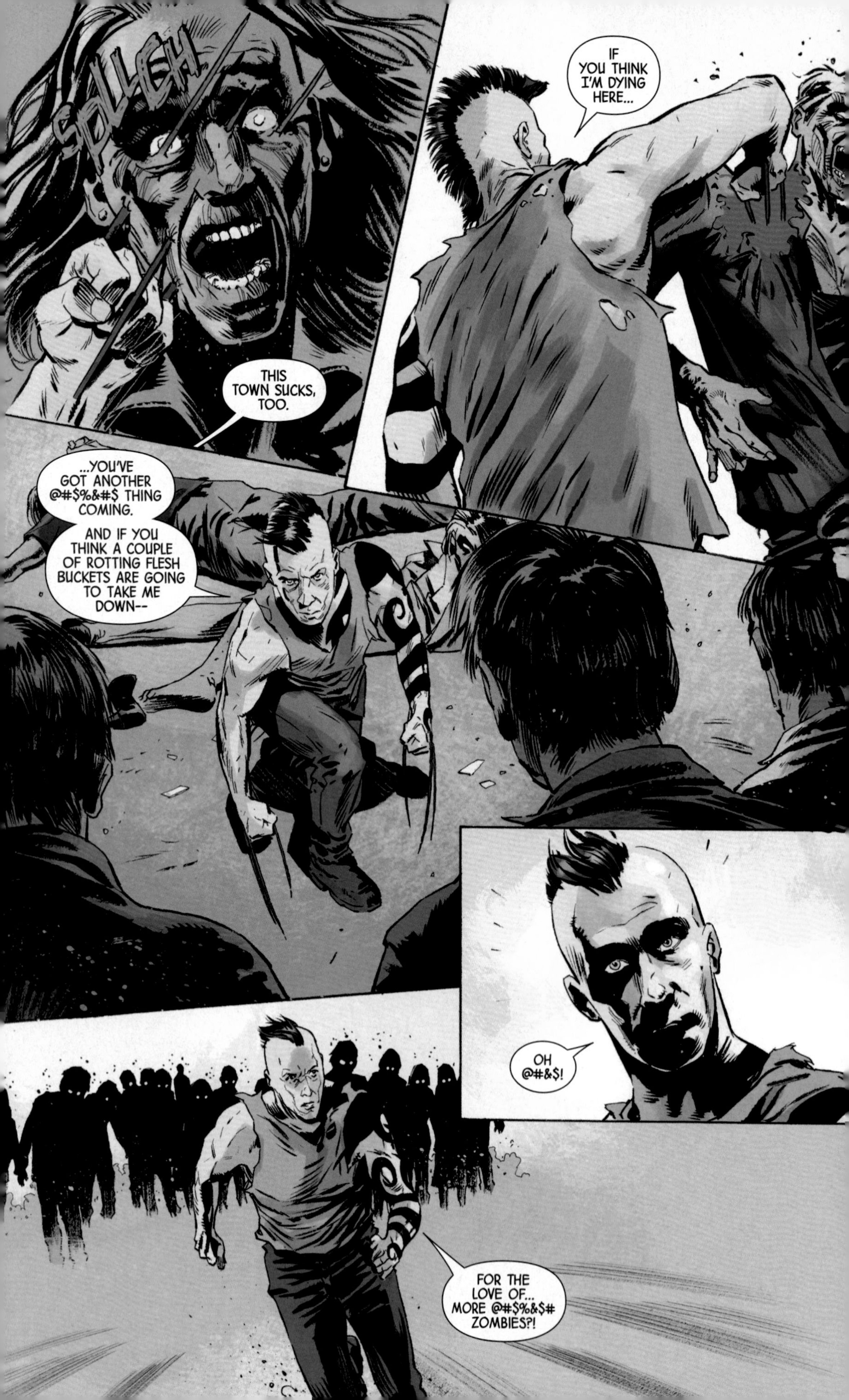
SPLLCH
THIS TOWN SUCKS, TOO.
IF YOU THINK I'M DYING HERE...
...YOU'VE GOT ANOTHER @#$%&#$ THING COMING.
AND IF YOU THINK A COUPLE OF ROTTING FLESH BUCKETS ARE GOING TO TAKE ME DOWN--
OH @#&$!
FOR THE LOVE OF... MORE @#$%&$# ZOMBIES?!

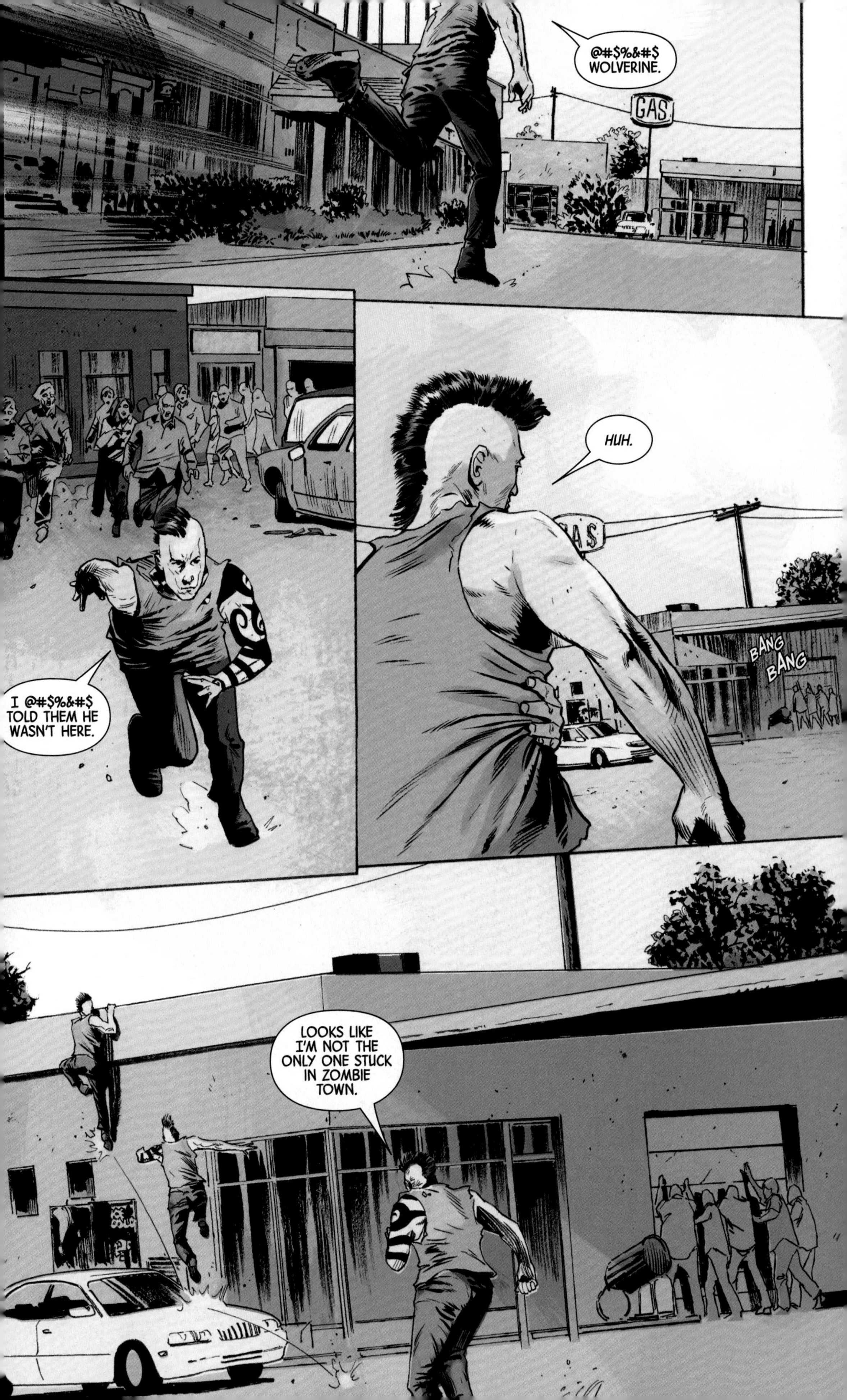
@#$%&#$
WOLVERINE.
GAS
I @#$%&#$
TOLD THEM HE
WASN'T HERE.
HUH.
GAS
BANG
BANG
LOOKS LIKE
I'M NOT THE
ONLY ONE STUCK
IN ZOMBIE
TOWN.

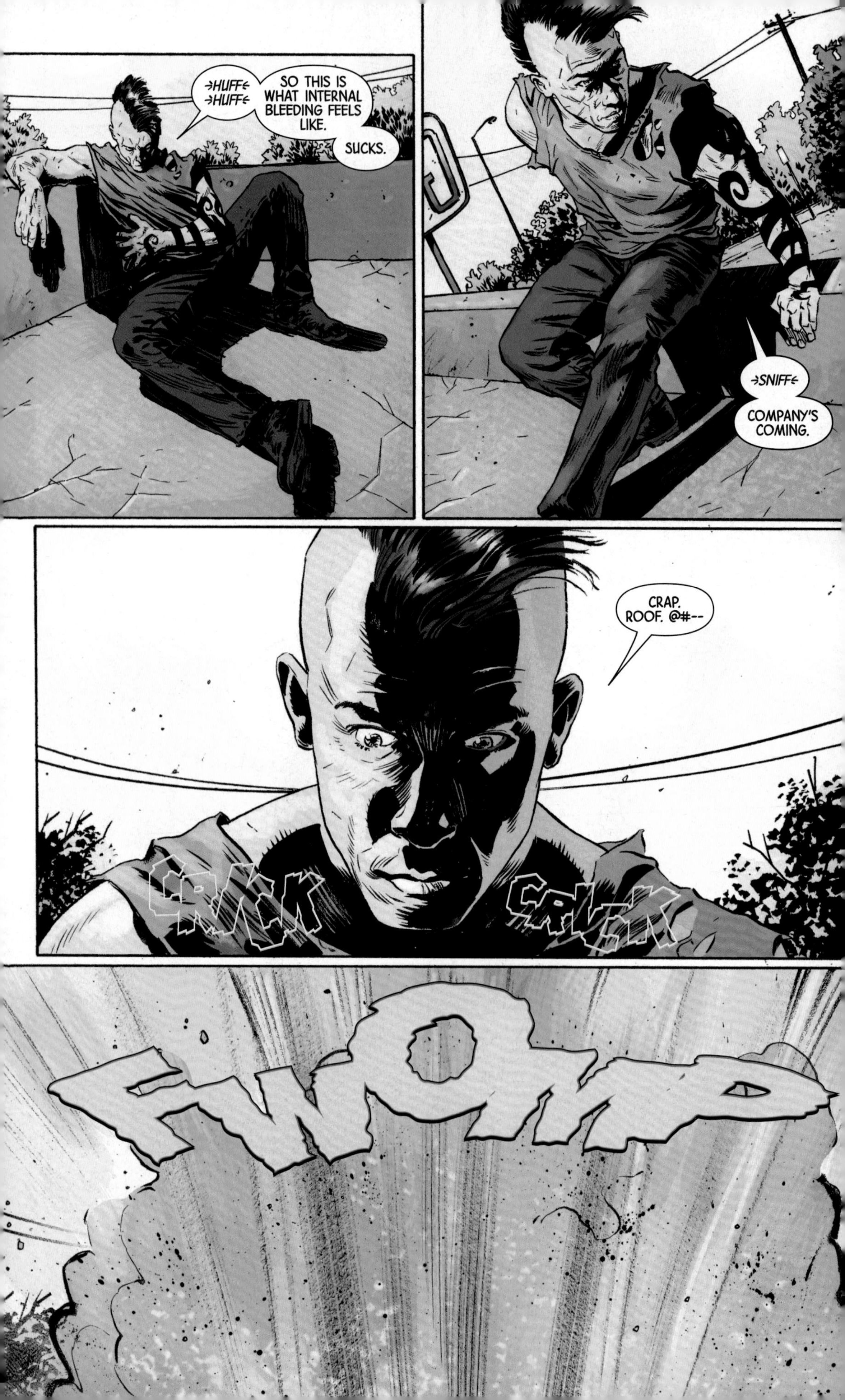

→HUFF← →HUFF←
SO THIS IS WHAT INTERNAL BLEEDING FEELS LIKE.
SUCKS.
→SNIFF←
COMPANY'S COMING.
CRAP. ROOF. @#--

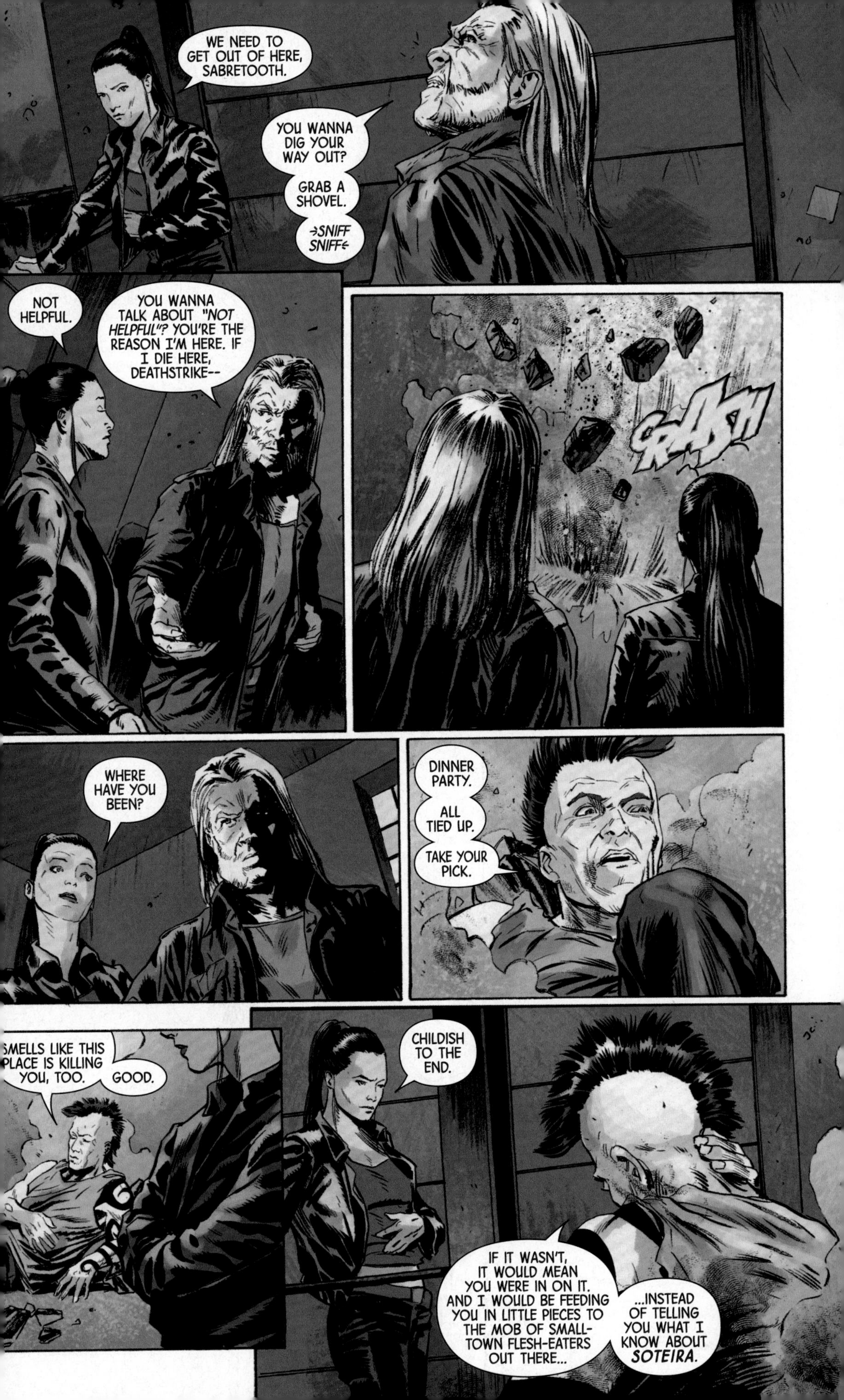
WE NEED TO GET OUT OF HERE, SABRETOOTH.
YOU WANNA DIG YOUR WAY OUT?
GRAB A SHOVEL.
→SNIFF SNIFF←
NOT HELPFUL.
YOU WANNA TALK ABOUT "NOT HELPFUL"? YOU'RE THE REASON I'M HERE. IF I DIE HERE, DEATHSTRIKE--
CRASH
WHERE HAVE YOU BEEN?
DINNER PARTY.
ALL TIED UP.
TAKE YOUR PICK.
SMELLS LIKE THIS PLACE IS KILLING YOU, TOO.
GOOD.
CHILDISH TO THE END.
IF IT WASN'T, IT WOULD MEAN YOU WERE IN ON IT. AND I WOULD BE FEEDING YOU IN LITTLE PIECES TO THE MOB OF SMALL-TOWN FLESH-EATERS OUT THERE...
...INSTEAD OF TELLING YOU WHAT I KNOW ABOUT SOTEIRA.

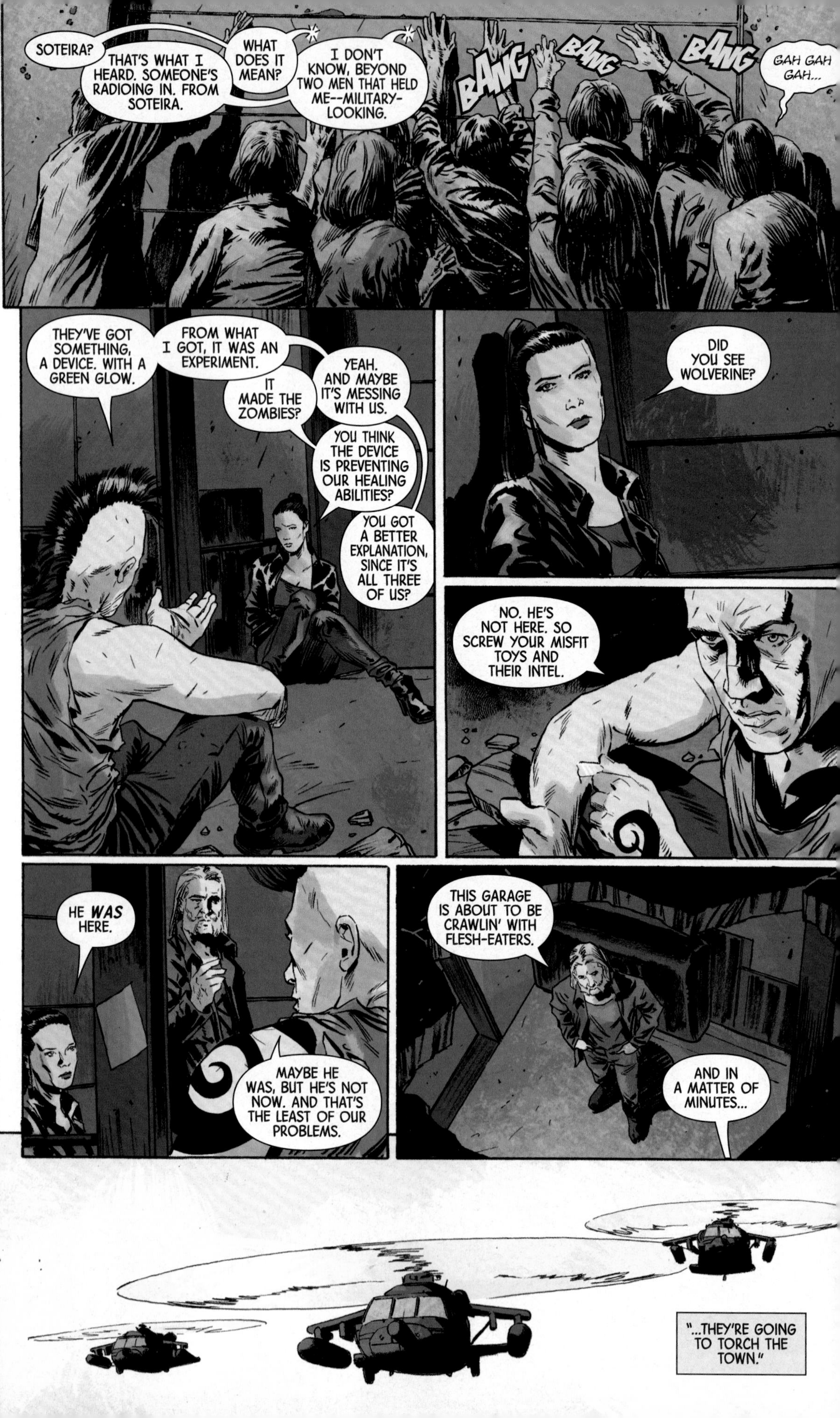
SOTEIRA?
THAT'S WHAT I HEARD. SOMEONE'S RADIOING IN. FROM SOTEIRA.
WHAT DOES IT MEAN?
I DON'T KNOW, BEYOND TWO MEN THAT HELD ME--MILITARY-LOOKING.
BANG
BANG
BANG
GAH GAH GAH...
THEY'VE GOT SOMETHING, A DEVICE. WITH A GREEN GLOW.
FROM WHAT I GOT, IT WAS AN EXPERIMENT.
IT MADE THE ZOMBIES?
YEAH. AND MAYBE IT'S MESSING WITH US.
YOU THINK THE DEVICE IS PREVENTING OUR HEALING ABILITIES?
YOU GOT A BETTER EXPLANATION, SINCE IT'S ALL THREE OF US?
DID YOU SEE WOLVERINE?
NO. HE'S NOT HERE. SO SCREW YOUR MISFIT TOYS AND THEIR INTEL.
HE *WAS* HERE.
MAYBE HE WAS, BUT HE'S NOT NOW. AND THAT'S THE LEAST OF OUR PROBLEMS.
THIS GARAGE IS ABOUT TO BE CRAWLIN' WITH FLESH-EATERS.
AND IN A MATTER OF MINUTES...
"...THEY'RE GOING TO TORCH THE TOWN."

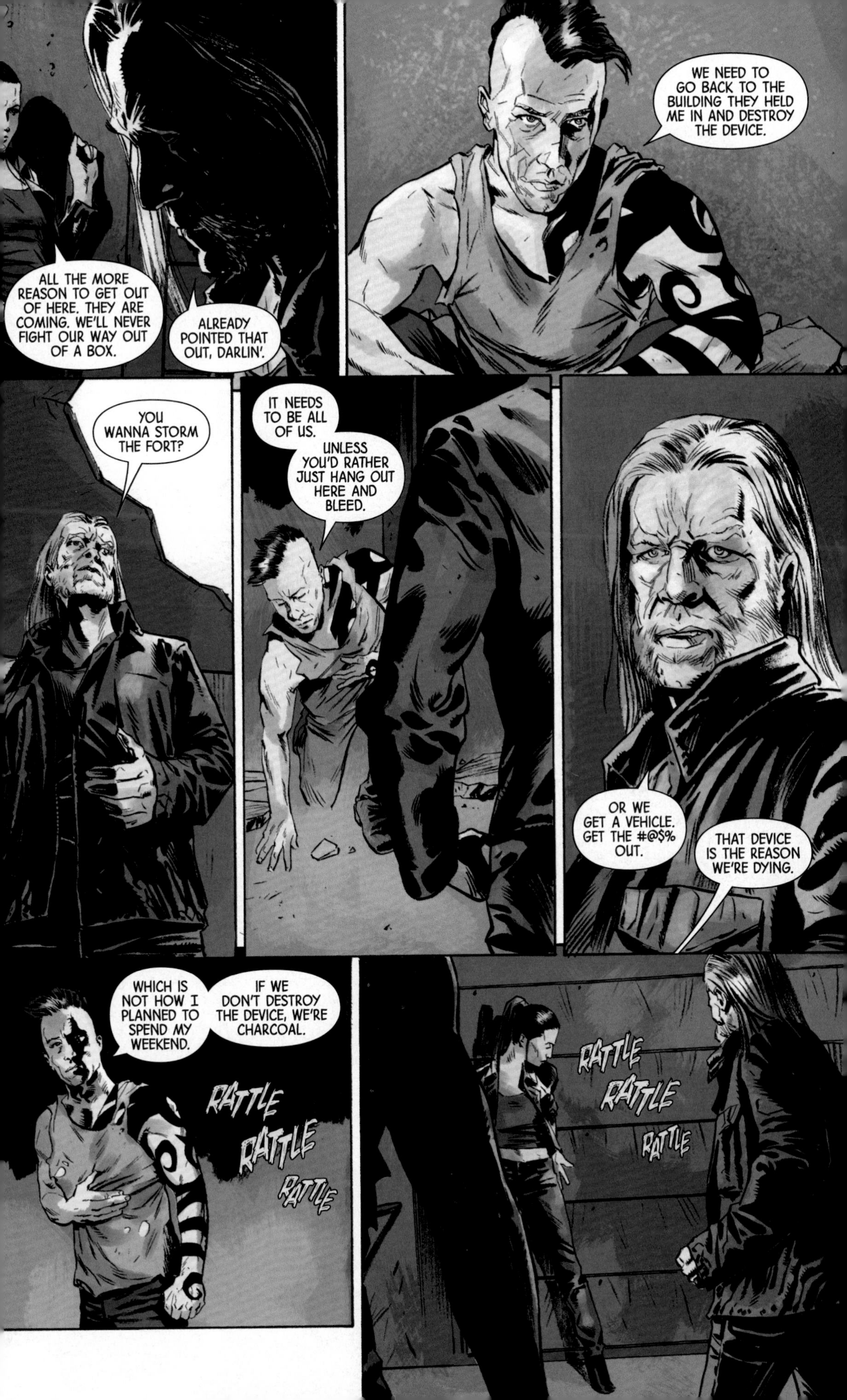

ALL THE MORE REASON TO GET OUT OF HERE. THEY ARE COMING. WE'LL NEVER FIGHT OUR WAY OUT OF A BOX.
ALREADY POINTED THAT OUT, DARLIN'.
WE NEED TO GO BACK TO THE BUILDING THEY HELD ME IN AND DESTROY THE DEVICE.
YOU WANNA STORM THE FORT?
IT NEEDS TO BE ALL OF US.
UNLESS YOU'D RATHER JUST HANG OUT HERE AND BLEED.
OR WE GET A VEHICLE. GET THE #@$% OUT.
THAT DEVICE IS THE REASON WE'RE DYING.
WHICH IS NOT HOW I PLANNED TO SPEND MY WEEKEND.
IF WE DON'T DESTROY THE DEVICE, WE'RE CHARCOAL.
RATTLE
RATTLE
RATTLE
RATTLE
RATTLE
RATTLE

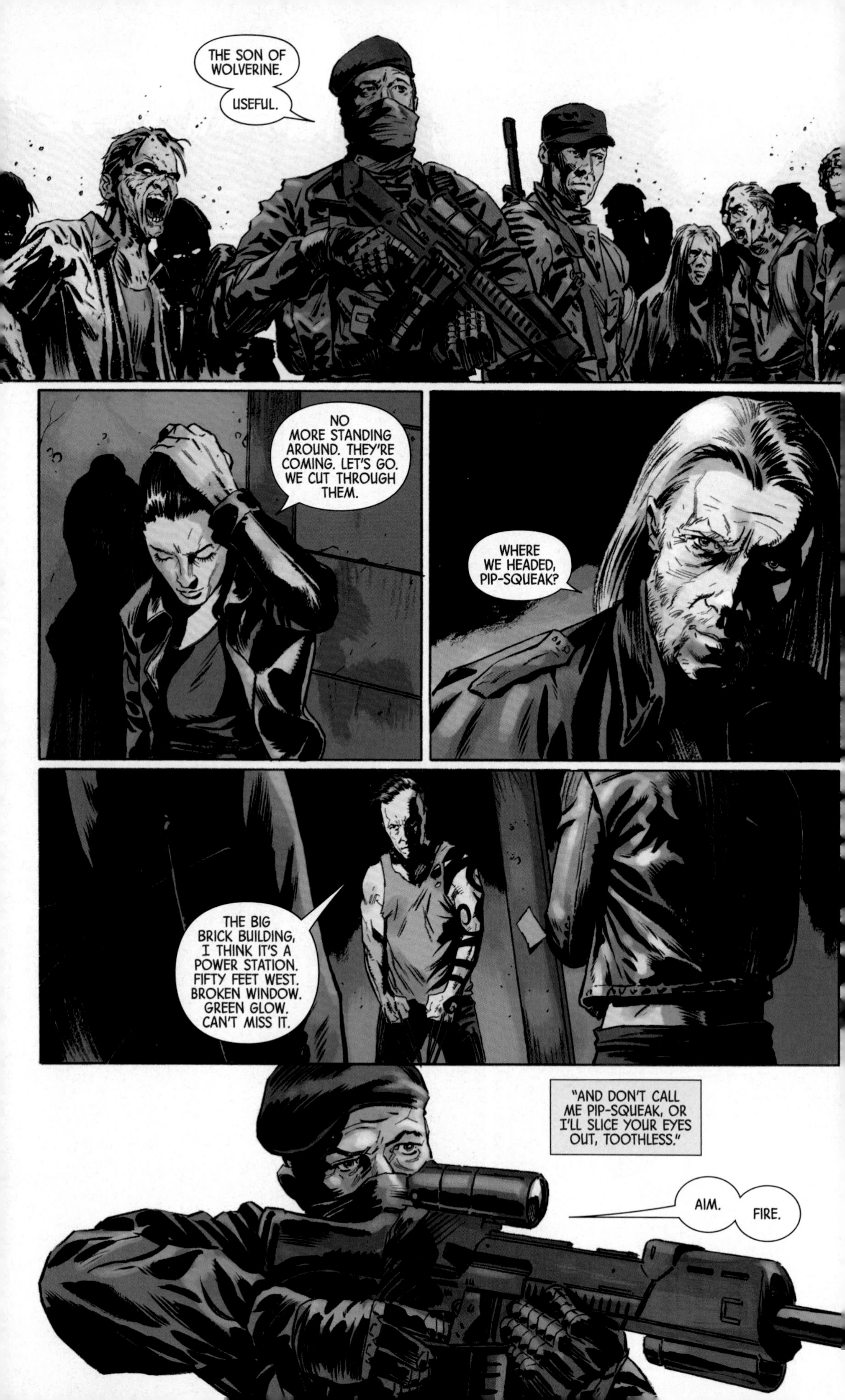
THE SON OF WOLVERINE.
USEFUL.
NO MORE STANDING AROUND. THEY'RE COMING. LET'S GO. WE CUT THROUGH THEM.
WHERE WE HEADED, PIP-SQUEAK?
THE BIG BRICK BUILDING, I THINK IT'S A POWER STATION. FIFTY FEET WEST. BROKEN WINDOW. GREEN GLOW. CAN'T MISS IT.
"AND DON'T CALL ME PIP-SQUEAK, OR I'LL SLICE YOUR EYES OUT, TOOTHLESS."
AIM.
FIRE.

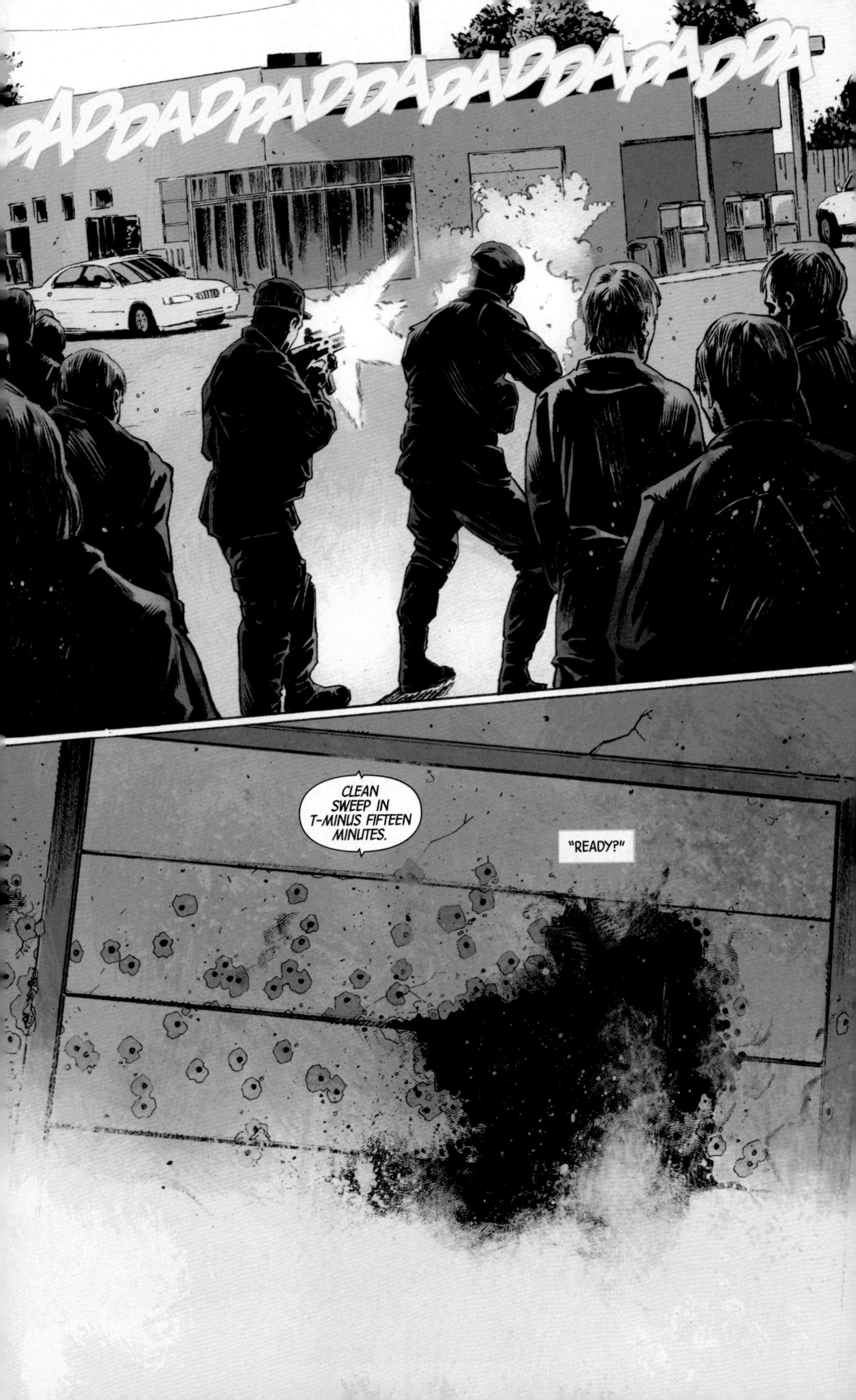
DADDADDADDADDADDADDADDADDA
CLEAN SWEEP IN T-MINUS FIFTEEN MINUTES.
"READY?"

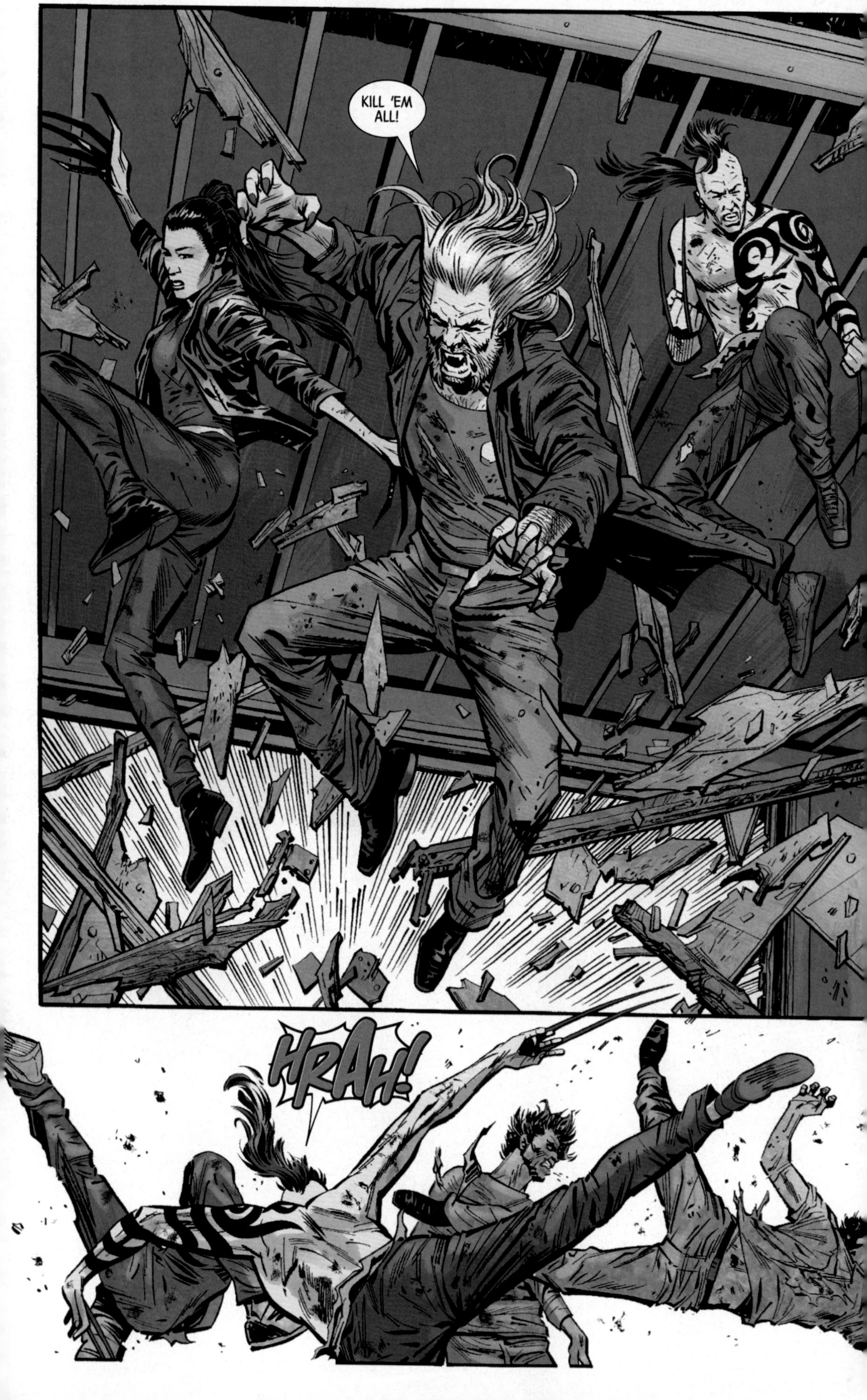
KILL 'EM ALL!
HRAH!

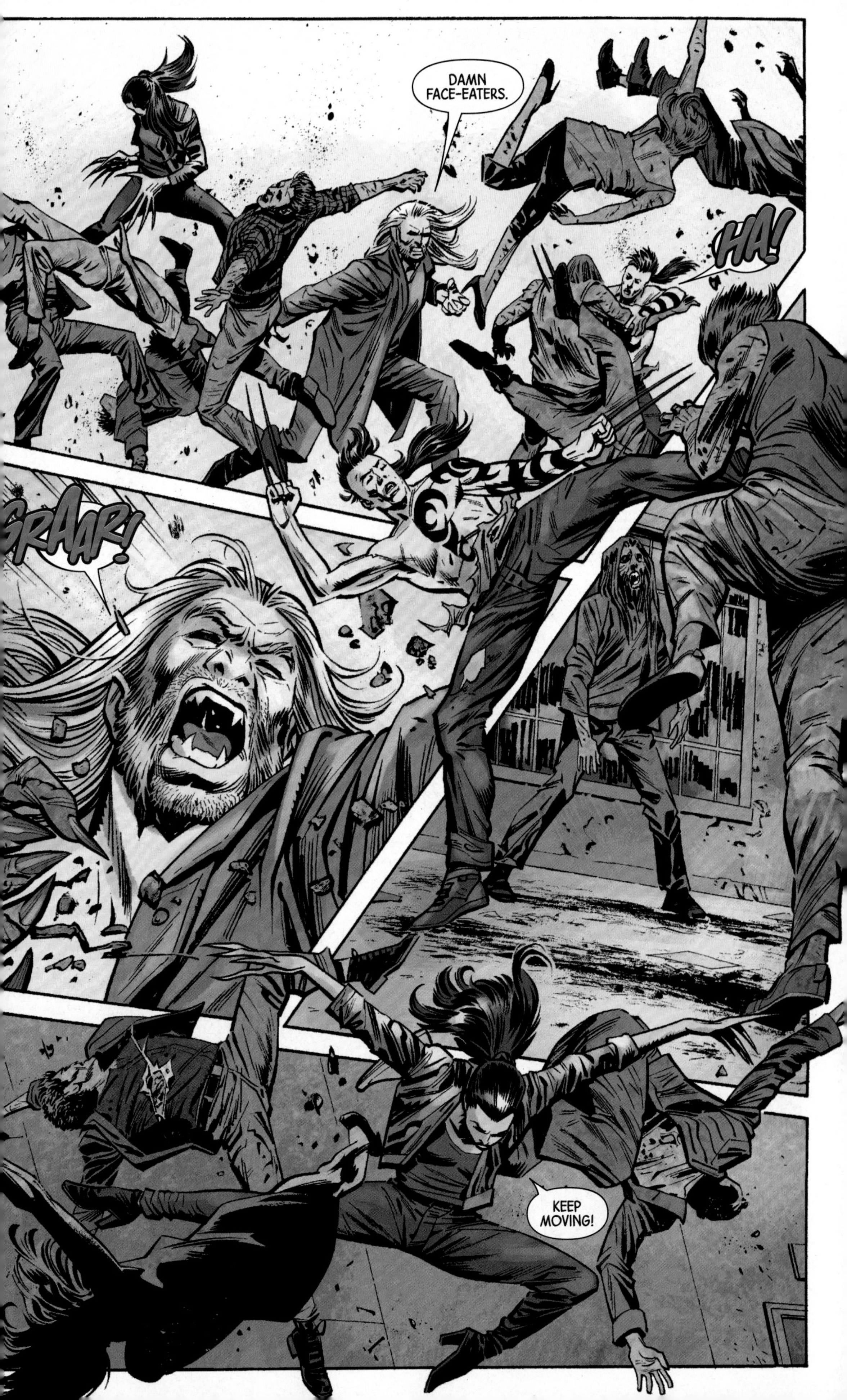
DAMN FACE-EATERS.
HA!
GRAAR!
KEEP MOVING!

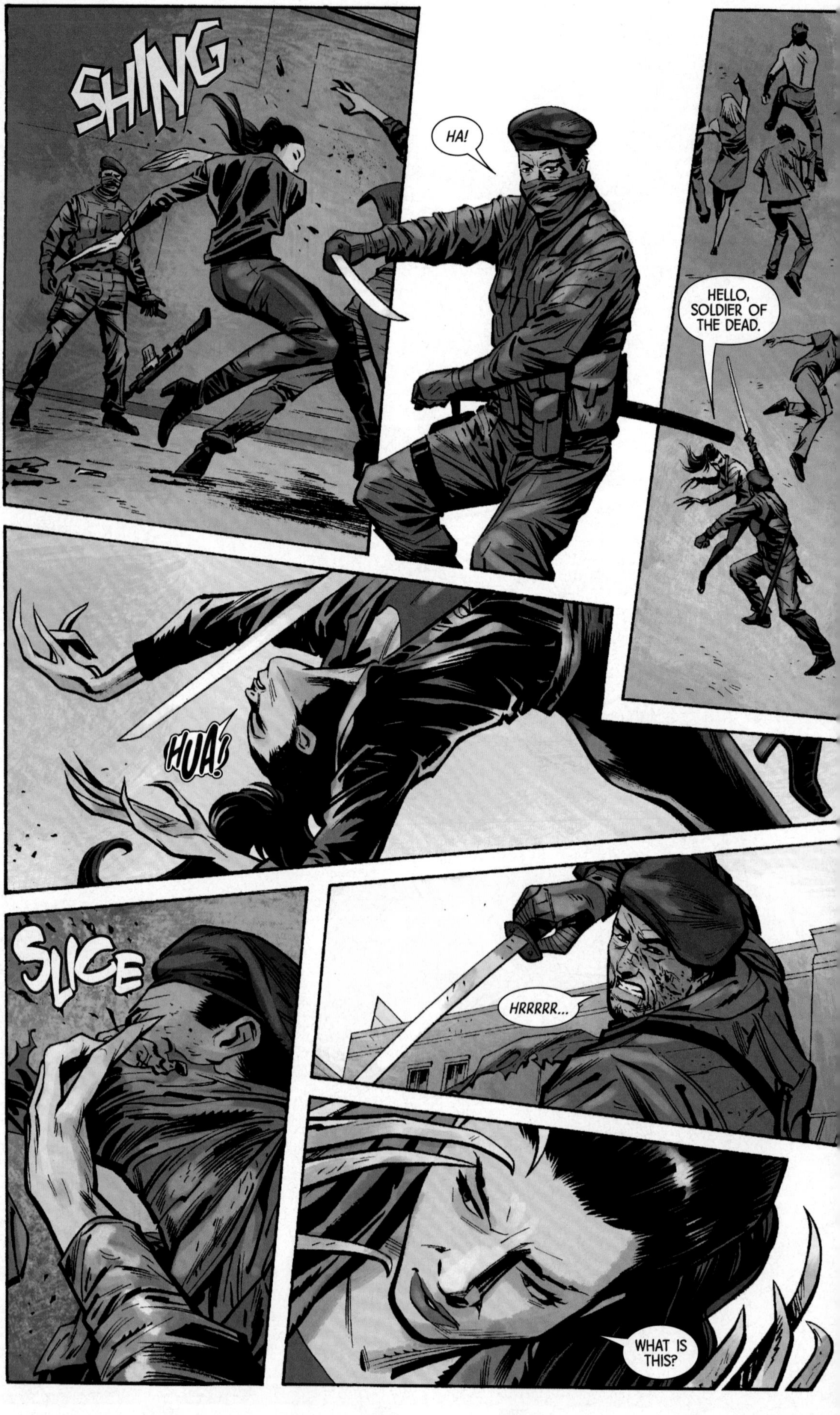
SHING
HA!
HELLO, SOLDIER OF THE DEAD.
HUA!
SLICE
HRRRRR...
WHAT IS THIS?

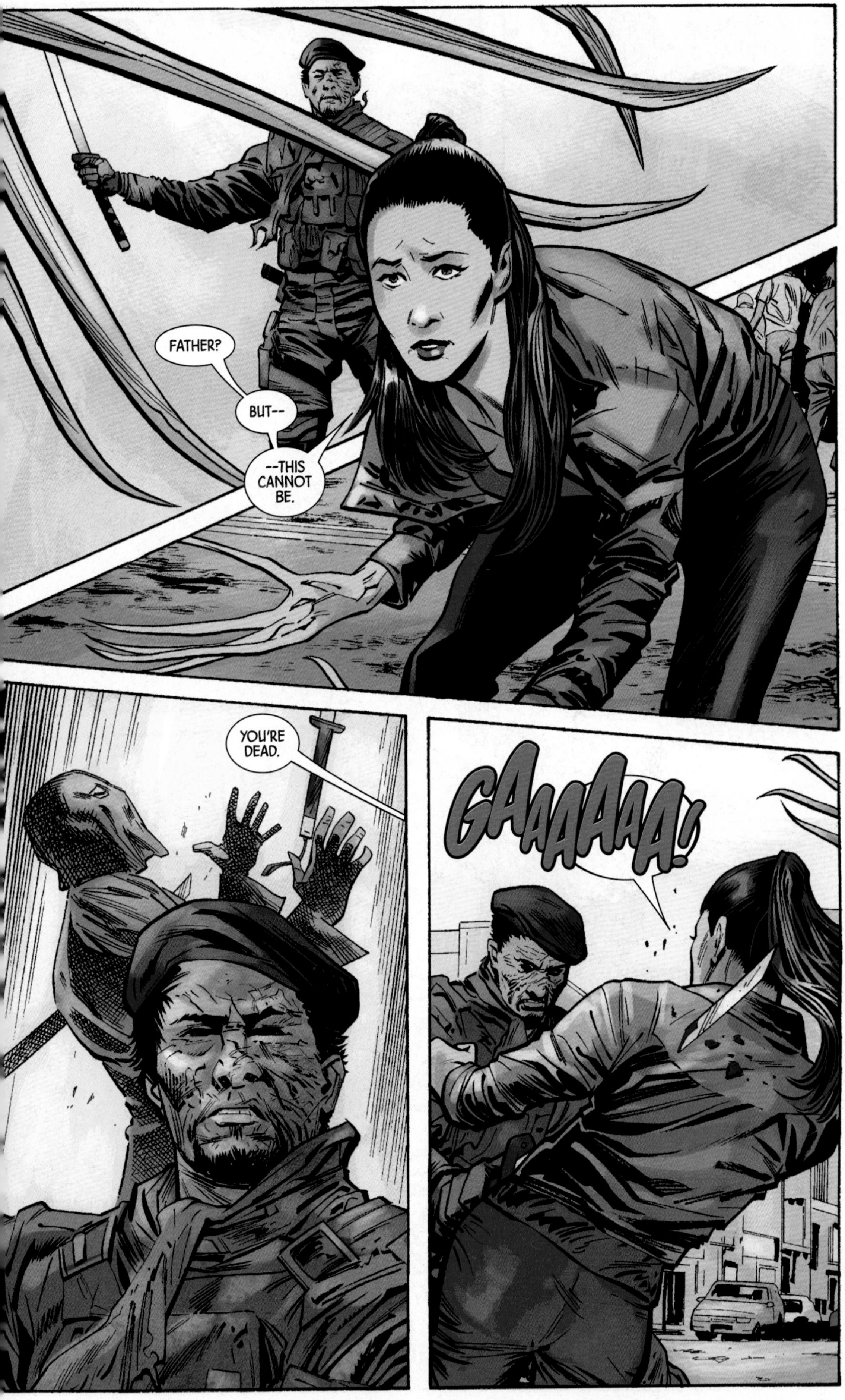
FATHER?
BUT--
--THIS CANNOT BE.
YOU'RE DEAD.
GAAAAAA!

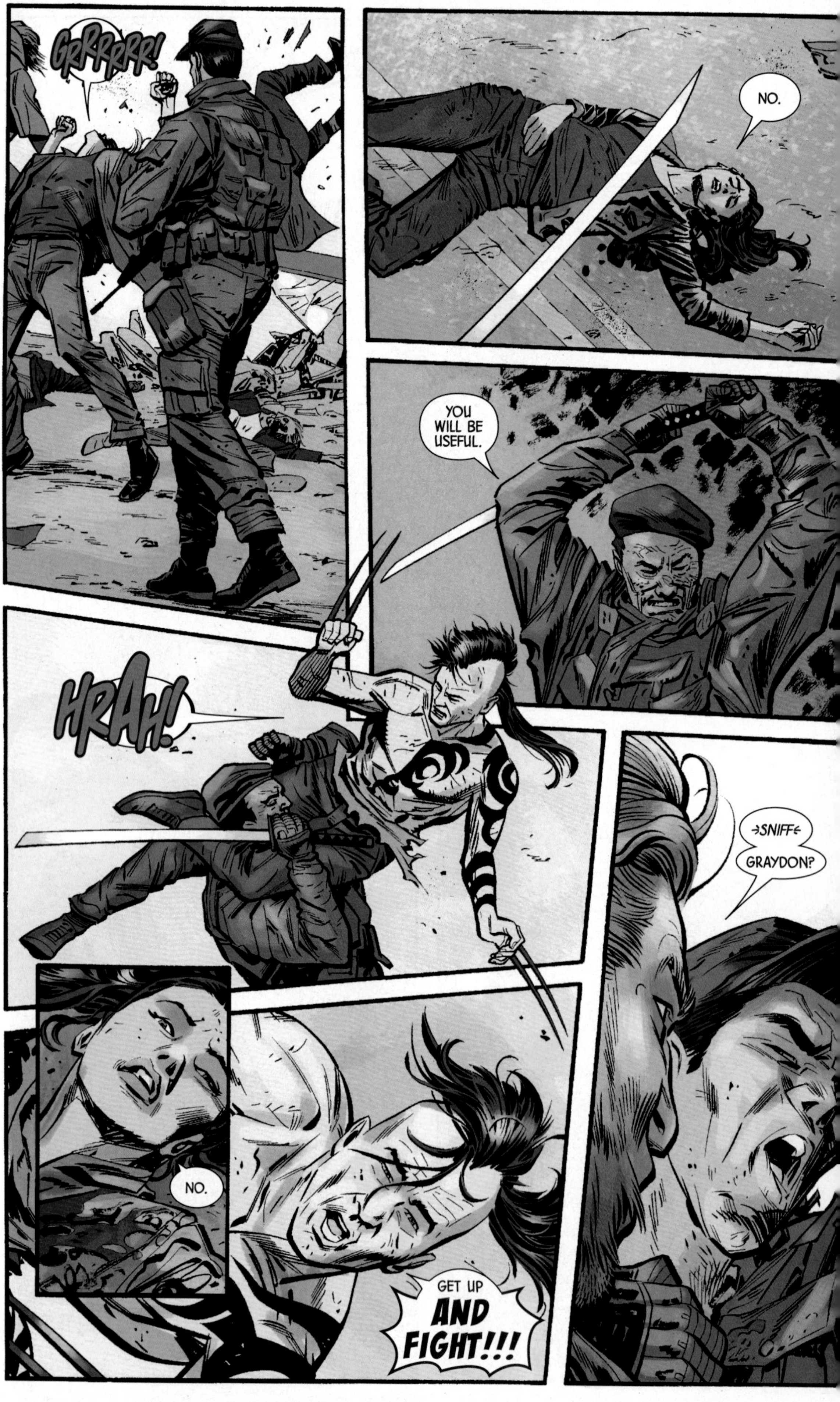
GRRRRRR!
NO.
YOU WILL BE USEFUL.
HRAH!
→SNIFF←
GRAYDON?
NO.
GET UP
AND
FIGHT!!!

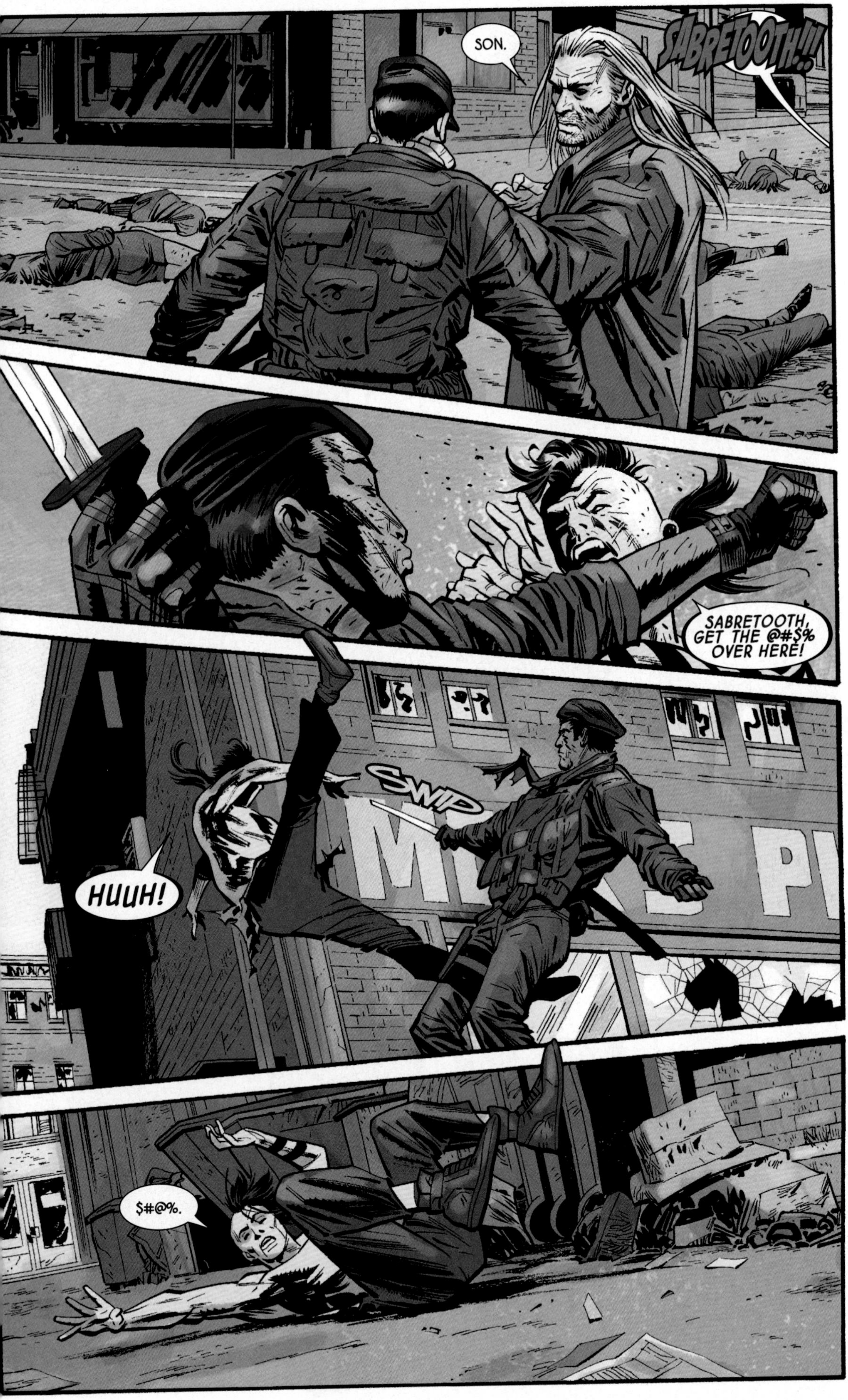
SON.
SABRETOOTH!!!
SABRETOOTH, GET THE @#$% OVER HERE!
SWIP
HUUH!
$#@%.

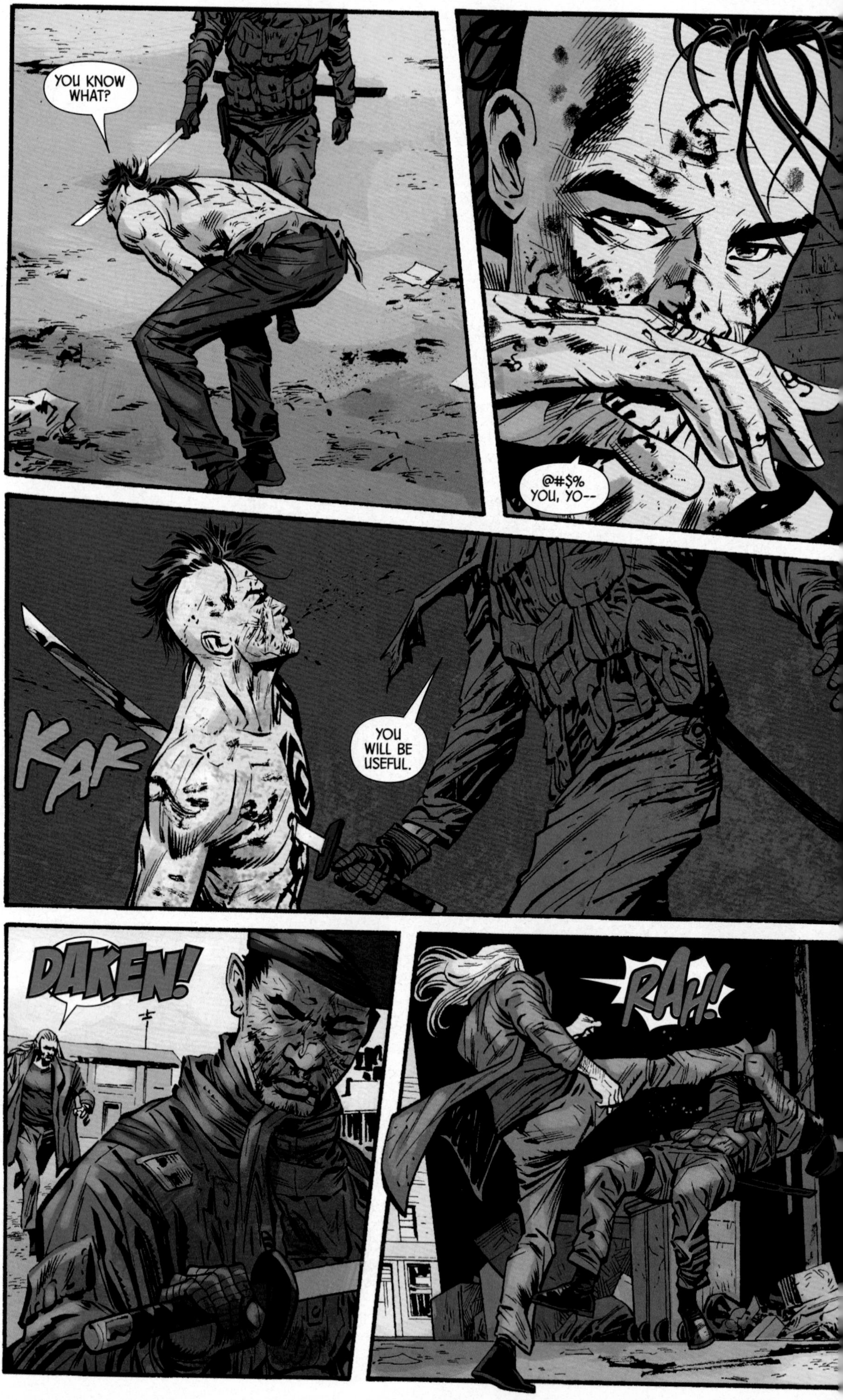
YOU KNOW WHAT?
@#$% YOU, YO--
KAK
YOU WILL BE USEFUL.
DAKEN!
RAH!

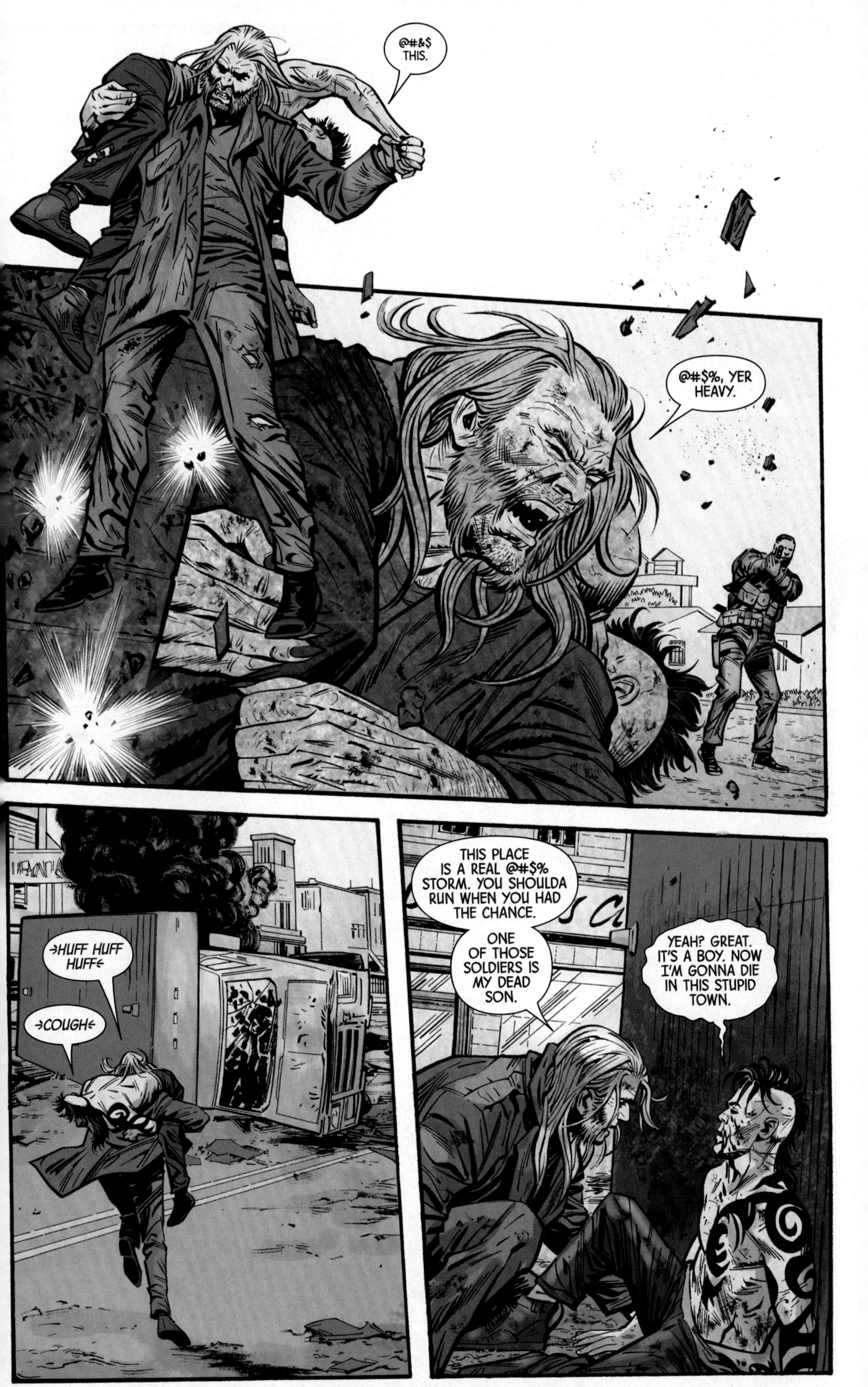
@#&$ THIS.
@#$%, YER HEAVY.
→HUFF HUFF HUFF←
→COUGH←
THIS PLACE IS A REAL @#$% STORM. YOU SHOULDA RUN WHEN YOU HAD THE CHANCE.
ONE OF THOSE SOLDIERS IS MY DEAD SON.
YEAH? GREAT. IT'S A BOY. NOW I'M GONNA DIE IN THIS STUPID TOWN.

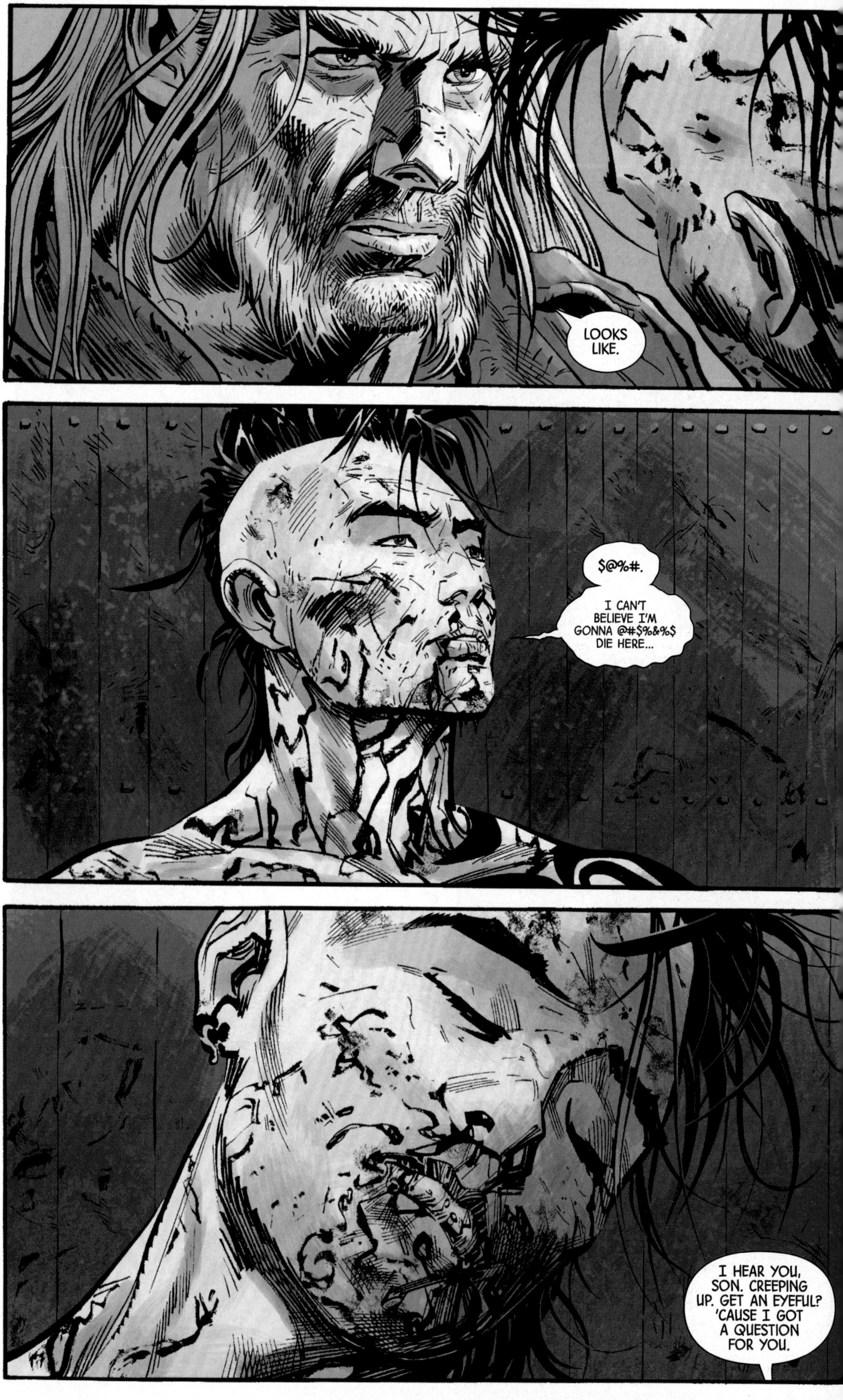

LOOKS LIKE.
$@%#.
I CAN'T BELIEVE I'M GONNA @#$%&%$ DIE HERE...
I HEAR YOU, SON. CREEPING UP. GET AN EYEFUL? 'CAUSE I GOT A QUESTION FOR YOU.

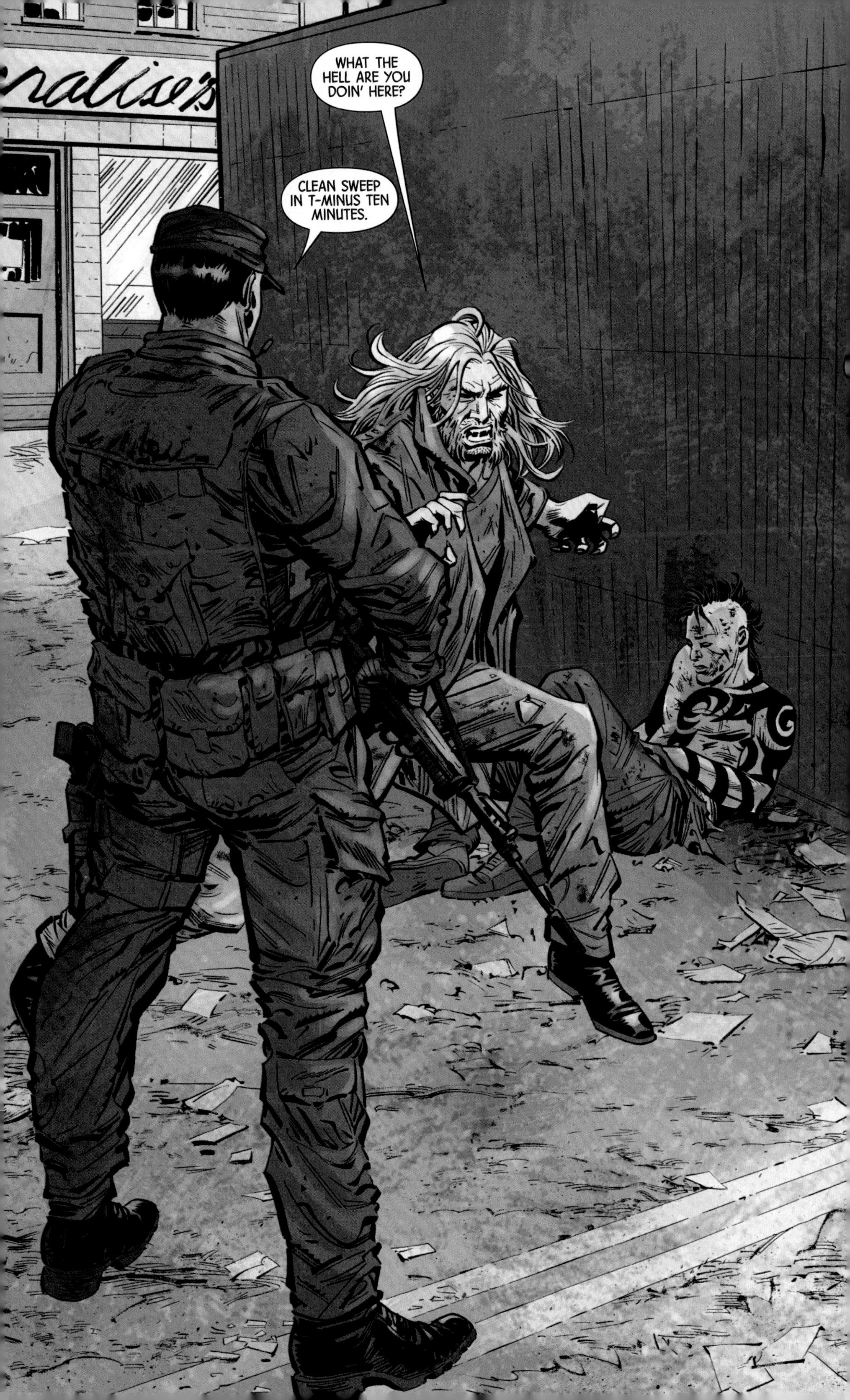
WHAT THE HELL ARE YOU DOIN' HERE?
CLEAN SWEEP IN T-MINUS TEN MINUTES.

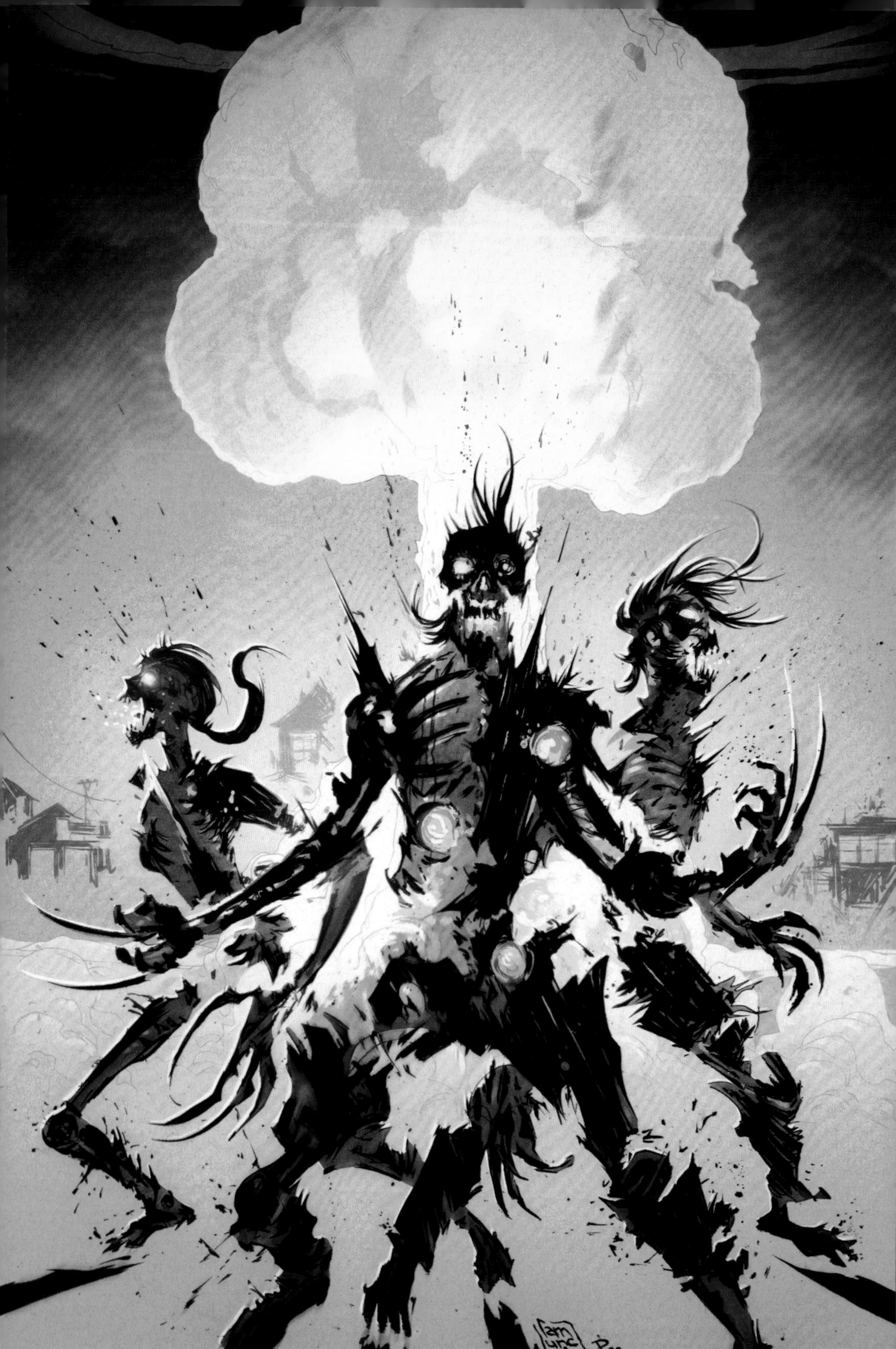

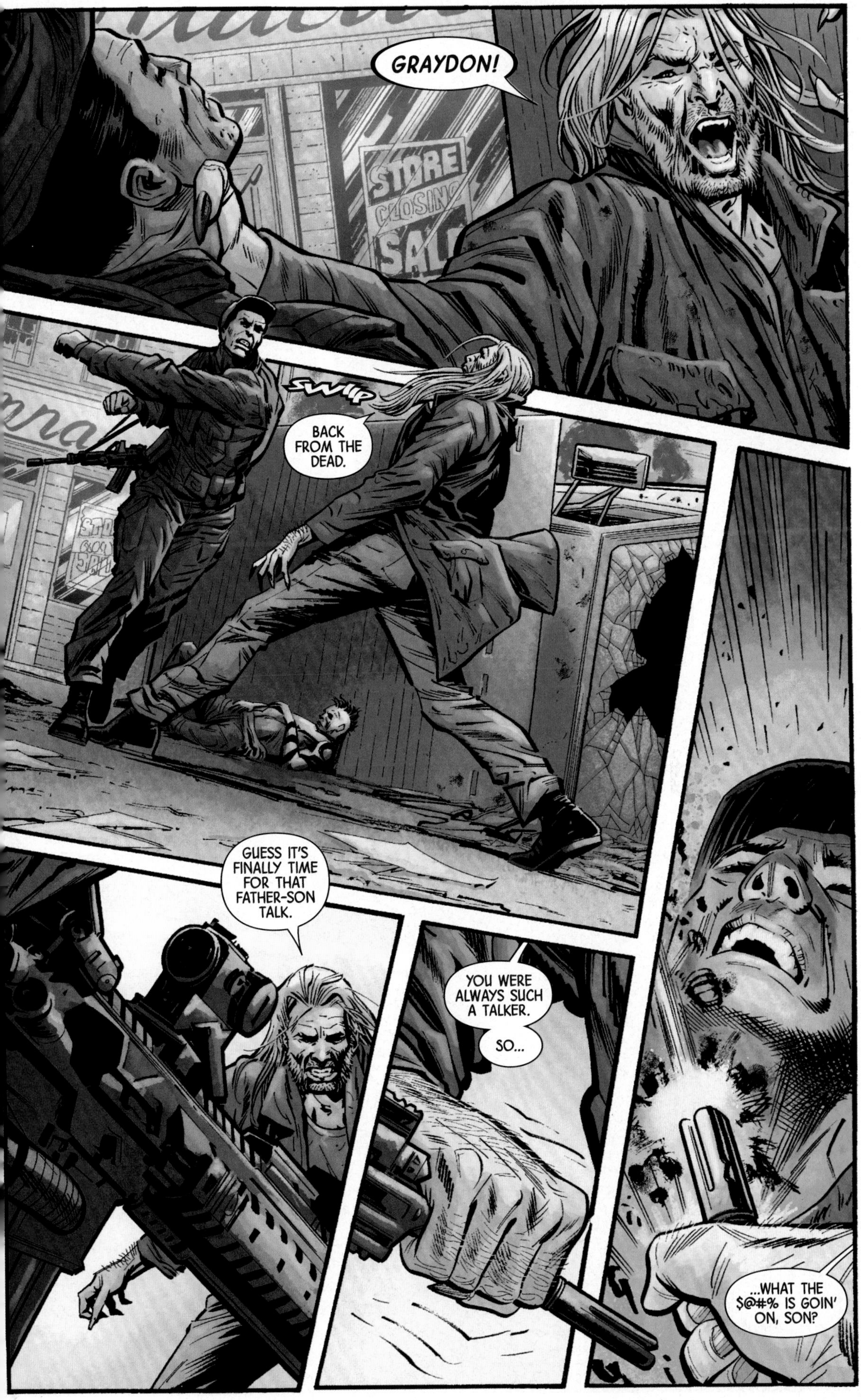
GRAYDON!
STORE
CLOSING
SALE
SWIIP
BACK FROM THE DEAD.
GUESS IT'S FINALLY TIME FOR THAT FATHER-SON TALK.
YOU WERE ALWAYS SUCH A TALKER.
SO...
...WHAT THE $@#% IS GOIN' ON, SON?

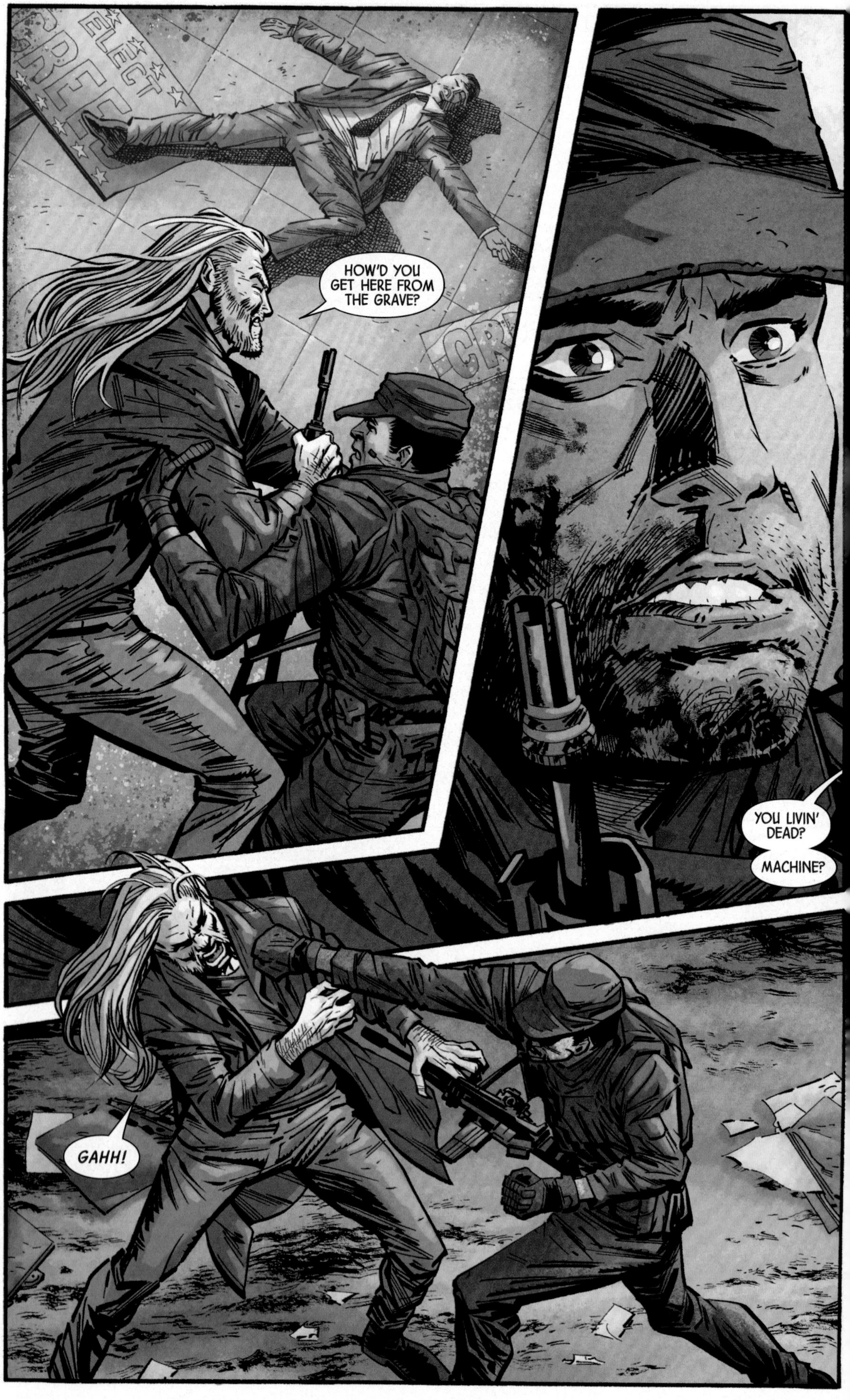
HOW'D YOU GET HERE FROM THE GRAVE?
YOU LIVIN' DEAD?
MACHINE?
GAHH!

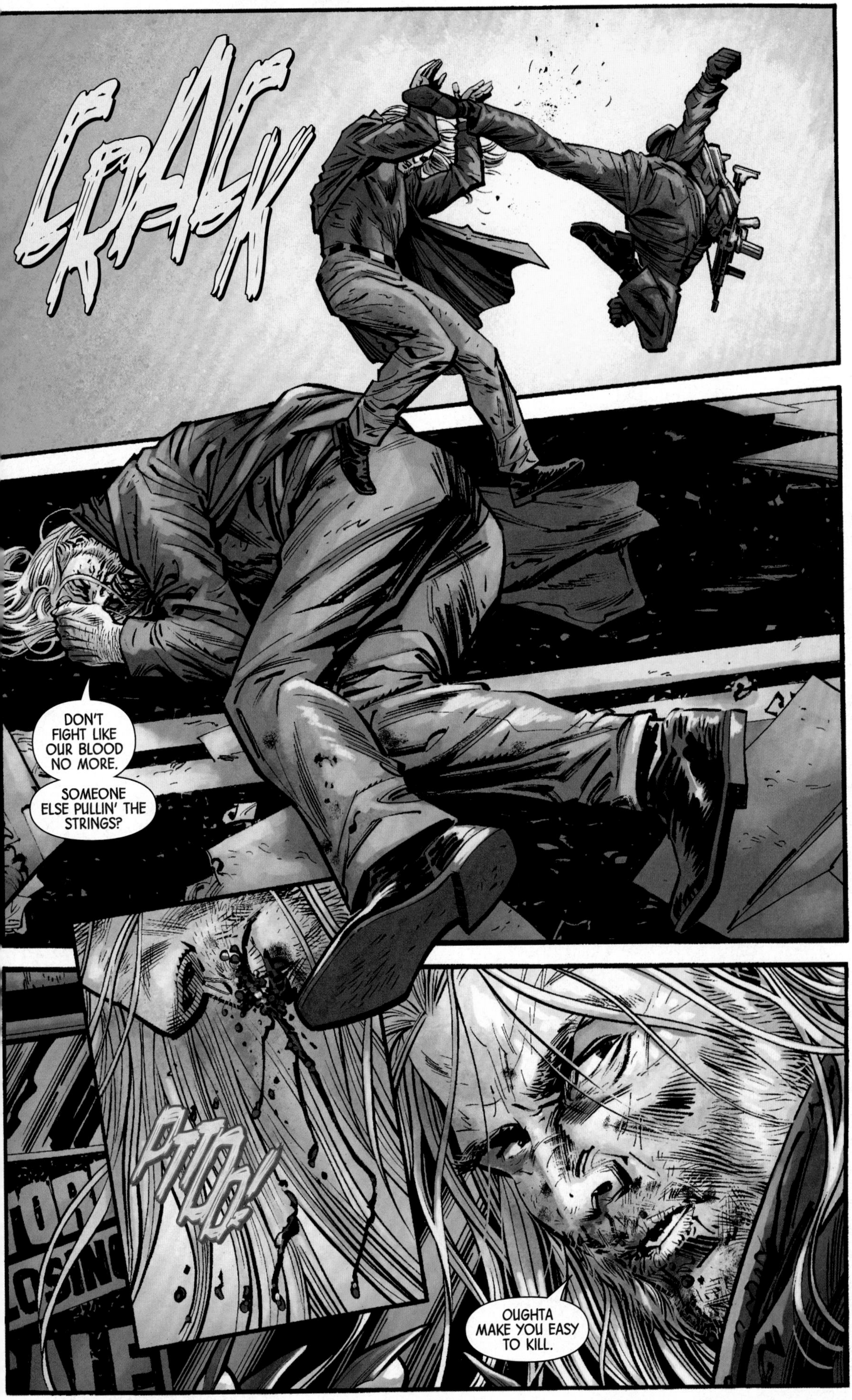
CRACK
DON'T FIGHT LIKE OUR BLOOD NO MORE.
SOMEONE ELSE PULLIN' THE STRINGS?
PTOO!
OUGHTA MAKE YOU EASY TO KILL.

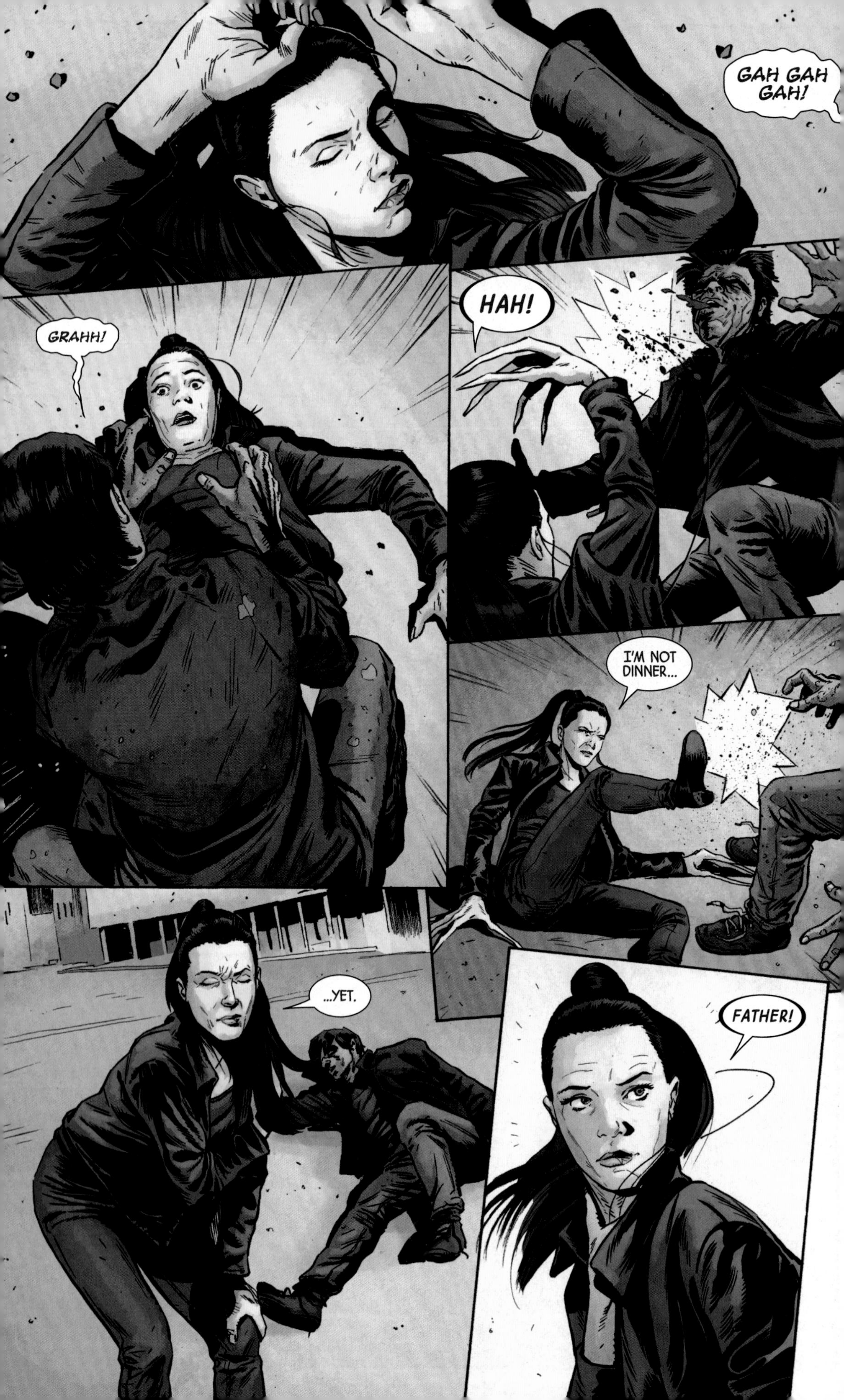
GAH GAH GAH!
GRAHH!
HAH!
I'M NOT DINNER...
...YET.
FATHER!

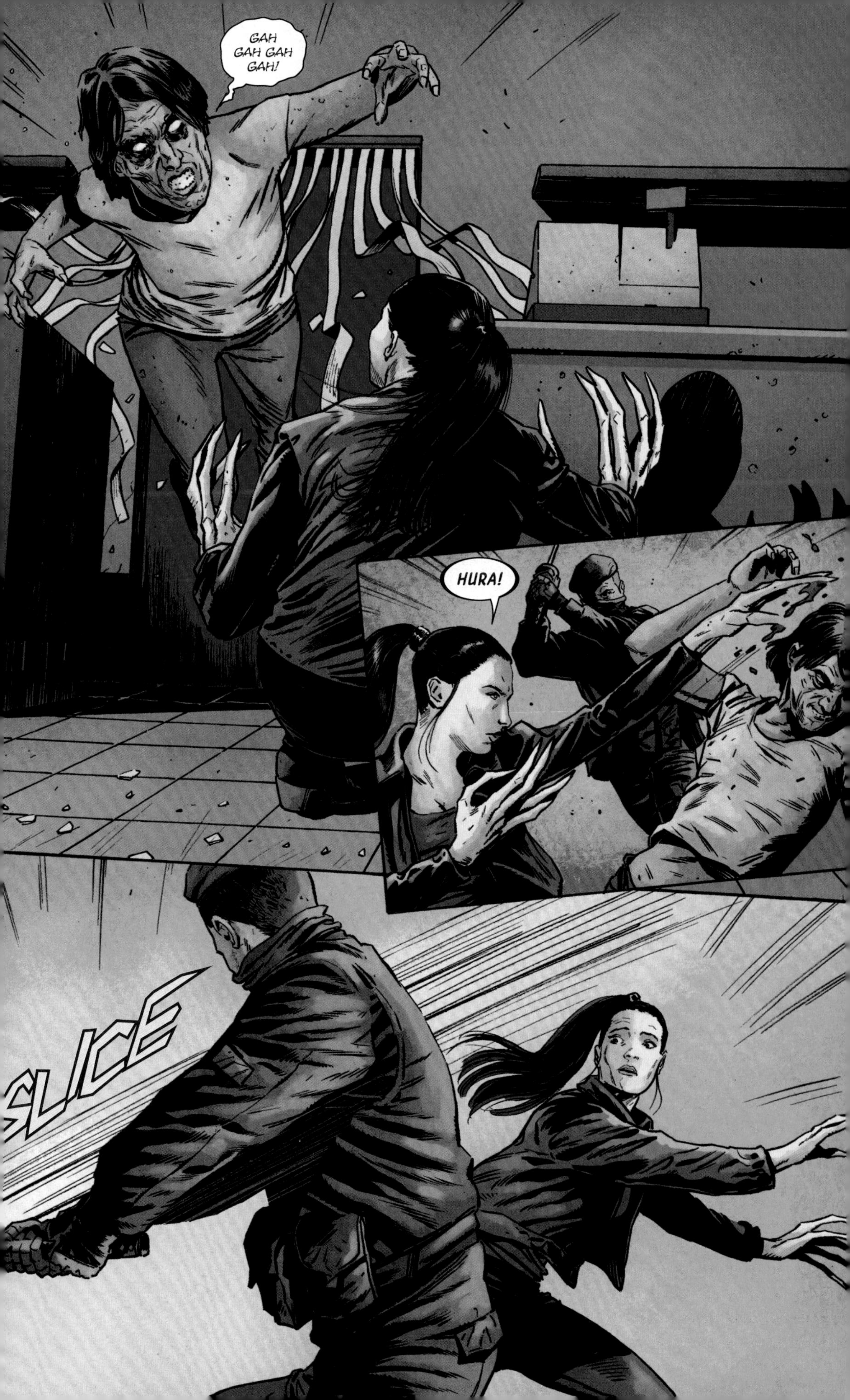
GAH GAH GAH GAH!
HURA!
SLICE

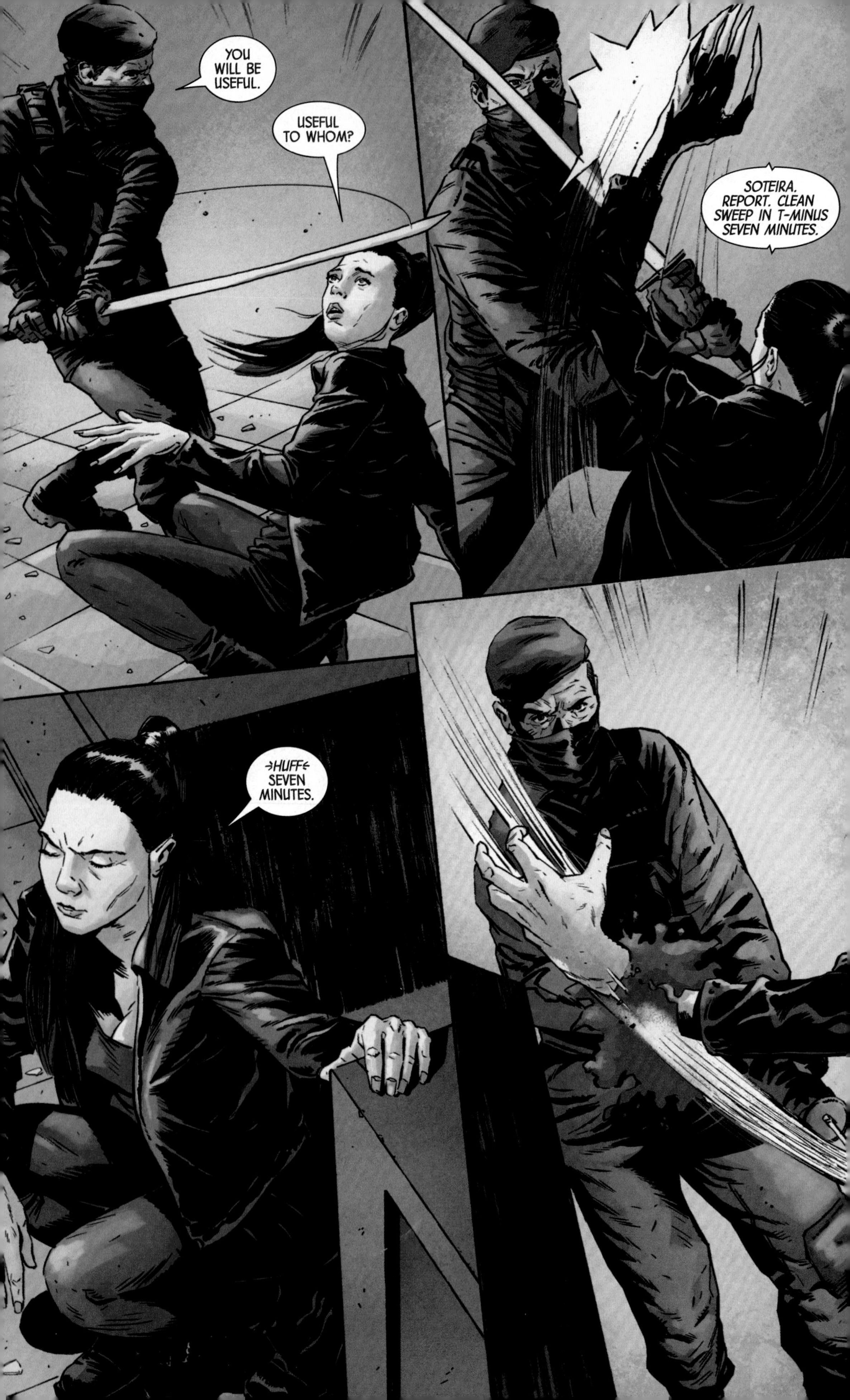
YOU WILL BE USEFUL.
USEFUL TO WHOM?
SOTEIRA. REPORT. CLEAN SWEEP IN T-MINUS SEVEN MINUTES.
HUFF SEVEN MINUTES.

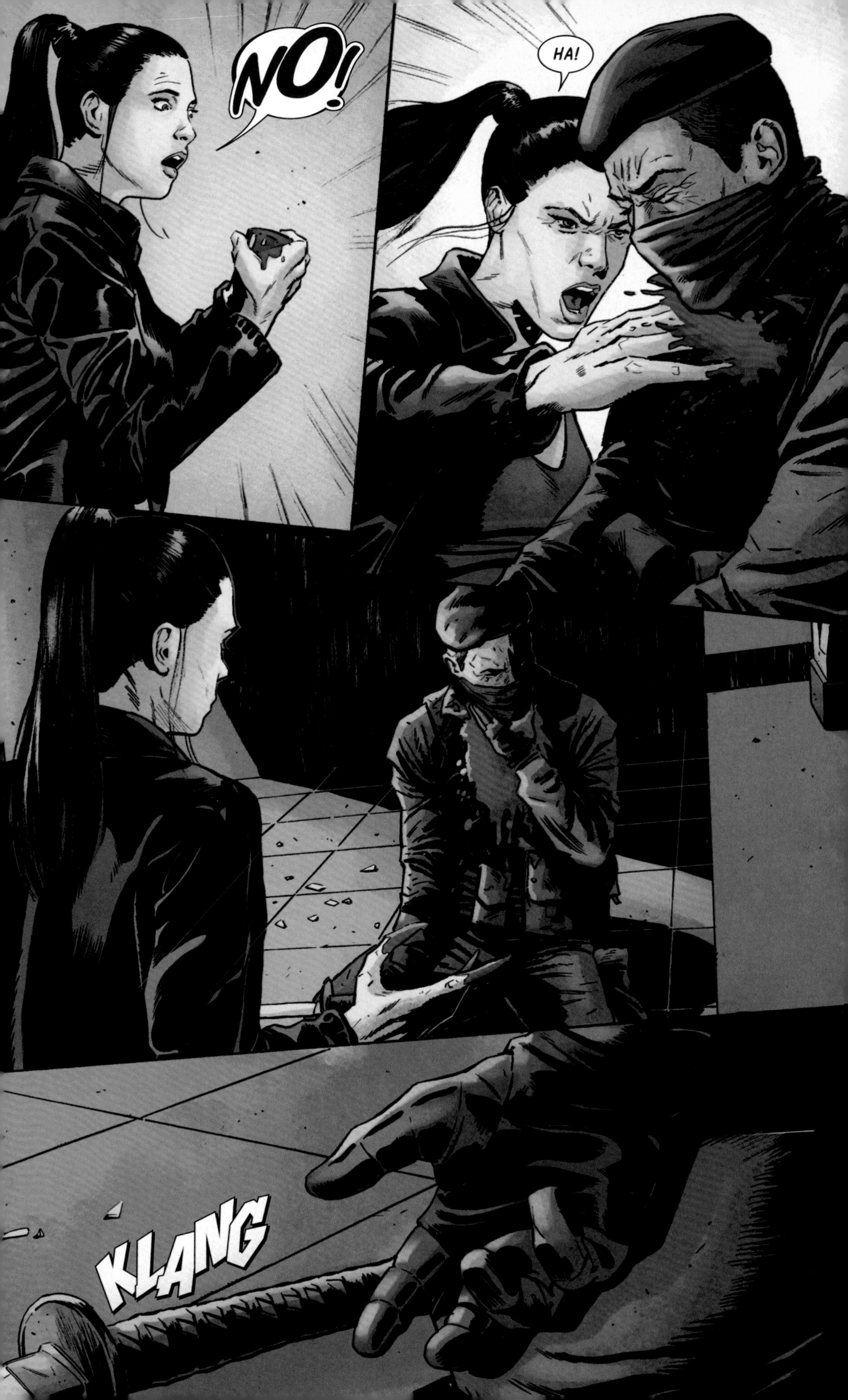
NO!
HA!
KLANG

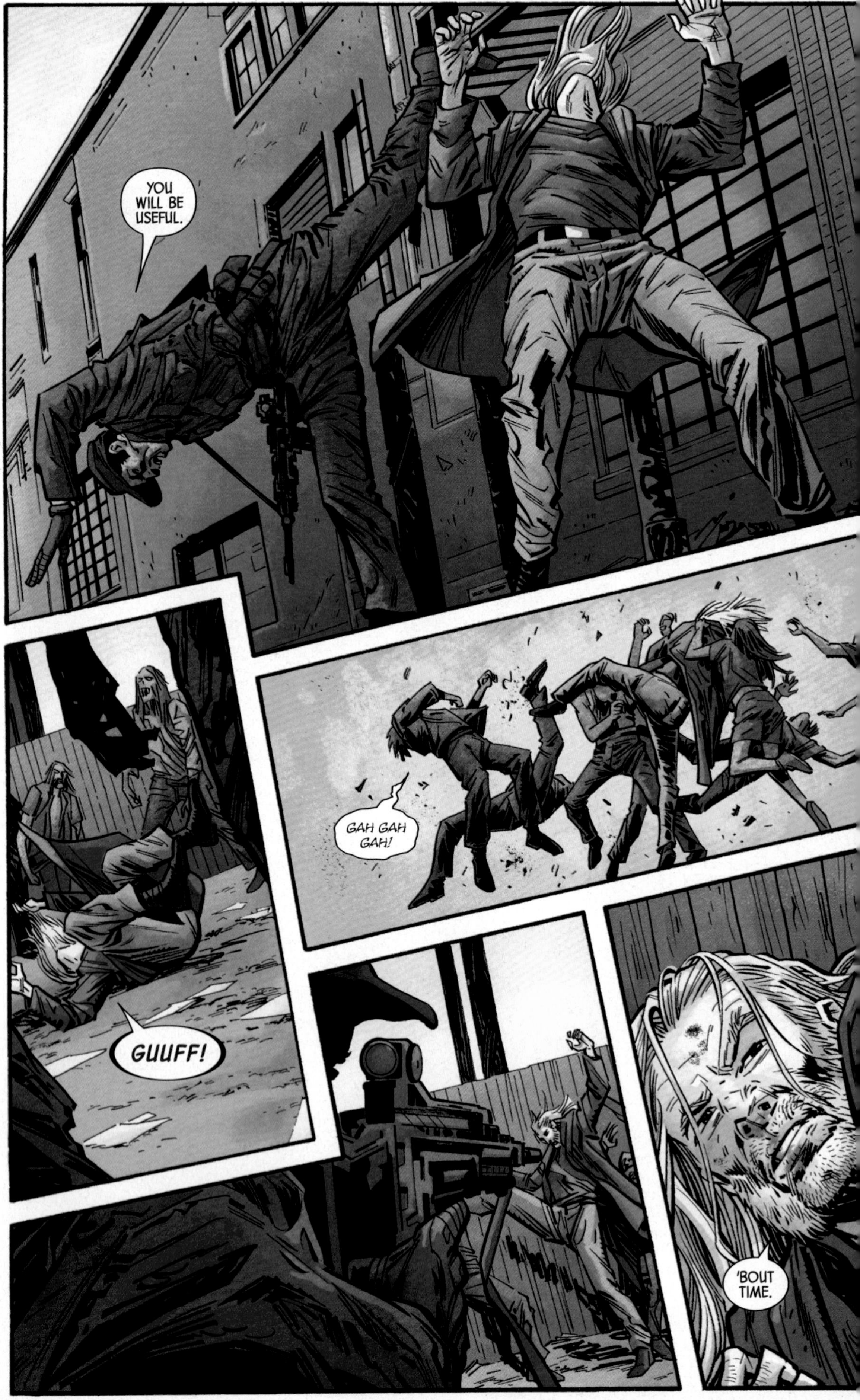
YOU WILL BE USEFUL.
GUUFF!
GAH GAH GAH!
'BOUT TIME.

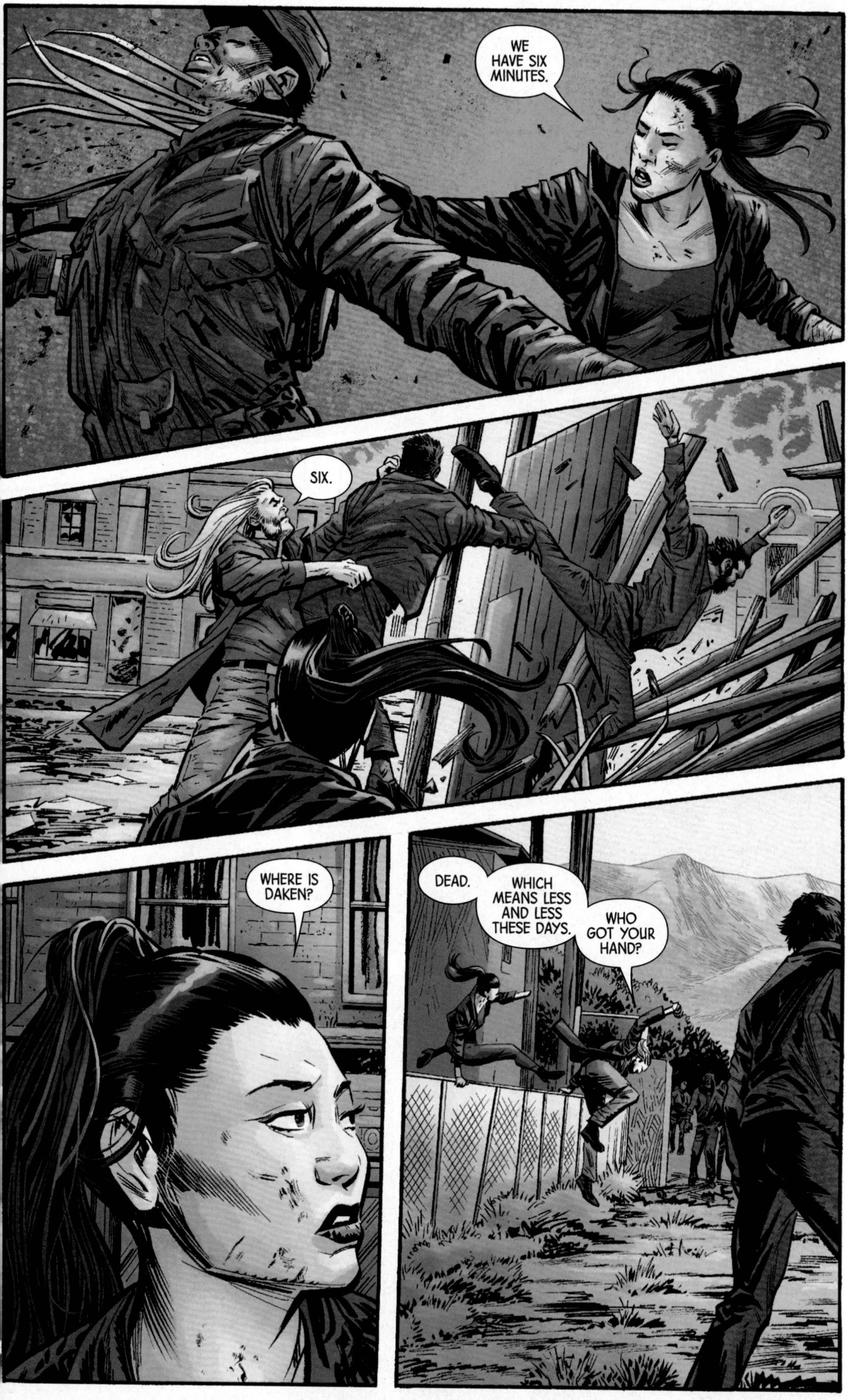

WE HAVE SIX MINUTES.
SIX.
WHERE IS DAKEN?
DEAD.
WHICH MEANS LESS AND LESS THESE DAYS.
WHO GOT YOUR HAND?

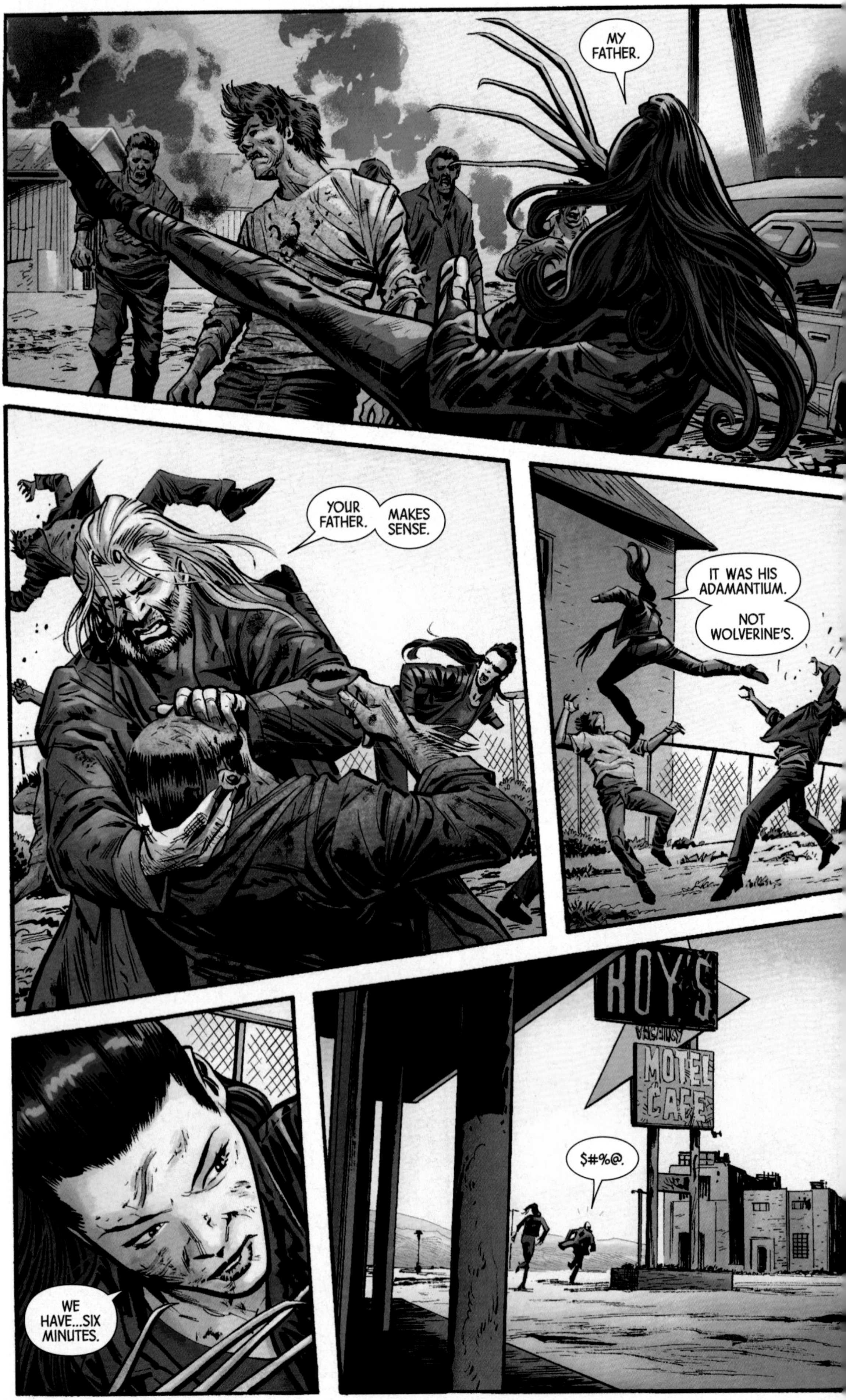
MY FATHER.
YOUR FATHER.
MAKES SENSE.
IT WAS HIS ADAMANTIUM.
NOT WOLVERINE'S.
ROY'S
MOTEL CAFE
WE HAVE...SIX MINUTES.
$#%@.

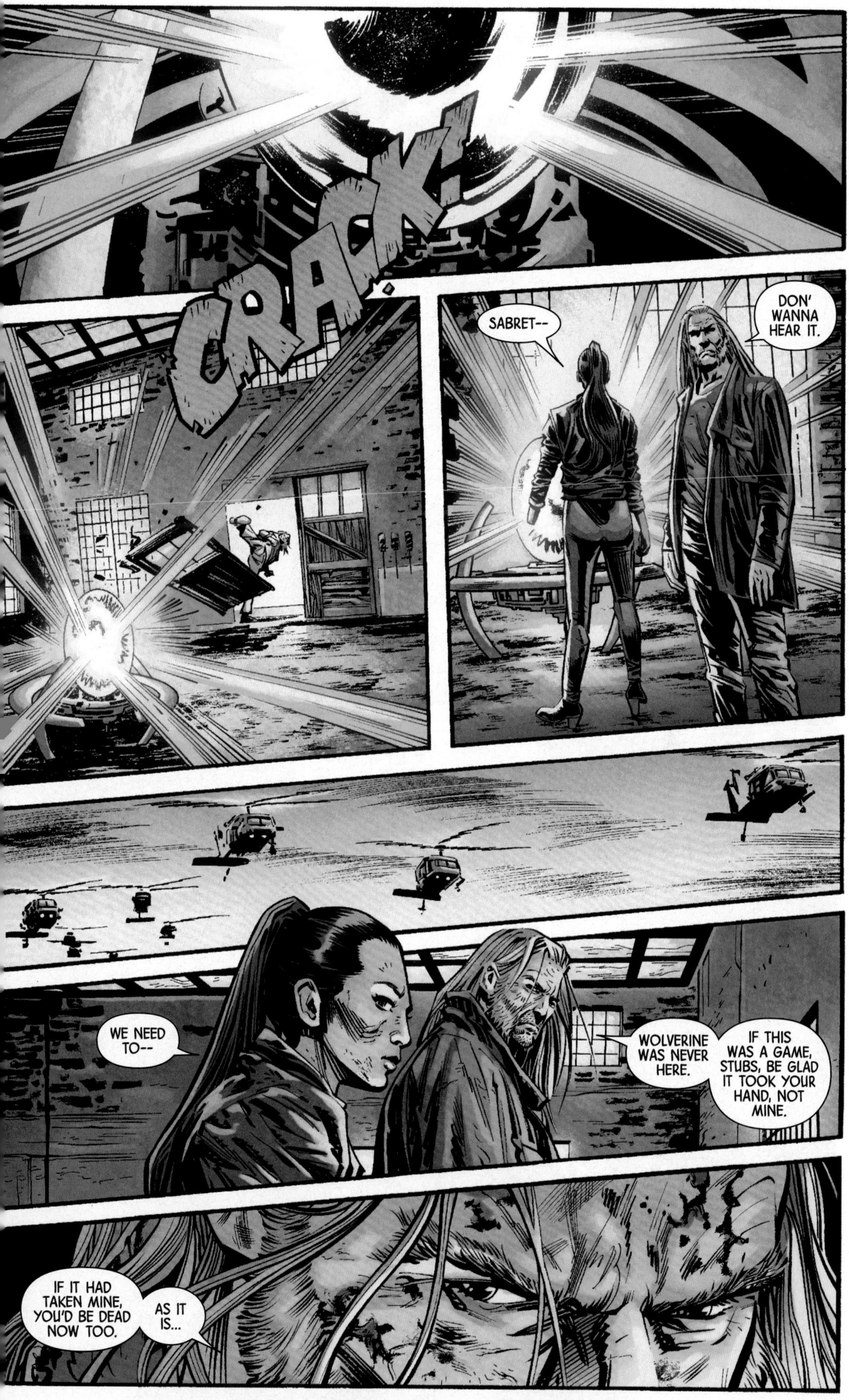
CRACK!
SABRET--
DON' WANNA HEAR IT.
WE NEED TO--
WOLVERINE WAS NEVER HERE.
IF THIS WAS A GAME, STUBS, BE GLAD IT TOOK YOUR HAND, NOT MINE.
IF IT HAD TAKEN MINE, YOU'D BE DEAD NOW TOO.
AS IT IS...

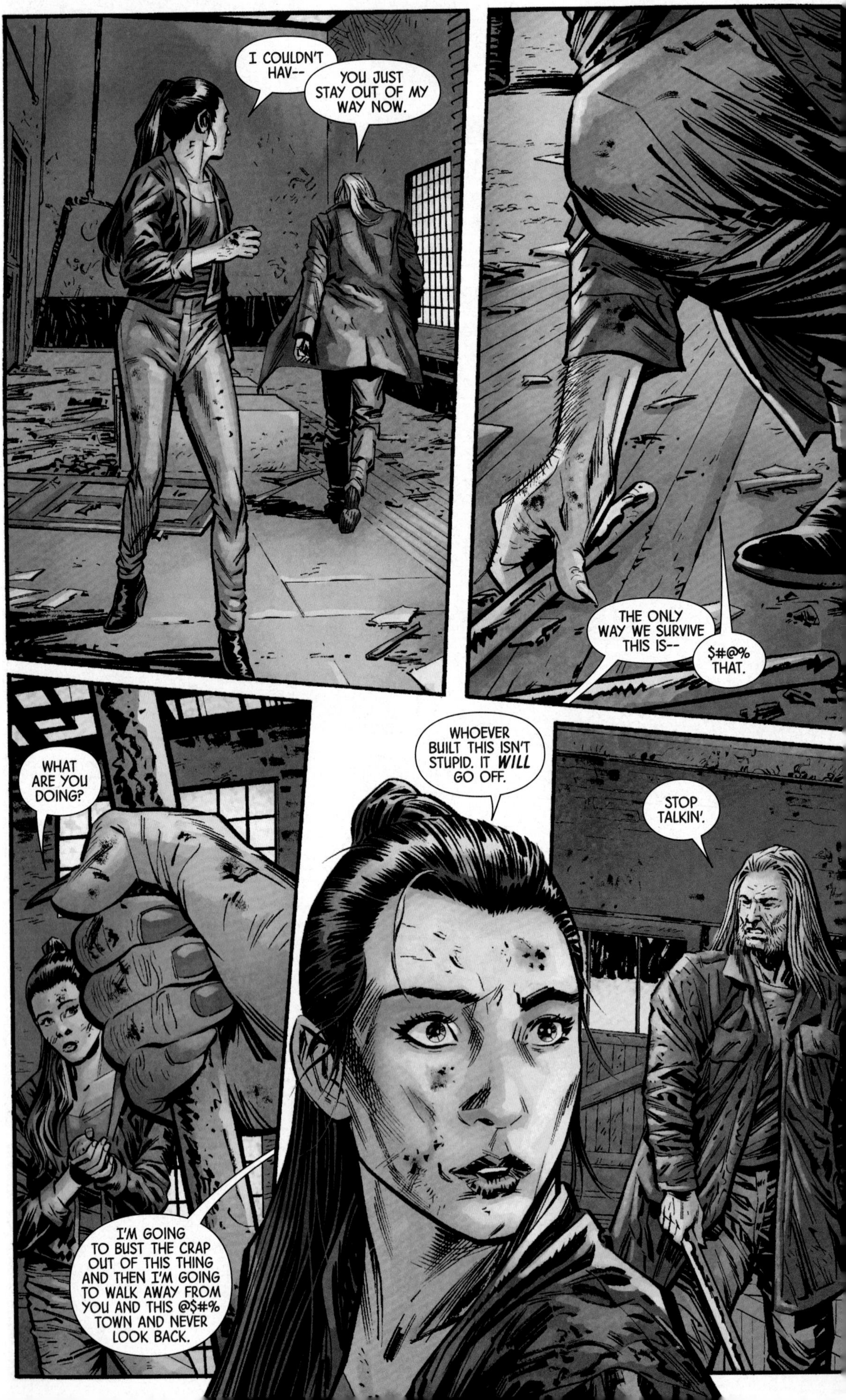
I COULDN'T HAV--
YOU JUST STAY OUT OF MY WAY NOW.
THE ONLY WAY WE SURVIVE THIS IS--
$#@% THAT.
WHAT ARE YOU DOING?
WHOEVER BUILT THIS ISN'T STUPID. IT WILL GO OFF.
STOP TALKIN'.
I'M GOING TO BUST THE CRAP OUT OF THIS THING AND THEN I'M GOING TO WALK AWAY FROM YOU AND THIS @$#% TOWN AND NEVER LOOK BACK.

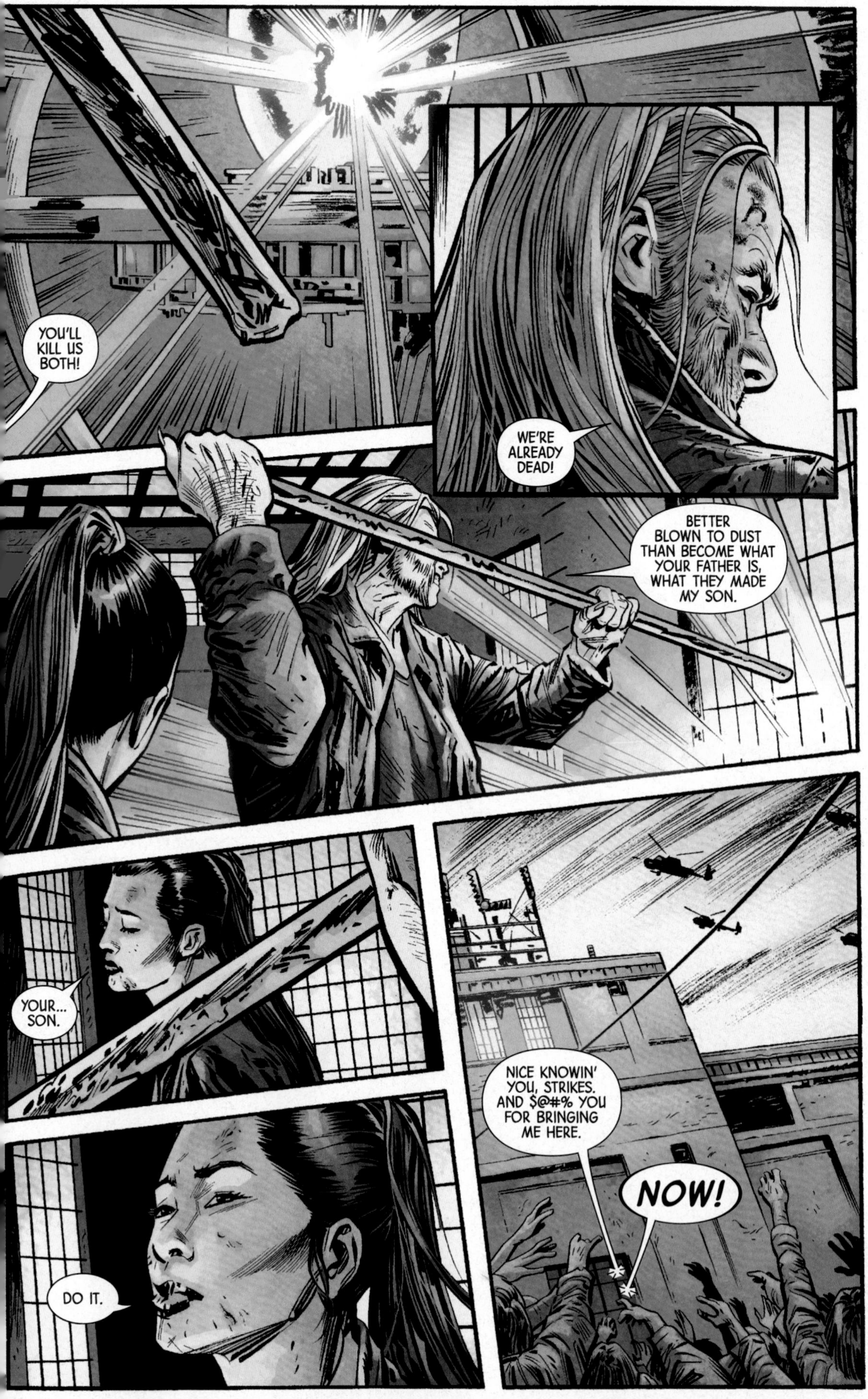
YOU'LL KILL US BOTH!
WE'RE ALREADY DEAD!
BETTER BLOWN TO DUST THAN BECOME WHAT YOUR FATHER IS, WHAT THEY MADE MY SON.
YOUR... SON.
NICE KNOWIN' YOU, STRIKES. AND $@#% YOU FOR BRINGING ME HERE.
DO IT.
NOW!

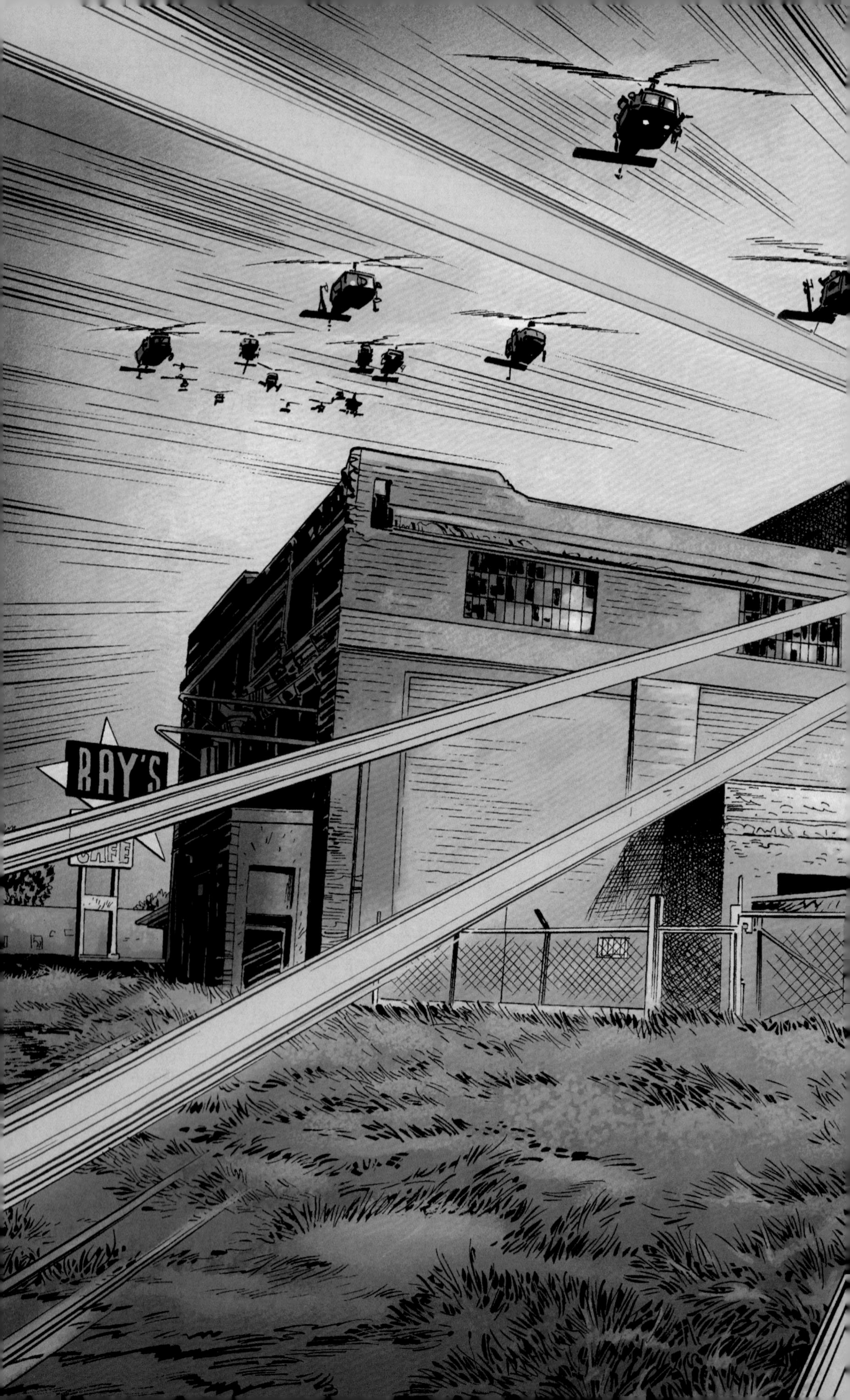
RAY'S
CAFE

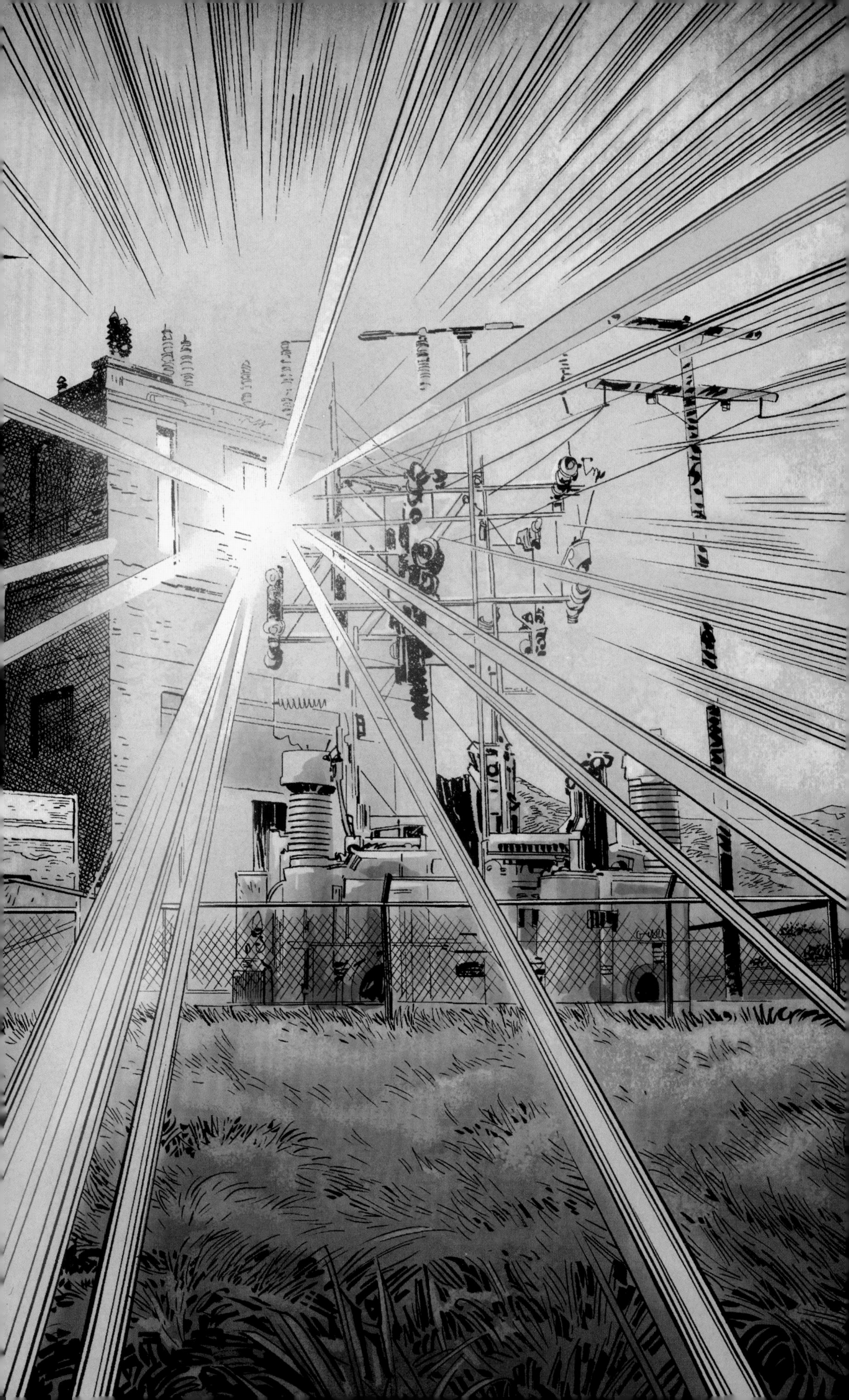

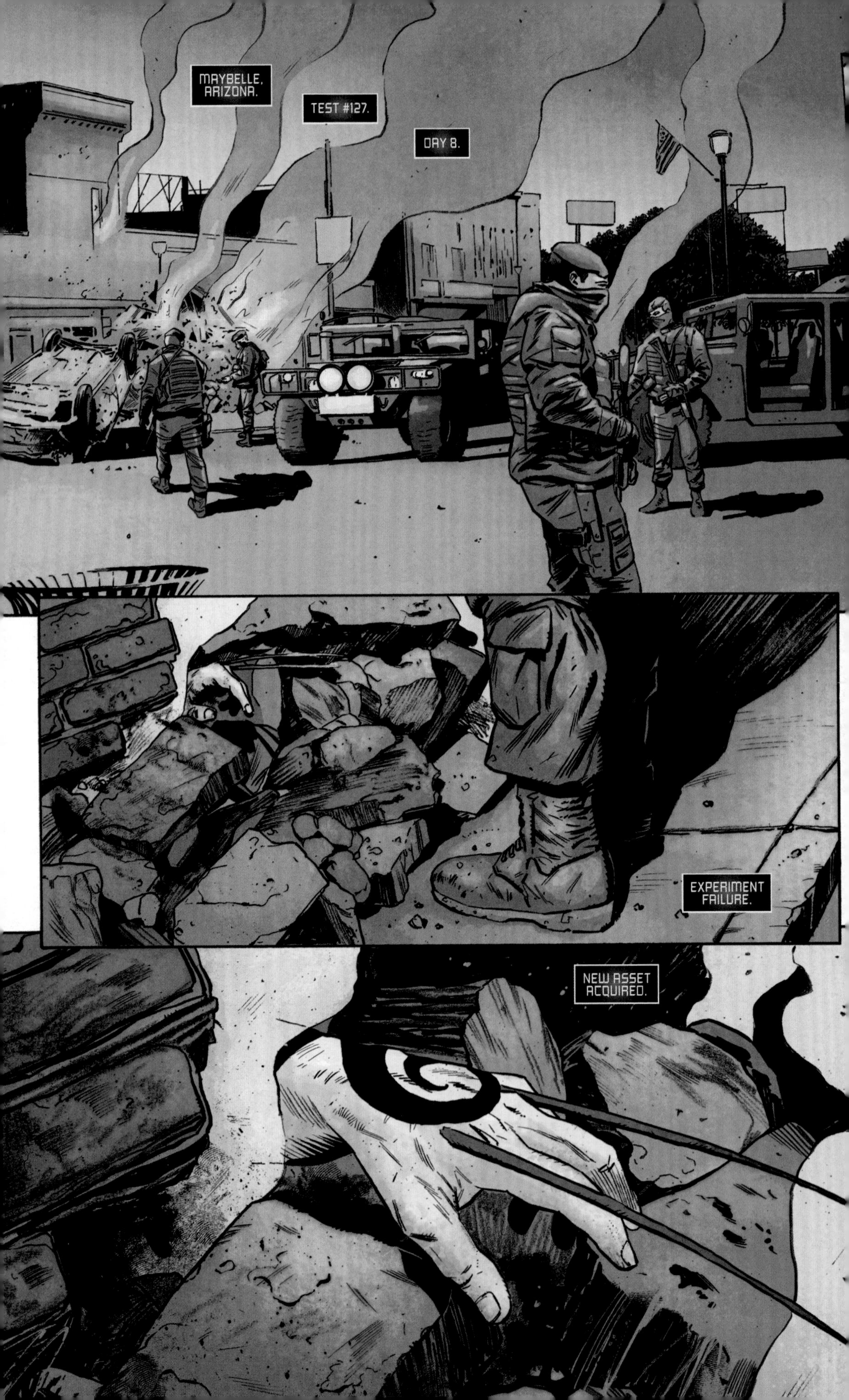

MAYBELLE, ARIZONA.
TEST #127.
DAY 8.
EXPERIMENT FAILURE.
NEW ASSET ACQUIRED.

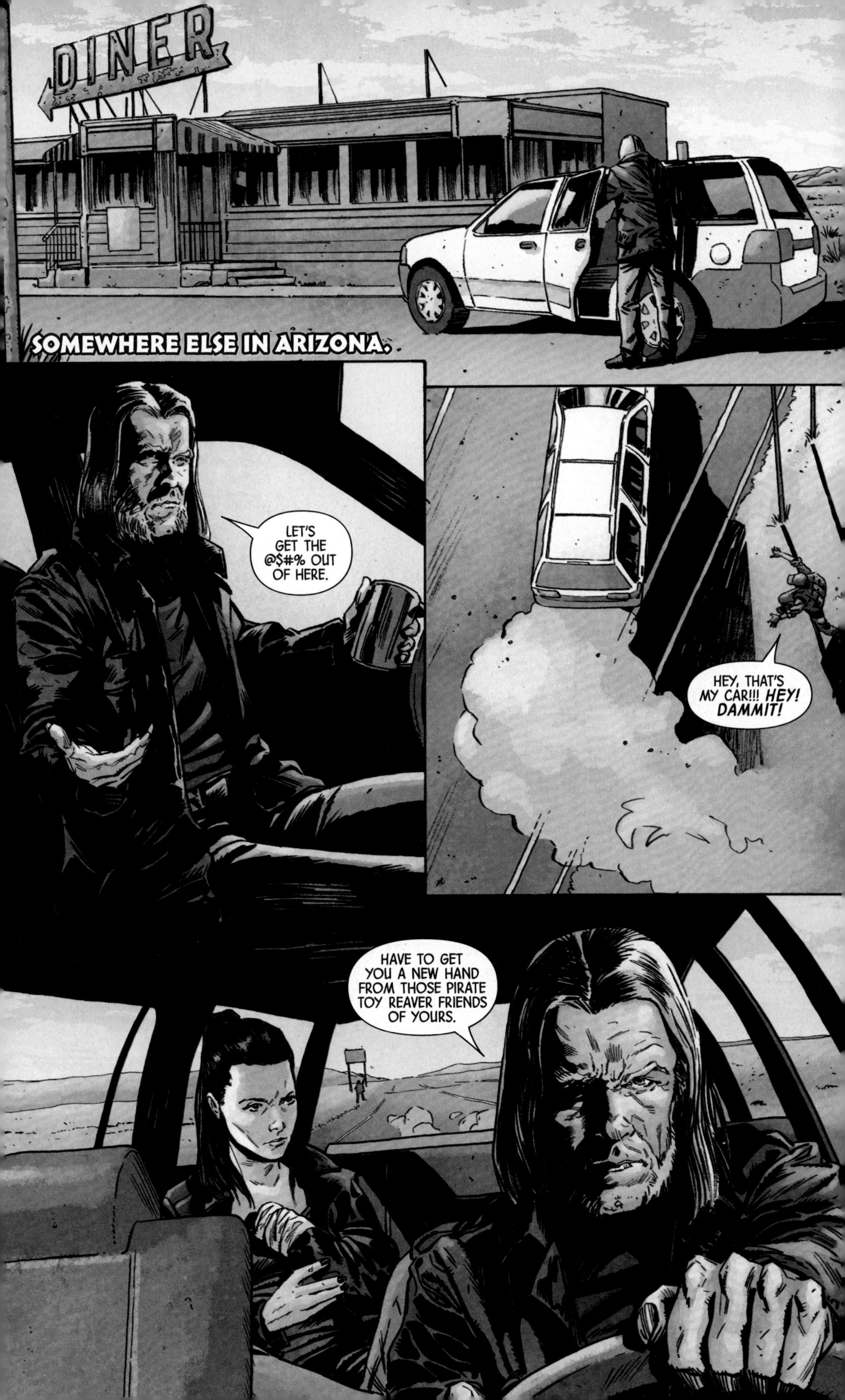
DINER
SOMEWHERE ELSE IN ARIZONA.
LET'S GET THE @$#% OUT OF HERE.
HEY, THAT'S MY CAR!!! HEY! DAMMIT!
HAVE TO GET YOU A NEW HAND FROM THOSE PIRATE TOY REAVER FRIENDS OF YOURS.

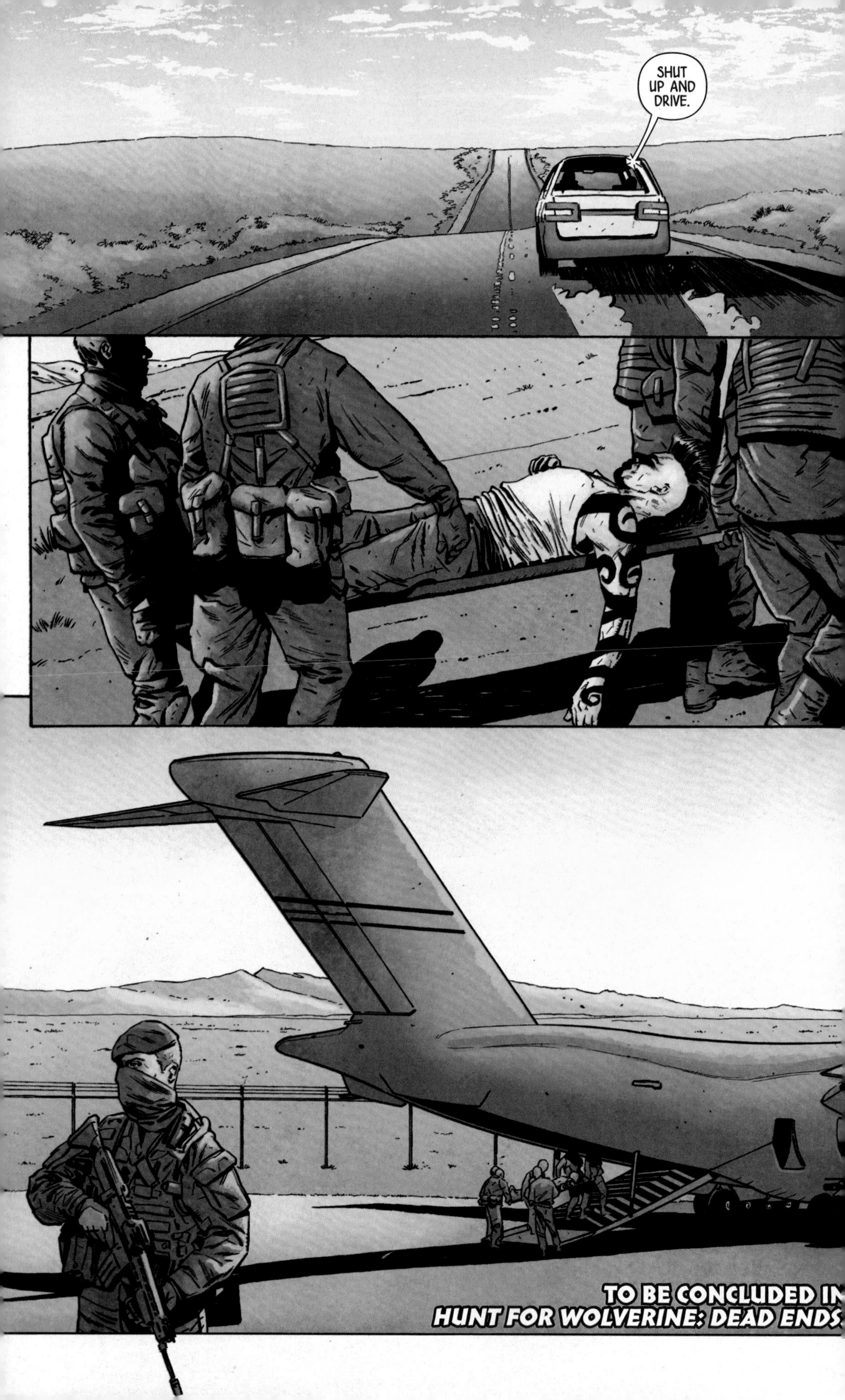
SHUT UP AND DRIVE.
TO BE CONCLUDED IN
HUNT FOR WOLVERINE: DEAD ENDS.

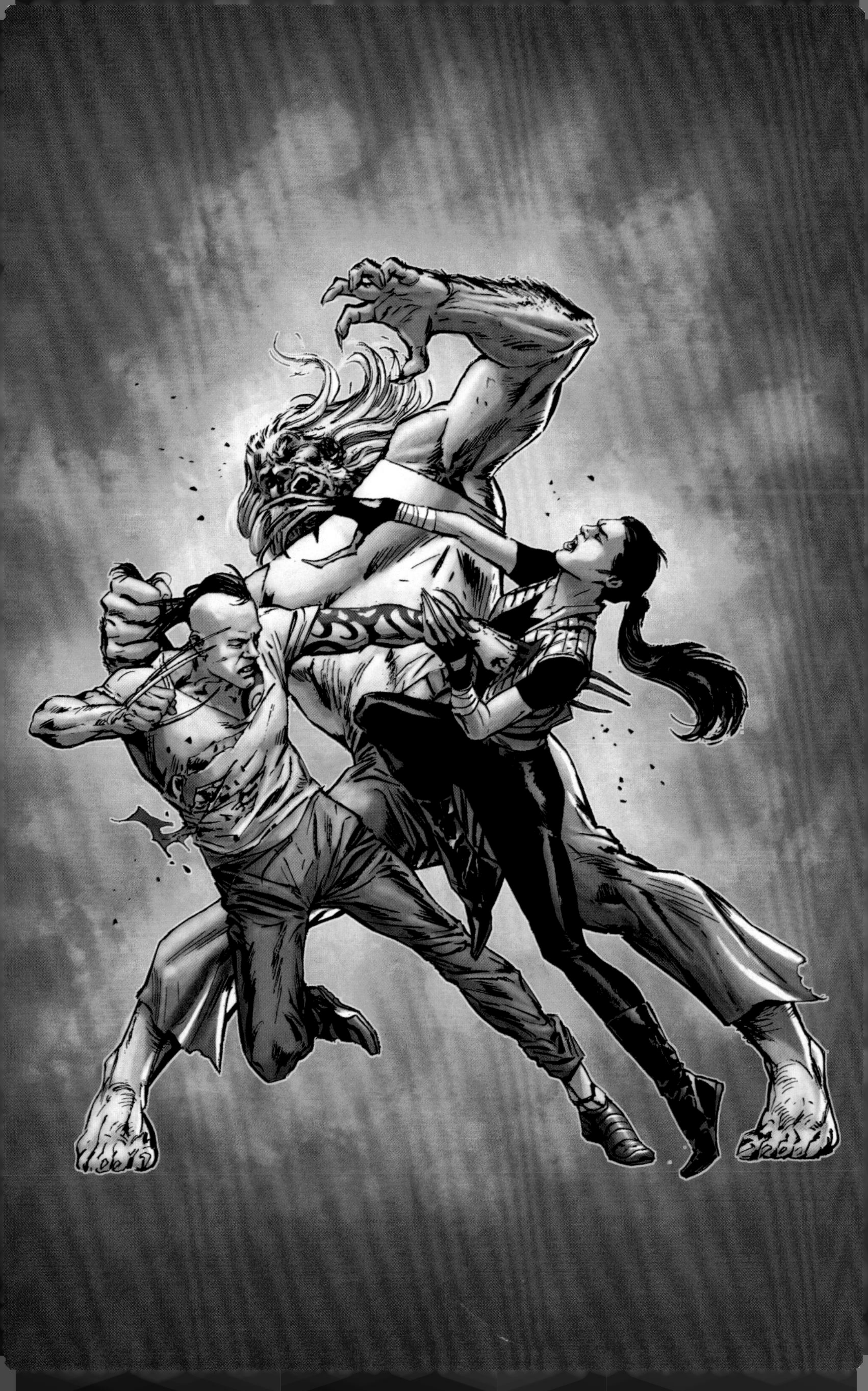

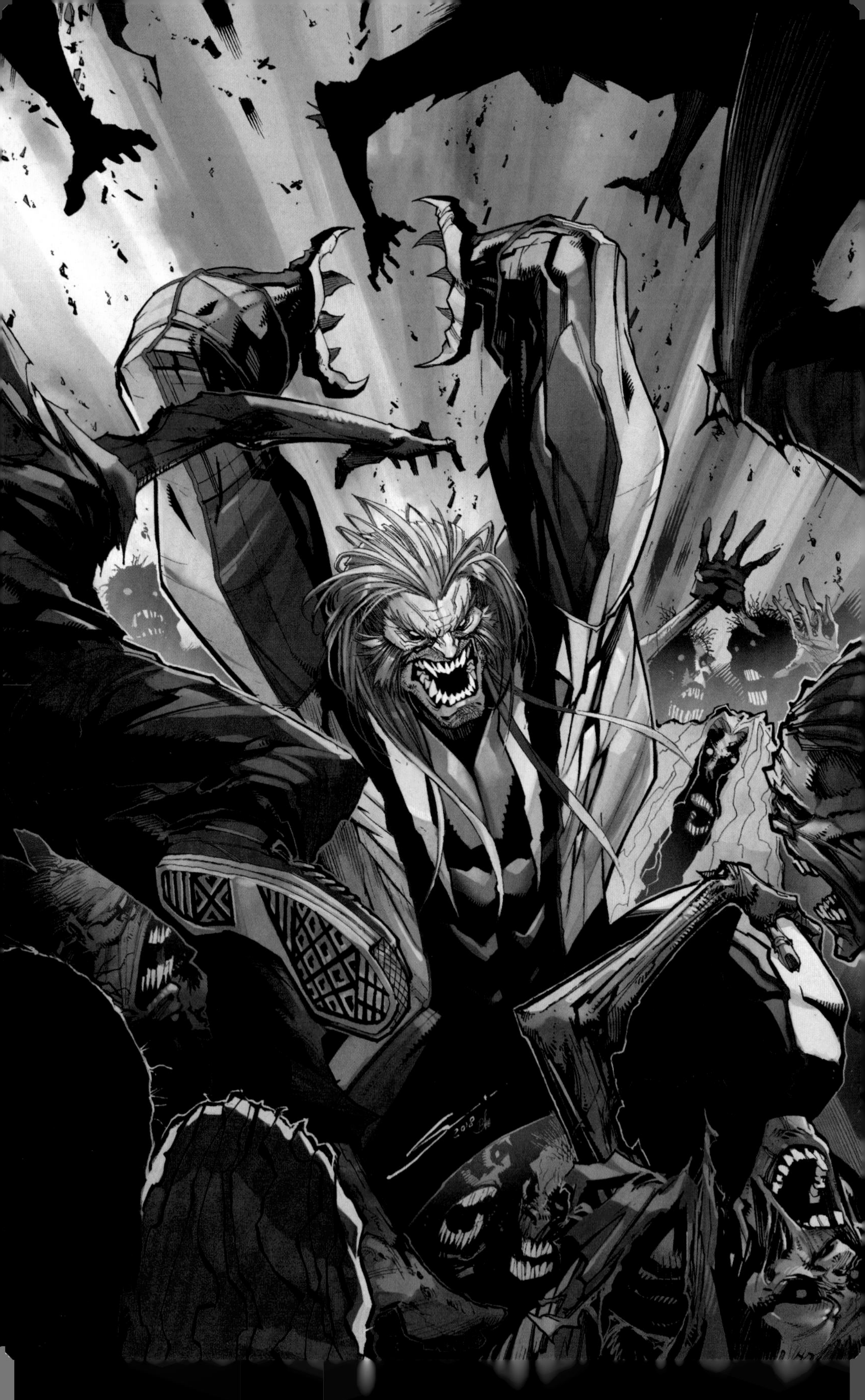

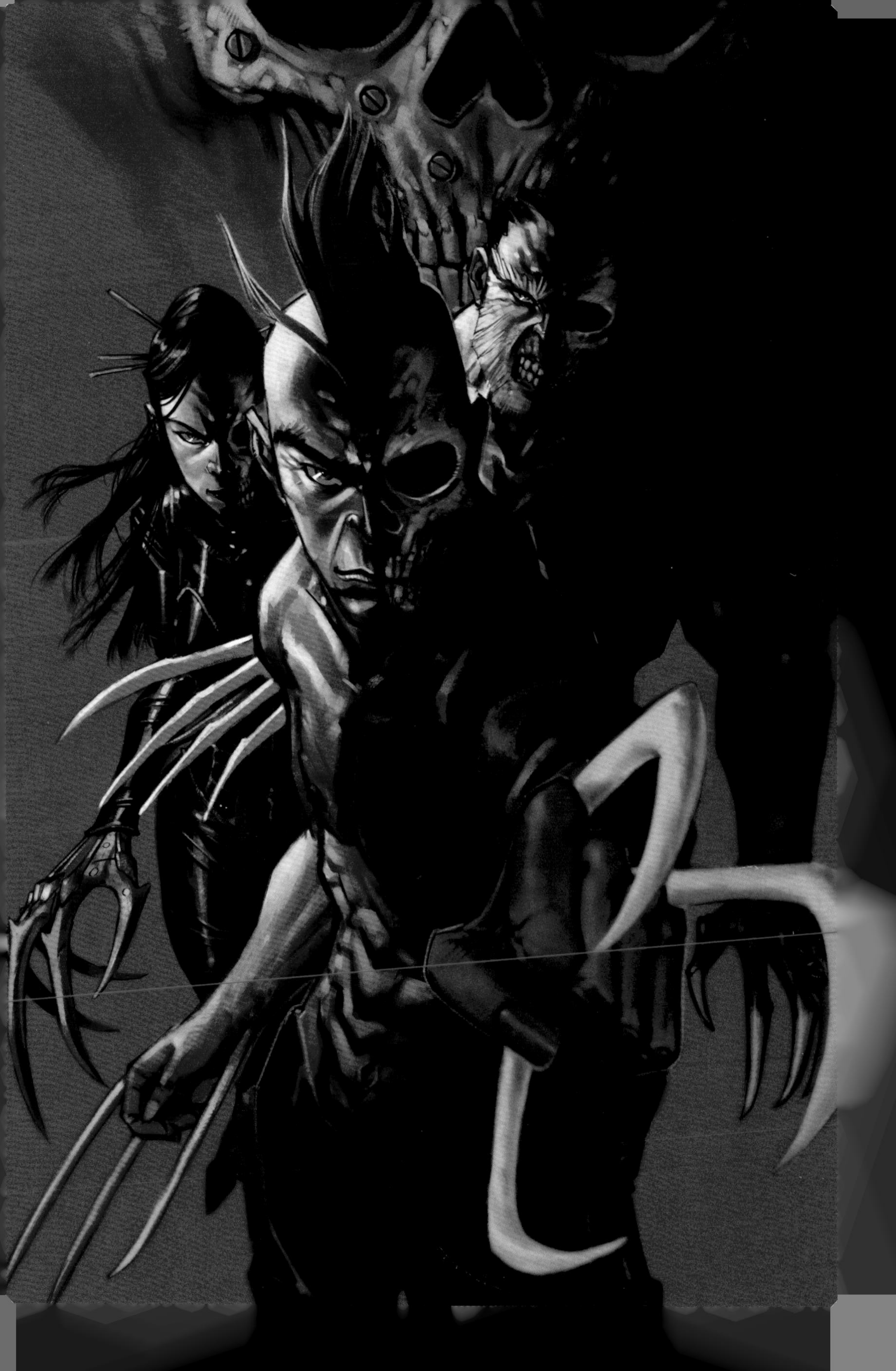

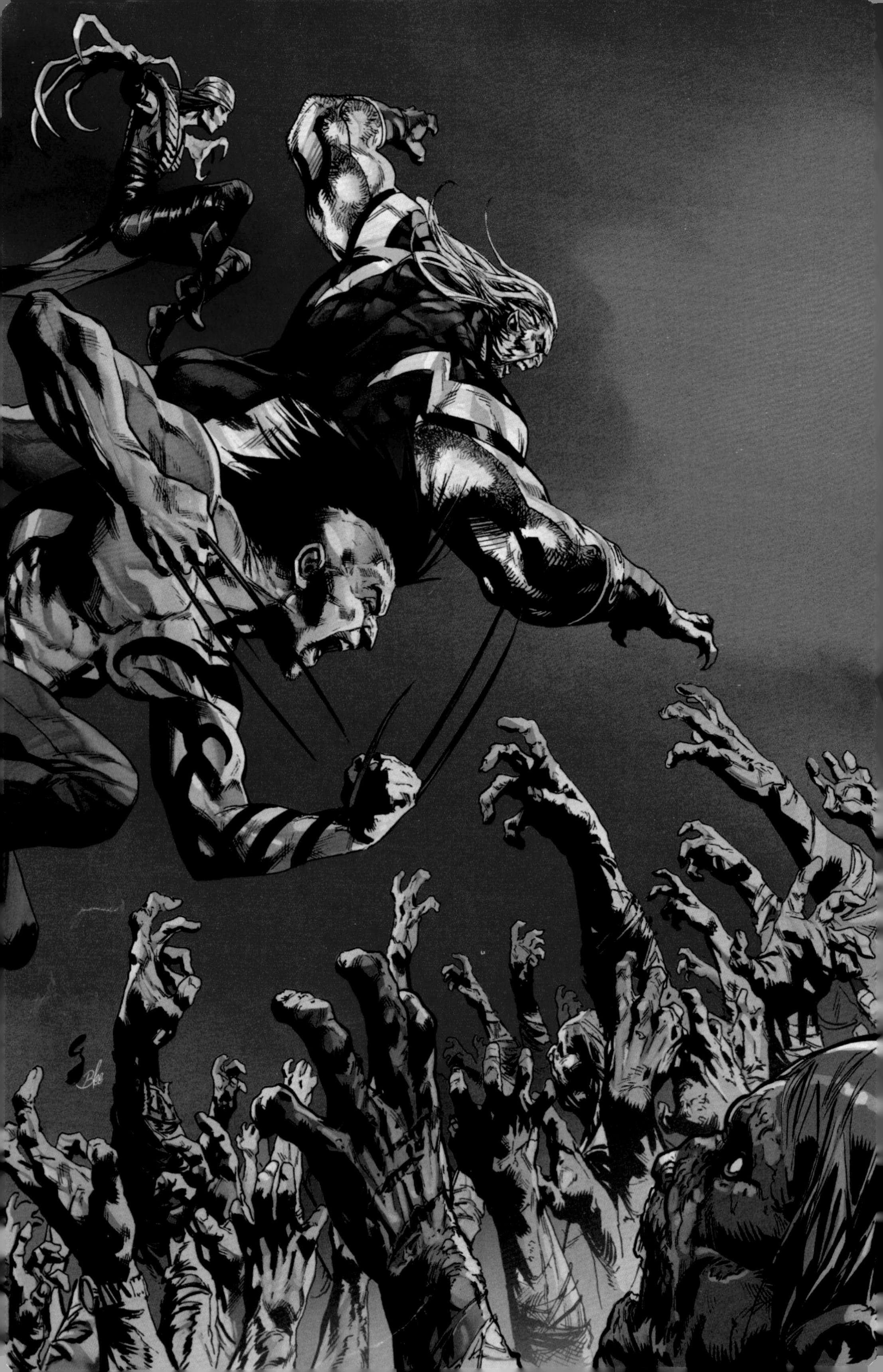